D1600694

FLYING THE ANDES

To Dick Denidinger
a good friend —
and a great
professional in
every respect!
Best Regards
Bill Knuson
10. 30. '97

Flying the Andes, Bill Krusen took this photo from the cockpit of a DC-3.

FLYING THE ANDES

The Story of Pan American-Grace Airways
and Commercial Aviation in South America
1926-1967

by
William A. Krusen

with Stephen Morrill

Based on the Journals of General Harold R. Harris

University of Tampa Press
Tampa, Florida
1997

While we have endeavored to report the information and anecdotes in this book as accurately as possible, we have in some cases relied upon stories and incidents told to us by those who were there. We have not attempted to verify all accounts, and recognize that events may have changed somewhat in retelling over the years as memories fade. All photographs are reproduced by permission from the collections of William A. Krusen, Harold R. Harris, and Charles Beatley.

Copyright © 1997 by William A. Krusen,
Harold R. Harris, and Stephen Morrill
All rights reserved
Manufactured in the United States of America

ISBN 1-879852-53-5
ISBN 1-879852-56-X (paperback)

Library of Congress Cataloging-in-Publication Data

Krusen, William A., 1920-
Flying the Andes : the story of Pan American-Grace Airways and commercial aviation in South America, 1926-1967 / by William A. Krusen with Stephen Morrill ; based on the journals of Harold R. Harris.
    p. cm.
Includes index.
ISBN 1-879852-53-5
ISBN 1-879852-56-X (paperback)
1. Pan American-Grace Airways–History. 2. Aeronautics, Commercial–United States–History. 3. Aeronautics, Commercial--South America–History. I. Morrill, Stephen, 1945- .
II. Harris, Harold R. III. Title.
HE9803.P35K78 1997
387.7'098–dc21   96-51257
CIP

CONTENTS

ACKNOWLEDGMENTS

The Panagra story could not have been told without the meticulous notes, photographs, and background information collected by General Harold R. Harris, and generously shared by his children, Alta Mae Stevens and Harold Harris, Jr. Their support and encouragement have meant a great deal to me.

Stephen Morrill did a masterful job in tying together the information and stories which have been in many Panagra memories for so long, and in the editing of those stories into the finished book.

My friends and fellow pilots at Panagra were a great help. I am particularly indebted to Tommy Grimm, who hosted my one-on-one meeting with General Harris; to Richard Witt and Charles Beatley, my Panagra housemates in Lima in the '40s, who added their insight and photographs; and also to John Brumbaugh, whose photographs were especially important in detailing the sequence of Panagra aircraft over the years.

I am also indebted to many other Panagra personnel, especially Tom Kirkland, Tommy Jardine, Loyal Domning, Frank Havelick, J. R. McCleskey, Chuck Schultz, Howard Caldwell, Hilliard Hicks, Chuck Curl, Paul Willey, and others whose names will appear as the story unfolds, and to R. E. G. Davies and Bob van der Linden of the Aeronautics Department of the National Air and Space Museum, Smithsonian Institution, for their review and comments on the manuscript.

Special thanks to my daughter, Pamela Krusen Meyjes, for her many hours of editing and for her enthusiasm.

Dr. Richard Mathews, Director of the University of Tampa Press, has offered creative advice for developing the book and making it more readable, and I am grateful to him, and to Ellen White and Ana Montalvo for their parts in bringing this first edition into print.

The project certainly would not have happened without the encouragement and understanding of my wife, Margo, as well as our three sons, Andy, Christopher, and Charles.

With deep appreciation and thanks to all of you.

DEDICATION

This story is dedicated to General Harold R. Harris, Sr.,
and to all the Panagra personnel, on the ground and in the sky,
who made it possible to create the finest airline in the world.

William A. Krusen and General Harold R. Harris, May 1986, photographed at the home of Tommy Grimm, a Panagra pilot.

PREFACE

BY WILLIAM A. KRUSEN

I have always wanted to document the story of one of the great airlines of the Golden Age of scheduled transportation, the story of Pan American-Grace Airways–Panagra–from its founding in New York and Lima in 1928, to its purchase by Braniff Airways in 1967.

This is a story about people: the early airline operators, the pilots, the ground personnel, and the mechanics. They were pioneers. They were adventurers, and they were all characters.

Today, it is difficult to imagine starting up an airline without state-of-the-art aircraft, sophisticated avionics, let alone without meteorological advice, with minimal navigational aids, and rudimentary airports. Gradually, Panagra put together an elementary infrastructure in Latin America, in countries with frequent changes of government, many of whose officials did not speak English. A basic schedule was started, originally with a single-engine Fairchild monoplane, and later, DC-2s and DC-3s. Over time, Panagra became one of the finest scheduled operations in the world.

General Harold R. Harris, who managed Panagra from its inception until he was called back to military duty during World War II, was certainly a character. A U.S. Army test pilot before he came to Panagra, Harris held many aviation records. He was the first pilot to jump out of an aircraft to save his life–the founding member of the Caterpillar Club, whose members have had their lives saved by parachutes made of silk.

When I started to prepare this book, I got a call from Tommy Grimm, a friend and a pilot for Panagra in the early years. "The story you're talking of writing about Panagra is causing some consternation with Harold Harris," Tommy told me. "He thinks you're trying to up-stage his story. I think you need to talk to him."

In early 1942, I had been hired for Panagra by General Harris, although he was based in New York at the time, and I did not actually meet him until after he had retired. Tommy set up the meeting between General Harris and me at Tommy's home in Connecticut. The General and I left that meeting very good friends. He told me that he wanted me to incorporate his reminiscences, photos, and maps into the story of Panagra. "You tell it; you get the job done," he told me. I promised I would.

Shortly after that, General Harris passed away. His daughter, Mrs. Alta Mae Stevens, called me and offered me the use of whatever I needed, with the condition that all materials and a copy of the finished book were to be sent to the Air Force Museum in Dayton, Ohio. I gladly agreed, and this book was underway.

For me, Panagra was a peak experience of sorts. I had wanted to fly ever since my grandmother told me about Lindbergh flying over the Atlantic. That got me hooked! I was only about six years old at the time. Then one day my father bought me a ticket on an open cockpit biplane, and we flew around Daytona Beach for about an hour. I watched the instruments, and the pilot let me handle the controls that moved the plane up and down, and I knew then that I really wanted to be a pilot.

Later, in 1939, when I was an undergraduate at the University of North Carolina, they ran what they called a Civilian Pilot Training Program. I signed up. For $35–and that was mostly for the medical coverage–I got a private pilot's license. Out of the group of fellows I went through training with–there were 20 of us–they picked two or three to take what they called their Advanced Training. I was one of them, and then I became a flight and ground instructor at Chapel Hill. I probably had about 150 hours in the air, a lot of pilot-testing, and I was teaching people how to fly. I was also teaching ground school, navigation, and civil air regulations. I was learning as fast as I could teach.

I was hired by Braniff in the summer of 1941, even before I had earned my instrument rating. My good friend, Ernest P. Spence, who was at UNC with me, and who was as crazy about flying as I was, went with me to Braniff. He stayed there–for the next 40 years–but I couldn't; it was too routine. Ernie said, "I know *you* won't stay here . . . this is too dull for you. You're going to go somewhere else." When I told him I was going to work for Pan American-Grace Airways in South America, I asked him if he wanted to come with me. "No," he said. "I don't want to go with you. I'm happy where I am. You ought to be, too, but I know you're not."

And I wasn't. I wanted something more.

So I went to work for Panagra when I was 21 years old. I was impressed with the opportunity to fly the biggest airplanes that were available at that time. In effect, I had the chance to do some pioneering, as opposed to the more predictable routine with Braniff. They ran tight schedules. You checked in and out ahead of time, and you made your flight plan. The Braniffs, the Americans, the Uniteds–all those fellows were really state-of-the-art in the aviation field. Panagra was certainly state-of-the-art in pioneering route structures that had never been operated before on a scheduled basis–and in pure survival.

The history of Panagra started with aviation pioneer Harold Harris and his meetings with businessman Juan Trippe, who ran operations for Pan American. Harris and Trippe put it together, and the W. R. Grace people put in money. Grace at that time controlled the economy of the west coast of South America. They were very powerful, since back then they had all the shipping lines. They had been operating sailing ships, private steamships, freighters, and passenger ships. This airline was just a small segment of their holdings. Juan Trippe was able to provide most of the operational side, while W. R. Grace, by offering financial backing and the political influence in various countries, helped pave the way.

Juan Trippe came and stayed with us a few years ago–the year before he died, as a matter of fact–and I asked him to tell me his side of what we did during the war. He said that Franklin Roosevelt had asked him to come to Washington. There Trippe heard from the President–in great secrecy, obviously–of the problems the U.S. military saw with German infiltration into South America. Our government believed there was a necessity to build a strong U.S. commercial aviation presence there, which could be immediately converted to military use if needed, and also to help move the Germans out, because they were a threat.

So Panagra got the best airplanes, and we got pilots from other airlines. We expanded very rapidly in South America partly because the United States government needed to take over what had been German territory in the north part of South America: Brazil, Colombia, Venezuela, and to a certain extent, Ecuador and Peru.

In the spring of 1942, I arrived in Lima to join Panagra. I flew with many talented pilots, in the beginning as a co-pilot, then as a first pilot on DC-2 freight runs, then as a captain on DC-2s and DC-3s on most of Panagra's passenger routes. Eventually, I flew the Panagra routes from Panama to Lima to Santiago, and across the Andes to Buenos Aires via La Paz, Bolivia.

In 1944, I took two weeks off to go to Dallas to marry Margo Sauer. It wouldn't have been easy to move most American girls to this environment, but Margo spoke Spanish fluently, got along with everybody, and knew just how to do things. We enjoyed living in Lima; our daughter, Pamela, was born there in October 1945.

In December 1945 I came down with typhus and yellow jaundice. I took a leave of absence to come back to the States for medical treatment and, unfortunately, never returned to Panagra.

I have wonderful memories of the years that I spent with Panagra in South America and of the people I met and associated with during that time.

Here is their story.

PREFACE

BY STEPHEN MORRILL

Before I could get decently started into this project, and before I had actually met him face-to-face, General Harold R. Harris died. I regret the loss of so fine a mind and such a good memory, but Harris himself planned for this, as he did for most things in his life, in a meticulous manner. He left behind prodigious notes, written histories, correspondence, even minutes from congressional subcommittee meetings. Most importantly, he left behind his own just-completed summation of Panagra's history.

At the last, perhaps knowing the end was near, he redoubled his efforts, finishing his rough draft just days before the end. In preparing the published version, Bill Krusen and I have rearranged some parts of Harris's work for continuity with other materials we have added, and polished up a word here or there, but Harris was an educated man, perfectly capable of writing his own book, had he but the strength and time to continue.

In amplifying some of Harris's journals and remarks, I received crucial assistance from more people than I can name here (but most of their names are included elsewhere in the book). I owe a debt of gratitude to everyone, but especially to the Panagra pilots for whose accomplishments I have the utmost respect.

I did one more thing as part of my contribution to assembling this book. I put General Harold R. Harris back into his own book. Despite his outgoing appearance, he was a shy man in some ways, and his version of the history hardly mentioned his own place in the formation of Panagra.

Though Bill Krusen and I have finally brought this story of Panagra to completion, in essence it was written by Harold R. Harris, with the help of a host of Panagra friends, then polished by still more friends. Any mention of Harris in the book is an addition by his friends, not a sign of ego on his part. Any mistakes—and there are probably many—are the fault of myself.

General Harold R. Harris: December 20, 1895-July 28, 1988.

INTRODUCTION

BY GENERAL HAROLD R. HARRIS

If you were to approach the average air travelers–even experienced ones–in any of today's air terminals, and ask them, "What does Panagra mean to you?" not one in a hundred would know what you were talking about.

But from the late 1920s through 1967, Panagra linked together the countries of South America's west coast, and linked the west coast to the east. The sight of an airplane overhead would elicit the exclamation, "There goes Panagra" in any of the nine countries in which the airline operated. The airline was so ubiquitous that to stone-age tribesmen in the Peruvian and Ecuadorian jungles, "Panagra" simply meant "high." Back country peasants, buying the cheaper balcony seats at the theaters in larger towns would joke about sitting in the "Panagra seats."

Panagra, the musical acronym for Pan American-Grace Airways, was the first U.S. carrier to operate on another continent. It was the first U.S. carrier to schedule its operations across the equator anywhere in the world. It was the first airline to operate regular scheduled passenger, mail, and freight service across the high Andes, between the coasts of South America.

During its entire history, this pioneer air service enjoyed the undeniable good will of each of the countries in which it operated. For many years, Panagra provided the only air service for passengers, mail, and freight over some of the world's most forbidding and impassable terrain.

Despite these and many more firsts, Panagra fought a continuous and almost fruitless battle to operate into and out of its own home country.

This history is compiled to keep alive the memory of the people, the daring exploits, and the dependable service of Panagra, whose very name was synonymous with aviation throughout much of South America for decades. From the most primitive aborigines in the Andes mountains to the most sophisticated urban dweller, the wings of Panagra were, figuratively and literally, a passport to the rest of the world.

THOUGHTS OF MY FATHER

BY ALTA MAE STEVENS

Daughter of General Harold R. Harris

Throughout most of my life, thoughts of my father were always associated with memories of watching planes take off–first from Lima's Limatambo airport, and from countless other airports ever since. In the early days it was always an unparalleled thrill to see that small silver body hurtling across a dusty field, gathering speed for its final vault into the sky. Would it make it or would the sky demons this time rudely thrust it back onto the ground?

My family inhaled flight, spooned it up in our breakfast cereal. The one truly amazing thing is that, given this circumstance, neither my brother, Harold Jr., nor I ever became pilots. However, there is no doubt that the involvement of our father with flight shaped our earliest consciousness. Not long ago, my brother and I compared notes about one of our earliest thrills–taking off and landing in the early Panagra seaplanes. This is what I wrote a few years ago about that experience:

> It is dying in perfect safety–
> this churning of green water
> boiling up over the windows
> as we, in a dry womb
> a thin metal sack, press
> madly across the ocean's breast.
> We are consigned to death.
> On each takeoff
> resurrection comes
> as a complete surprise.

While living in Nova Scotia, my husband, children and I made a point of visiting Baddeck, Alexander Graham Bell's summer home for many years. There in 1907, when Daddy was 12 years old, Bell and some colleagues, including F. W. "Casey" Baldwin, John A. D. McCurdy, both Canadian engineers, and Glenn Curtiss, then a famous motorcycle racer billed as "the fastest man in the world," had organized themselves into a group known as the Aerial Experiment Association. They built and flew four airplanes, the most famous of which was the Silver Dart. When I stood overlooking the beautiful Bras d'Or lake, I thought of how ordinary mortals were in absolute awe of these early pilots, daring adventurers into the new realm of sky. I imagined that some day, Daddy—who had personally met only Baldwin—might join them, and I wrote the following:

A Dream of Dead Pilots

(My father at Baddeck, Nova Scotia)

One day at Baddeck you will rendezvous
with Baldwin, Curtiss and McCurdy
in the Silver Dart, legendary biplane

skimming Bras d'Or, the glassy lake,
lined with frowning pines.

When they lift you from the beach,
you will hear the thrum—
strong wind in the strut wires—

you will feel the lurch,
the ripping loose from firmament.

You will reclaim
the broaching of the blue
when pilots all were young.

and others, dwindled earthlings,
stared upward at the sun.

At intervals through his life, Daddy churned out articles for various aviation magazines on his early adventures. His articles were like the stories he told my children—always exciting and focused on the event rather than on his or anyone else's personal reaction to it.

Once I said to him in exasperation, "Daddy, do you realize that all of the hairbreadth escape stories end the same way? While you are flying it, the plane develops a serious problem. You manage to correct it enough to land. The mechanic examines the plane and tells you that another twenty minutes in the air and you would have crashed. You walk away, and the next day you fly in another plane. But how did you *feel?* How did those around you *feel* when they heard this? Surely it wasn't that commonplace to lose pilots?" And, I should have added, "How, after you were married, did your wife *feel?*"

So, when I went on to comment poetically on the experience of typing for him the text of a speech to the Dayton Stamp Club in which my father described the circumstances surrounding his making the first emergency parachute jump over McCook Field, I simply filled in what I considered the essential details he had omitted. ("Fairchild," by the way, was Muir Fairchild, a fellow test pilot and close personal friend who was flying the other plane that day.)

Starting and Stopping at the Wrong Places

He should have begun with the Wrights'
kites or the first international airshow
for dirigibles, balloons and airplanes
in a Los Angeles field.

He played hookey to watch, and there was only
one fatality that day.

But he began with two planes: his
one-winged (an experimental model)
and Fairchild's, two.

We have to assume the prairie
golden fan flipped wide
to accommodate a speckless October sky.

the farmer, his head later severed
by some lowflying pilot's wheelbrace,

busy among the dead cornstalks
clattering in a light breeze.

Since he spoke of pheasants,
ground squirrels, rabbits, eyes

squeezed shut against
the exploding prop wash,

we must imagine them, too;
the coffee cup, half-empty
left on the hangar sill;

the bulky flying suit
crammed grudgingly and
at the last minute
in an undersized parachute harness,

the jaunty thumbs-up
to Fairchild next to him.

The Dayton Stamp Club knows
two Army pilots went up to test ailerons.

They executed mock combat. His plane crumpled.
He jumped. After four frantic tries,
his parachute opened.

He floated into history and never thought
to mention Muir Fairchild's

joyous smile at finding him alive,
though bruised, in a military infirmary.

When John Glenn circumnavigated the earth at an altitude higher than any man had ever gone, our Dad was working at the business of promoting financing for small airplane companies that were, literally and metaphorically, simply trying to get off the ground. I remember watching Glenn's thrilling ride on TV and phoning Daddy in New York to tell him that I was thinking of what he represented as a living embodiment of almost the entire American experience with flight. I had no sooner launched into my story than Daddy stopped me. "Thank you, dear, for calling," he said abruptly, "but I'm really busy right now."

So, when it came time to ask my son Alex to draw a suitable illustration for the cover of my father's 85th birthday celebration invitation, I wrote this:

I said to my son, give me
some illustrations, something
to epitomize the career
of a business man who,
when notified of John Glenn's
bold leap outwards, said simply
thank you, but I'm busy right now

meaning that he had been caught
in midflight, mindflight
between vectors and passenger
capacity, not that his soul
was ever anywhere but in
the pure empyrean
where the towering cumulus

dazzle and torment, walking
like silent giants noiselessly
beside the silver craft—
needles in a blue haystack.

I talked of parachutes and biplanes
cartoon-style. My son who bathed
early in the jetstream.,
knew better, drew instead
the bright eyeblink in the clouds
signifying heaven.

In *Wind, Sand and Stars*, Antoine de Saint Exupéry, whom Daddy met when the famous author was flying a mail route in Brazil, wrote:

> The events of a life are not notches on a perpendicular bar, one above the other. They are not embedded in one spot in time. They are more like horizontal threads in a tapestry. That red thread that appears only at one point in your life, the red center of a flower–has it not been there all the time, hidden underneath, on the back side of the tapestry, waiting till it should find its place in the pattern, disappearing once it had fulfilled its role; but there underneath all the time, forming part of the whole firm, intricate, varied, structure of the woof?

There is no doubt but that Daddy's red thread was flight. Always optimistic, always looking into the future, he followed its unerring path. I think he still does.

This poem, I titled "Flying the Time Line":

It is chilly in the cockpit.
The pilot, resting his eyes,
pushes up his goggles, presses
gloved fingers against the lids.

Cold air needles stab his face.
Except for the engine's regular
shudder, he is alone.
Checking location, he looks down.

Below, undulating lazily,
flows a red line. He turns
his gaze. Behind, lost in clouds,
their pilots pinned inside,

lie a million twisted wrecks.
Ahead, in the new dawn,
a handful of bright stars.
Towards these he sets his course.

FLYING THE ANDES

Panagra's first airplane on Lima's Santa Beatríz racetrack with pilot Daniel Tobin in the cockpit and Henry Elliot standing under the wing. It was the first U.S. scheduled flight operated south of the Equator anywhere in the world, and the airplane now hangs in the National Air and Space Museum, Smithsonian Institution.

The single-engine Panagra plane sits poised for its inaugural flight on September 13, 1928, at the Lima racetrack.

Crowds at the Lima racetrack for the inauguration of the first Panagra flight from Lima to Talara include President Leguía and U. S. Ambassador Moore.

PROLOGUE

The morning of Tuesday, September 13, 1928, had been foggy, as was common in Lima, Peru, at that time of year. But by mid-morning, as Peruvian President Augusto Leguía and other dignitaries arrived at the Santa Beatríz racetrack, the fog had cleared and the sun shone brightly. It would be another fine day in this City of the Kings, built by Francisco Pizarro, the Spanish herdsman-turned-conquistador. Pizarro, who was nothing if not a showman himself, would have appreciated what was to happen that day.

Sitting at one end of the racetrack's infield was a tiny airplane, a single-engine Fairchild monoplane. Operated as a mail-and-passenger service, it would that day usher Peru into the aviation century. The remainder of the South American west coast would soon follow.

For this was the era of "those daring young men in their flying machines," when almost no one had flown. To fly was glamorous, rare, maybe even a bit dangerous. In South America it was macho. Not surprisingly, every dictator on the continent wanted to do it or to be seen shaking hands with those who did.

But no self-respecting leader wanted to go out to the dusty cow pasture where the nation's tiny air force might have a few biplanes in working order. Instead, a racetrack, the gathering place of the nation's wealthy and beautiful, would be pressed into service as a temporary stage.

And the highest official present, Peruvian President Augusto Leguía, was in a cheerful mood. He chatted with Chief of the Peruvian Army, Colonel C. J. Bazo, with the American and British ambassadors, with various local businessmen, and with an assortment of aides-de-camp and governmental ministers.

Peruvian Postmaster General H. G. Hanrott and Benjamin Romero, an editor for Lima's afternoon newspaper, *El Comercio*, were less enthusiastic. They had drawn the privilege of flying as the first passengers. The airplane carried one pilot and four passengers, or, as was the case with today's flight, two passengers, who shared the tiny cabin with a pile of canvas mailbags. Hanrott was accompanying his mail. Romero was there to be a part of the news, either as a successful passenger or as a casualty. Which it was to be probably did not matter much to the young reporter who was on hand to record his employer's departure.

Supervising the preparations were Harold R. Harris and C. E. Woolman, chief entomologist and vice-president of Huff Daland Dusters. Harris had first dreamed of an American airline in South America just a year earlier, and today he was seeing the first wobbly steps of his newborn creation. Woolman's own dream was just taking root. He would some day found Delta Air Lines, naming it after the Mississippi River delta.

At 10:35 a.m. William Howell, a stenographer with the W. R. Grace Company's steamship section, arrived with the mail, pulling his truck alongside the Fairchild. He found the pilot, Daniel Tobin, engaged in what was to become an all-too-familiar ritual: on-the-spot repairs.

"Tobin said to us, 'I've got a little bit of a gas leak here, right over the cabin door, but I don't think it's much,'" Howell recalled. "He rolled some soap up with a band of tape, covered the leak, stepped back to survey the result, and said, 'That's got it.'" Howell transferred five mailbags, four small ones and one large, heavy one, to the ground beside the Fairchild's right front tire. Howell then moved his truck back and joined the crowd.

"Tobin, who piloted that first flight from the racetrack, was a Huff Daland pilot occasionally loaned to Panagra," Loyal Domning, a later Panagra pilot, recalled. "In early 1931 he got too close to the ground while doing aerobatics during a fiesta at Pedro Beltrán's *hacienda.*"

President Leguía walked over and one by one picked up three of the smaller bags and threw them through the open cabin door onto the floor. The American ambassador picked up the last small bag and heaved it, then turned to the crowd and launched into a speech. Leguía answered in kind. *Señores* Hanrott and Romero clambered up into the cabin, somewhat clumsily because of the mail bags on the floor, and sat down. President Leguía shook their hands as they did so, then turned to Tobin and shook his hand, too, for good measure.

Then everyone backed off and watched with bright-eyed interest. Tobin looked down at the last, biggest and heaviest bag. He looked around. He picked up the bag, staggered to the door, shoved it in, climbed in himself, and shut the door. He started the engine and warmed it up for a few minutes with a thunderous roar. Then he turned the nose of the plane toward the far end of the racetrack and started his takeoff roll. That his tail—and prop wash—swung toward the crowd *might* have been coincidence.

"The plane took off in a cloud of dust," Howell recalled. "We were a week shaking ourselves out." At 10:45 a.m., after a 100-meter run, the Fairchild lifted off, banked to the northwest, and headed for Talara, on the Peruvian seacoast some 560 miles away, with stops to be made at points en route. Leguía and entourage retired to the nearby Jockey Club, where they washed down the dust with champagne and toasted the success of Peru's new national air service.

Out on the racetrack the cloud of dust filtered away toward town as attendants picked up the litter and raked the track clear of tire marks. They paused occasionally to gaze to the north at a slowly-dwindling speck in the clear blue sky. Neither the racetrack attendants, nor Daniel Tobin, nor even Harold Harris, had any idea that one day that same aircraft would hang, as Panagra Aircraft Number P-1, in the Smithsonian Institution's National Air and Space Museum in Washington, D.C.

But they all knew, as that faint drone faded into silence, that a new era had come to South America, that the face of a continent would soon be changed forever.

One of the first Panagra Fairchild monoplanes crossing the Andes about 1928. Mt. Aconcagua, highest peak in the western hemisphere, is in the background.

Captain C. H. Lesesne, Jr., took this shot of the Peruvian Andes between Huancayo and Lima from the cockpit of his Ford Tri-Motor, August 13, 1936.

An early photograph of a Panagra Fairchild (FC2-W2) on the outskirts of Lima.

CHAPTER 1

1926

The western coast of South America in the 1920s was a land of great promise, isolated by deserts and torrential rivers and sealed off from its better-known eastern side by the towering mountains of the Andes *cordillera*.

Rising in the fjords of southern Chile and climbing immediately to towering heights near Santiago, the Andes continued north all the way into the fringes of southern Panama. At the modern junctions of Bolivia and Argentina and Bolivia and Peru, the massive mountains divided, as a stream divides to flow around an island, and that island was the *altiplano*, or high plain. The flow of mountains merged again in central Peru and continued northward as three parallel ranges into and through Colombia, where the ranges fanned out, like the fingers of a hand, before running to the ocean. The towering mountains utterly dominated western South America; you could never avoid their climatic effects, and only rarely were they not visible.

Between the mountains and the sea, little rain fell. In Peru, and especially around Lima, frequent heavy fogs brought some moisture, but farther south was a desert some 1,800 miles long–equal to the distance from New York City to Denver–and 80-120 miles wide. In the Atacama desert of northern Chile, rain had never been known to fall. The Atacama bore, with egalitarian equanimity, the footprints of ancient Spanish conquistadors marching south to look for gold and those of 19th century Chilean troops marching north during the War of the Pacific to visit disaster upon the Bolivians and humiliation upon the Peruvians.

The rivers are almost all useless for transportation, descending from the nearby mountains as rushing torrents. Only the Guayas River in Ecuador permits even limited traffic beyond its mouth.

The net result of this conspiracy of geography, until the twentieth century, was an absolute lack of transport for anything too heavy for a burro, horse, or llama–or, more often, a man's back. Progress brought a few railroads and some very bad roads. The cost of constructing even these was prohibitive. South America needed a way to link its communities without having to span every canyon, grade every mountain pass, or pour concrete and steel over an earthquake-prone land.

Into this mixed and inadequate transportation scene came an American military pilot-turned-businessman. It was 1926, and Harold R. Harris was 30 years old when he arrived in South America to supervise airborne cotton-dusting operations for the Huff Daland Dusters Company. A graduate of the California Institute of Technology and of the Army Air Corps Engineering School, Harris had first learned to fly in Italy during World War I, then returned to the States as a military test pilot out of McCook Field—now Wright-Patterson AFB—near Dayton, Ohio.

Harris soon became the Army Air Corp's chief test pilot and head of its flight test work. He accumulated twelve world records for flight at various altitudes, speeds, and with various weights. He was the first—indeed, the only—man to fly the "Barling Bomber," by far the largest aircraft ever flown at the time. (Typical of the whimsical nature of aircraft design in those early years, the Barling was a ridiculous example of too much of a good thing, with engines, wings, and wheels in profusion, all laced together with guy wires, almost as though someone had decided that to make a big bomber, all you had to do was to wire together a dozen Spads. Needless to say, the wind resistance was tremendous.)

Aircraft testing today is a carefully controlled business with much planning going into each flight. In the early 1920s, things were simpler. "You took off," Harris explained. "You flew around a while. You landed. It was an accomplishment."

Test pilots did not always accomplish the last part, however; there were more successful takeoffs than there were successful landings.

On October 20, 1922, Harris became the founding member of the "Caterpillar Club," that organization of pilots whose lives had been saved by the grace of the silkworm when their aircraft failed them. Silk was used for the first parachutes.

Harris was testing some new ailerons on a Loening PW-2A pursuit monoplane when the aircraft began to vibrate violently from what we now know as "aileron flutter." Harris did not know about aileron flutter. He *did* know his legs were being beaten black-and-blue by the thrashing of the control stick.

Desperately, he throttled back, but the wing bracing collapsed, and the wings began to flap uselessly. The aircraft went into a dive.

Although a few brave souls had deliberately, and under controlled conditions, jumped from various heights with the new parachutes, no pilot had ever leapt from a damaged aircraft and lived to tell about it, though quite a few had tried, and even more had fallen by accident. Just seven months earlier another test pilot, Frederick Niedermeyer, had "augured-in" at McCook Field under similar conditions when his Fokker PW-5 lost its wings. Then, before the horrified eyes of McCook personnel, Niedermeyer grimly rode the disintegrating aircraft straight into the ground.

Harris, who admitted that he hadn't intended to wear his new-fangled parachute that day because it was a tight fit in the cockpit of that particular aircraft, had put the thing on to show an interested civilian how it worked and had decided to leave it on.

No one had ever discussed the exact procedure for bailing out, but Harris needed to get away from the viciously thrashing control stick anyway, so he climbed out onto the fuselage where, at 2,500 feet, the wind conveniently blew him off. He was barely clear of the aircraft when it disintegrated entirely. Harris pulled once, twice, three times on what he thought was the ripcord before realizing he had hold of a leg strap. He located and pulled the correct ring, and his parachute snapped open just 500 feet–three seconds falling time–above the ground. Harris fell through a grape arbor behind a house in suburban Dayton, unhurt but for badly bruised legs. The site of this first successful use of a parachute to save the life of a pilot is today a part of the "History of Aviation" tour in Dayton, and is marked with a plaque.

In 1925, Captain Harris took a leave of absence from the military to work with Huff Daland Dusters on a boll-weevil dusting program in the Southern states. It was to be a long leave of absence, for Harris would not put his uniform on again for seventeen years.

Huff Daland, with its headquarters at Ogdensburg, New York, was formed in the early 1920s by Thomas Huff and Elliott Daland with the intention of manufacturing aircraft. The company was modestly successful, making aircraft for the U.S. Naval Air Service and for the U.S.

Crop dusting, Louisiana, 1926.

Army Air Service. Harris, then Chief of Flight Test Branch, Engineering Division, for the Army Air Service, flew the Huff Daland aircraft and got to know and like the firm's principals.

In 1924, Huff suggested that the company form a crop-dusting division as a way of broadening its portfolio, and twelve dusting planes were built. But, if he were to "commercialize" fully on the use of his planes, Huff realized that he needed to put his dusting operation in the hands of someone with a lot of flying and management experience. He went to Washington to talk to Major General Mason Patrick, head of the U.S. Army Air Service. The two men agreed that Harris would be given a year's leave of absence to work with the dusting company. After a year, he could decide if he wanted to resign his commission and stay with the company, or return to the Air Service. Only after these arrangements had been made did Huff go to Dayton to notify Harris. It was probably history's first hijacking of an airplane pilot.

Harris joined Huff Daland in February, 1925, to supervise "commercialization." At this time virtually the only use for aircraft in the United States was in the military services. Some commercial photographic mapping was being carried out in aircraft built by the Sherman Fairchild company, but it was not a significant business. A transcontinental air mail service had been operated by the post office as early as 1919, using surplus WWI aircraft and pilots willing to fly them, but it was a very costly endeavor, and, of course, they carried no passengers.

Even though the Europeans had started immediately after the First World War, at this time no one in the United States had made any serious attempt to develop either commercial passenger traffic or the large transport aircraft needed to make such traffic an economic success.

Satisfied with the quality of the duster aircraft, Harris tried next to recruit some pilots. It wasn't hard to do.

"In those days, a graduate of the Army Flying School was not retained in active service but went directly into the inactive reserve upon graduation," Harris recalled. "There was no difficulty in securing good men who were delighted to have employment in flying, even though it was of a sort they had never thought of."

Not everyone Harris asked was eager to sign with Huff Daland. One graduate, Charles Lindbergh, decided after some thought that, since he happened to already own his own Standard (a training plane developed during WWI), he'd rather barnstorm around county fairs and make a lot of money than tie himself down with the dusting business.

If an executive and a knowledgeable chief pilot were essential to a dusting operation, an entomologist was even more necessary. C. E. Woolman was a "parish agent" in Louisiana (in any other state, he would have been called a "county agricultural agent"). The state of Louisiana lent Woolman to the U.S. Department of Agriculture, who in turn lent him to Huff Daland.

C. E. Woolman.

Woolman was more than a good entomologist, he was a natural salesman who could sip corn "likker" on the front stoop of a South Carolina shack or mingle with the upper crust of Peruvian aristocracy (the "forty families of Peru") with equal aplomb. Woolman also took to flying with such enthusiasm that, upon his return to Louisiana, he went on to found Delta Air Lines. Many years later, Woolman's old friend Harold Harris would be, among his many other activities, a Delta vice-president.

The Huff Daland Company began to carry out dusting contracts across the United States and down the west coast of Mexico. But there was a problem inherent in this line of work: it was dependent upon the growing season. It seemed obvious that in order to have work year-around, South American countries should be included, because the seasons were reversed there.

"At this time (1926), the cotton plants in Peru were being ravished by army worms," Harris recalled. "Planters in Peru arranged with Pedro Beltrán, owner of a large cotton farm and head of one of the "forty families," to come to the States to see what the U.S. Department of Agriculture could recommend." The USDA recommended dusting, adding that there was only one firm set up to do it. That company was Huff Daland. Woolman went to Peru to talk to Beltrán and his fellow growers. The rest of Huff Daland followed shortly. By December 1926, Huff Daland was in business in Peru.

The dusting went well, but Harris was particularly annoyed by the poor transportation facilities and the difficulty of obtaining spare parts from the United States. He also talked to a number of Peruvian businessmen who seemed in favor of some sort of air travel arrangement, if one could be arranged. He kept this in mind when, in 1927, he set out on a tour of South America to assess the markets for his dusters and for the aircraft manufacturing arm of Huff Daland.

Traveling by train, motorcar, and steamboat across South America, Harris soon realized something else. European nations were busily engaged in selling aircraft to the South Americans, usually for military purposes. The French, in particular, had an active schooling program for pilots, who, not surprisingly, preferred French aircraft when they returned to their South American homelands. The Germans concentrated not on the schools for young pilots, but on the trade connections with older Latin American statesmen and businessmen, and were rapidly penetrating the continent.

In Brazil the bigger states were still quite independent; some had their own separate air forces and armies. Visiting São Paulo, Harris was approached by a young Brazilian lieutenant who had heard that Harris was the first "caterpillar."

The Brazilian wanted to jump out of an airplane. The São Paulo Air Force owned one parachute, but no one knew how to pack it properly. Harris was a parachute expert. Could he help?

"Parachute expert, my foot," Harris recalled. "I knew nothing about parachutes except that I had once used one. Well, this fellow's friends wanted me to make sure it was packed properly before he made his jump. There weren't two 'chutes, just the one, and if it didn't work, you didn't get your money back. I hadn't packed a parachute since 1922, when I packed one just to try it. But I packed it for him with a great deal of determination because I didn't want to have a fatality on my hands. This lad went up a couple of thousand feet and jumped out, and the thing worked!"

Harris reported back to Huff Daland later in 1927 on the prospects for dusting and for selling aircraft. In his report, he included a map of proposed passenger and air mail routes. He focused on the west coast of South America because that was the shortest distance from the United States, and because Huff Daland was already operating in that area.

Harris was a methodical man, and he had already investigated such mundane things as the proximity of hotel accommodations for passengers. (Hotels were to remain a problem in smaller towns for a long time to come; Panagra often arranged for passengers and crews to sleep overnight in small guest houses.) He also looked into the availability and types of ground transport, both for passengers and for fuel and freight, the size and condition of landing "fields" (although they didn't deserve the name), and the availability of fuel.

He marked the route off into 600-mile segments because that was what he considered to be the practical range of an aircraft of the day with a full load and full tanks and leaving a bit of fuel aside for reserve. He included a discussion of the possibility of obtaining local government air mail contracts, and perhaps, in the future, tying these to U.S. air mail routes.

If the United States government did anything at all right in those days with respect to aviation, it was to encourage the use of air mail, and to assign air mail routes on the basis of which company seemed most capable of carrying out the contract, rather than on the basis of the lowest cents-per-mile bid. As a result, some scandalously wasteful contracts were let, and there were occasional complaints, both from the losers in the bidding and from congressmen concerned about the bidding process. But the excess money received usually went to develop the passenger side of each airline's operation so that, in effect, the U.S. Post Office was subsidizing the development of passenger transportation.

Possession of a mail route contract also assured an airline of a steady income, a profit base upon which to predicate future expansion into passenger traffic. Because the United States was the only aircraft-building country not intentionally fostering a subsidized national airline, the little help that came along occasionally from the post office was all the more appreciated.

While Harris was touring South America, the New York brokerage house of Hayden Stone acquired Huff Daland Dusters. Harris went to New York in the fall of 1927 and laid his map and his figures on the desk of Richard Hoyt, Hayden Stone's senior partner.

It was a fateful moment. Harris had no way of knowing, but Hoyt and the J.P. Morgan group were even then working on a plan to finance an airline from Key West to Havana, with plans to expand further into Latin America as opportunities developed.

Hoyt was considered an important man in aviation circles. He had put together the Curtiss-Wright merger, and he still served as chairman of the board of the Curtiss-Wright Aircraft Manufacturing Company. Between his own long-proven enthusiasm for aviation and the newer public enthusiasm for flight, generated by Lindbergh's New York-to-Paris odyssey earlier in the year, Hoyt felt the time was right to move, and move quickly, into South America.

Hoyt called Juan Terry Trippe, a young, well-connected businessman, son of a New York investment banker. Despite the coincidence of the Spanish first name, bestowed upon young Trippe in honor of an aunt named Juanita, Trippe never learned Spanish, hated the name Juan, and put up only grudgingly with his public relations department in their later attempts to exploit the name in South America.

Trippe was an aviation enthusiast himself who had trained during WWI as a bomber pilot but who had not seen action. He had already operated a couple of small airlines with mixed success and was working with Hoyt on this new project.

In June of 1927 Trippe had incorporated an airline called The Aviation Corporation of America. He had good financial backing—his old school chums had names like Morgan, Rockefeller, Vanderbilt—but no aircraft. A bigger drawback was that he had no serious prospects for any of the all-important mail routes. But another airline *did* have a license for a Key West to Havana mail route. This was Pan American Airways, Inc., a corporation formed earlier in 1927 by some Army Air Corps officers—Major Henry H. "Hap" Arnold among them—and some prominent civilians. Pan Am was organized with the intent of heading off a perceived German threat in Latin America by beating them to the commercial markets. Arnold, working as an intelligence officer in Washington, had been particularly disturbed by the success of SCADTA (Sociedad Colombo-Alemana de Transportes Aéreos) in Colombia, which was set up in December of 1919 with German ex-combat pilots backed by heavy German capitalization. In eight years, they had changed the lives of most Colombians, connecting for the first time the long valleys separated by those three Andean *cordilleras* and, in the process, ingratiating themselves with the Colombian people.

Now, laying his compass on his South American map, Arnold could see that Colombian airfields and SCADTA equipment were a scant hour from the Panama Canal as the bomber flew. Furthermore, the SCADTA equipment was manned entirely by pilots still active in the German Air Reserve.

Before Pan American Airways could do more than apply for and obtain the right to the one mail route from Key West to Havana, the Billy Mitchell affair occurred. General Mitchell, outspoken advocate of air power, was court-martialed on grounds of insubordination, after humiliating the Navy Department by showing that aircraft could sink even battleships. Hap Arnold and the other military officers of Pan Am decided to mind their own military business and leave the establishment of air routes to the civilians. Arnold, in fact, was to go on to become Chief of the Army Air Force during the Second World War.

So Pan American was an airline with a mail contract, but with no aircraft and no one willing to stay on as a company officer any longer than necessary.

Trippe stepped in, and, after some teeth-grinding negotiations, acquired the airline together with its mail contract. There were to be many other deals, many other tough negotiations, and many other airlines associated with Trippe, but this was the start of Pan Am as an international airline.

Trippe was one of the visionaries of early aviation. While others fought over domestic mail routes and short passenger routes, he saw money to be made in the long haul, across the world's oceans, linking countries together. He pushed forward on two fronts: he negotiated landing rights on foreign soil, and, in some instances, built his own bases. He also supervised the construction of huge flying boats with the fuel range necessary to span those oceans. He saw to it that the factories filled his orders first, even if that meant ordering aircraft into production well ahead of any plan for their actual use. Eventually, Panagra would benefit peripherally from Trippe's almost reckless planning; when Harris needed long-range flying boats in Panagra's early days, they were available, even when other airlines were begging for them.

The flying boats which Trippe supported were more than a way to transport enough passengers to make long distance routes pay for themselves; they became symbols of American power overseas. Flown by ex-Navy pilots and using former ships' navigators and celestial navigation to find their way, they so impressed themselves upon the consciousness of our society that even today's airline pilots still use some of their archaic nautical terms.

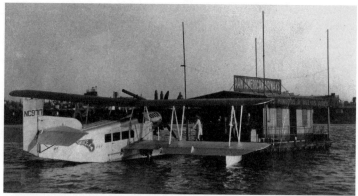

A Loening amphibian at Panagra's floating dock in Montevideo harbor, about 1929. While the small amphibian's main job was to carry mail, passengers could ride as well. A sign on the dock advertises, "75 minutes to Buenos Aires."

Trippe and Hoyt had barely begun their planning when Harris showed up on the doorstep at Hayden Stone, report in hand. Hoyt telephoned Trippe. "Trippe, come over here," he said. "There's a fellow I want you to meet. He's two years ahead of us."

Trippe showed up with Andre Priester, a short, balding, dour, Dutchman with the title of "chief engineer" at Trippe's tiny airline. Priester was known for his taciturn manner. He spoke little because he couldn't speak English very well. Also, he could not get along with anyone but Trippe, but he took his title seriously, driving ground crews to distraction with his insistence upon precise maintenance. Sometimes he seemed fanatical: brass fittings inside the engine nacelles, where no one could see them, had to be brightly polished. Toolboxes had to be neat and clean at all times. He also laid down tough requirements for pilots, too, insisting that they not smoke or drink in public. Flying, Priester insisted, must be done with precision and care for personnel, passengers, and equipment. Nothing less than perfection was good enough.

There was a long silence in Hoyt's office while Priester took his time studying Harris's maps. Then he pushed those aside and picked up Harris's notebooks and reports, reading them one by one with an expressionless face. Hoyt and Trippe watched Priester; Harris watched Hoyt and Trippe.

Finally, Priester put the last report down, looked up, and said, "Yah. Dis vill do."

It was high praise, though Harris, who had expected something more (and from someone higher in the organization), did not know it. With minor variations on the theme, Panagra's entire eventual route and passenger-mail profit mix for the next forty years was to follow the pattern laid out by Harris in 1927.

Top: Fairchild FC-2, Panagra's first plane, being picked up in Lima to be taken to the Smithsonian National Air and Space Musuem. Center: Wings could be folded within two minutes for storage or transport. Bottom: In hangar at Smithsonian.

CHAPTER 2

1927-28

Hoyt and Trippe sprang into action. A new company, Peruvian Airways Corporation (PAC), was formed by September 1927 to exploit the Huff Daland opening and to implement Harris's plan. Juan Trippe would be the president of PAC, while Harris would be vice president and general manager. The new airline could use the Huff Daland pilots and mechanics, at least to start, but passenger aircraft were needed. Harris went to the Fairchild factory with some definite ideas in mind.

The result was the model FC-2, a high-wing monoplane, a variation of a design that Sherman Fairchild had intended for his own aerial photographic company. It was a single-engine aircraft powered by a Wright Whirlwind engine of what Harris referred to as "an alleged 220 horsepower." The wings could be folded for storage, or unfolded and the aircraft prepared for flight in a few minutes. This was a major selling point in the days when aircraft had to be delivered to their new bases by ship and then assembled on the spot by untrained labor.

Partly because of this ease of transport and assembly, the Fairchild was to become a popular "bush" plane in remote parts of the world. On January 15, 1929, Admiral Richard E. Byrd became the first man to fly to the South Pole in his Fairchild FC-2-W2, the *Stars and Stripes*.

The standard configuration carried four passengers and the pilot, all in the same cabin. The cabin had windows that could be opened for ventilation. There were no brakes, no flaps, no control over the propeller pitch, and no reversible thrust. The plane had a cruising speed of perhaps 85 miles an hour, could not surmount high mountains, and was forced to remain at low altitude for lack of an oxygen system or cabin pressurization.

Vibration and noise were awesome. The pilots liked to shout over their shoulders as they passed particularly interesting sights, but the passengers rarely heard them. There was no cabin attendant, seats were uncomfortable, and the cabin was too low for many passengers to stand erect. Nevertheless, the Fairchild was arguably the finest passenger airplane then flying in all of South America. And it had one amenity that no other airline in the world could boast; Harris had insisted upon the installation of a toilet compartment. It's always good to have an airplane designed by an old test pilot.

Landing sites were equally primitive. Humorist Will Rogers's description of the average landing field in the United States at that time was, "a small open space, surrounded on three sides by high tension wires, and on the fourth side by a cemetery." In Peru, landing fields at first were usually soccer fields or straight stretches of roads. The racetrack extravaganza had been a publicity ploy only; Peruvian Airways, and later Panagra, oper-

Panagra Vice President Douglas Campbell.

ated from the military airbase at Las Palmas, on the other side of Lima, until November of 1935 when a civilian airport was built.

"The first Panagra plane I flew on was P-1 from Trujillo to Lima," recalled Douglas Campbell, who was eventually to replace Harris as vice president for operations. "We took off from the road. The road was hard stone, and that's where they landed. Then when they got the tri-motored Fords, they were too big to do that."

Away from the main cities and towns, landing sites were even worse, and pilots who had to contend with unpredictable weather, cranky engines, and the occasional empty fuel tank didn't always have the luxury of using even those. Often they had to make an emergency landing at any likely-looking level piece of ground.

Designated alternate fields were worse still. "With below-minimum weather at Tucumán, Argentina," recalled Panagra chief pilot Frank "Great Stone Face" Havelick, "I landed a DC-2 passenger flight at Cachi Yaco and quickly sank into the mud to the under surface of the wing. Besides being the designated alternate to Tucumán, Cachi Yaco was a cattle ranch, and it took all the gauchos, horses, and tractors on the *estancia* to extract me from the mud."

From the very first, Panagra planes had their distinctive bright yellow stripes on the wings. Green was the standard color for all equipment, lettering on the plane, and so forth. Chuck Beatley once taxied P-1 out onto the grassy runway at Lima, Peru, with the airfield's green-painted battery cart still attached to his aircraft. The battery cart was used to provide electric power until such time as the engine was started. Beatley started his takeoff run with the cart still trailing behind. Halfway across the field, the attaching cables broke and the cart tumbled off to one side. Beatley flew on.

Upon his return he was summoned for a chewing-out. "Why didn't you make sure the battery cart was disconnected before you took off?" he was asked.

"Well, the cart is painted green, right?"

"Yes."

"And the grass is green, the same color as the battery cart, right?"

"Yes."

"And on top of that, I had on my new green Ray-Bans."

Possibly the most abused equipment of all on those early aircraft were the undercarriages. One pilot, Hughie Wells, flying in the early 1930s, learned just how tough his Curtiss Condor's undercarriage really *was*.

Wells was pretty tough himself, as Panagra pilot Loyal Domning recalled. "He and Cliff Travis and 'Swede' Larson had brought two of the big twin-engine Condors down from the United States in 1933, smuggling them to the Bolivian government, then at war with Paraguay. Wells and friends neglected to secure U.S. State Department permission for this escapade, and the aircraft were impounded in Peru upon their arrival there.

"If they returned to the U.S., the pilots faced arrest for violating U.S. neutrality law. So they decided to settle down in South America. Cliff Travis joined Panagra and was sent to fly Ford Tri-motors from the Santiago, Chile, base. Swede was a copilot at Panagra's Lima, Peru base

A twin-engined Curtiss Condor.

for a while and then went to La Paz, Bolivia, where he flew for a gold mining company. Wells went to work for a Peruvian airline which had purchased the two Condors." When World War II broke out, Travis joined the U.S. Air Corps, and all was forgiven.

Wells and his Condor became a regular sight, flying cargo out of Lima to many of the more remote airstrips in the Peruvian hinterlands.

There was hardly a more remote spot than the oddly-bent strip at Januií. It was cut into and around the side of a mountain. With the steep hillside rising on one side and the equally steep ravine dropping off the other side, the airfield was so curved that a pilot on his takeoff run couldn't see around the corner in the middle of the airstrip. Nor could a pilot afford to wait until he had rounded the curve to go to maximum take-off power; the strip was too short. Thus it was that Wells, taking off in his usual overloaded condition, came skidding around Juanjui's midpoint bend to find himself in a dilemma.

Just beyond the middle of the runway was a scrawny burro that some local Indian had herded onto the field. "The Andean Indians disregarded completely any cautionary measures when crossing airports along their accustomed trails," Domning recalled. "After all, they were there first."

Wells had only seconds to make a life-and-death decision. *His* life or death; he didn't care about the burro.

A quick glance at his airspeed indicator told him that the odds of stopping were nil. He was already nearing takeoff speed and any attempt to stop the heavily-loaded Condor would probably win him a quick trip into the ravine below.

Wells tried some quick pedal-work. But an aircraft isn't supposed to have to dodge obstacles at the same time that it's blasting full-bore down a runway. There was a tremendous jolt as the left landing gear hit the fleeing burro. Wells managed to keep the Condor upright while trying to think of something else to do. Hitting pack animals just at rotation wasn't something covered in flight school. For that matter, bent runways weren't covered in flight school, either.

Despite the impact, the airspeed was still high, and the engines seemed untouched. Wells decided to go for broke and continued his takeoff.

With considerable reluctance, the Condor lifted off, and Wells, with a sigh of relief, turned toward Lima. The left landing gear wouldn't retract, which was hardly surprising, Wells thought, considering that it was now probably bent into about the same shape as the Januií runway. The Condor handled sluggishly, which didn't surprise Wells either. He had never before flown an overloaded biplane at too-high an altitude with one wheel stuck down into the airstream. He devoted his attention to keeping his airspeed up long enough to get to Lima.

Landing at Lima was easy. There was only one wheel to crank back down and only one way for Wells to find out if the other was still at-tached to the aircraft. The Condor slid in for a landing and touched down as well as could be hoped for, and without anything collapsing.

But as Wells taxied off the runway he saw airport personnel point-ing at him and at his landing gear. When the Condor shuddered to a stop, he leapt out to check the left wheel, expecting to find the sort of damage that could be seen at such a distance. What he found was to-tally unexpected. The burro he had hit had not been left dead on the Januií runway, mourned over by its native owner. Almost the entire carcass was firmly wedged into his left undercarriage. Word of the un-usual cargo, and its method of transport, spread rapidly. A crowd gath-ered to sympathize with Wells's unenviable task of cleaning up his air-craft, and soon a photographer arrived on the run from the local news-paper to film this most famous of Indian burros—and the only one ever to fly on a Curtiss Condor.

Wells was an itinerant, one of many, and some eccentricities may have been expected of him. But in fact, PAC, and later, Panagra, were also to become the home of the oddball pilot, of the man who did not fit into the rapidly-ossifying corporate structure of the big airlines in the States.

Aviation started with the individual and stayed with the individual as long as it was considered dangerous and unusual and as long as it didn't involve the public; in other words, up to and through the early mail routes, flown by half-crazed young men in underpowered old Curtiss JN-trainers, the famous "Jennys." But carrying passengers re-quired a big investment, both in expensive aircraft and in corporate infrastructure, and the goggles and scarves gave way to checklists and rules.

Another local character was "Slim" Faucett, an itinerant pilot who went on to found his own airline. There was no shortage of itinerant pilots after the Great War; but there *was* a shortage of itinerant pilots with management ability. The ones who could not fly well wound up in trees and on mountain slopes; the ones who could not balance their books found other jobs, and everyone sorted out quickly.

Douglas Campbell recalled the first time he met Slim Faucett. "My six-month-old son got a very bad case of dysentery, and I persuaded Slim to come up to Paramonga and fly us down to Lima to the hospi-tal. He was then operating a single-engine Curtiss Oriole, a biplane in which the pilot sat in the front seat and could take two passengers in the back, and he made a living flying all over Peru with that.

"He had been chief mechanic at a Curtiss Aviation School in Lima. Curtiss set up these schools in various parts of the world in the early 1920s to teach people how to fly. But this one went broke because they gave too many lessons on credit. In lieu of his back pay, they gave him this airplane.

"One of the first things he did was to fly over the Andes to Iquitos, an important river port of the Amazon River in eastern Peru. He won a $10,000 prize. It took about a year to do it, but he got there and back. He landed on a sand bar along one of the rivers east of the Andes and broke his propeller, and had to sit and wait for another propeller to be shipped down from the States. Then it was the wrong one, and he had to wait for another few months to get the right one. But he finally made it.

"In 1927 Slim lost his Oriole while landing in the dark at Bellavista, Peru. He landed on top of a burro that was walking across the field. The burro walked away from the accident, but the airplane was a total wreck. He bought two Stinson Detroiters, single-engine monoplanes with enclosed cabins that carried four passengers apiece."

Faucett later rebuilt one of the Stinsons, substituting a 750-hp engine for the original 450-hp one, and stretching the cabin to accommodate seven or eight passengers. The work was done entirely by Indian technicians in a local hangar and without any engineering studies. It turned out to be a very fine airplane to fly and performed throughout Peru, which was Faucett's territory at that time.

Airlines in South America, in China, and in other remote places seemed to attract the last of the maverick flyers. One reason for this was that the governmental supervision was not so strict. (As late as 1943 I was flying as a full captain, even though I was a year underage for the job according to the rules of the U.S. Civil Aeronautics Board—the CAB—which had jurisdiction over Panagra.) Not that safety was forgotten. Andre Priester might have been far away in Pan Am's office in Miami, but Panagra was to have some chief pilots of equally Draconian beliefs. And, perhaps because of the sheer difficulty of flying under the conditions that prevailed, pilots tended to be especially careful and cautious. You were your *own* CAB, chief pilot, and guardian angel all rolled into one. If you were careless for a moment, South America had many more ways to kill you than did the States.

Pilots rarely became careless; in forty years of flying over the highest mountains in the western hemisphere, through rapidly-changing weather with no meteorological data, and, at least in the early days, with homemade maps and no radios, Panagra suffered only nine accidents that killed a total of 24 crew members, but three of these also involved passengers, killing a total of 29. With radios and better weather data, not to mention better aircraft, accidents gradually became less frequent. The last death was in 1943; for the last twenty-four years of its existence, Panagra flew without an injury to passenger or crew. Few airlines today, for all their on-board computers, sophisticated weather modeling backed by satellite photos, and electronic navigation aids, could match Panagra's safety record.

Native dugout canoes escort a Sikorsky-43 at Tumaco, Colombia. Developed expressly for Juan Trippe's Atlantic and Pacific ocean routes, the S-43 could stay aloft more than 17 hours, and fly more than 2,500 miles.

But it would take more than careful flying to make Panagra a success; it would take careful management skills. And in the rapidly-expanding world of 1920s aviation, balancing profit against expansion was a problem. For Juan Terry Trippe it was more of a problem than for most; he wanted to expand faster than anyone else.

Trippe *always* had a problem with his dreams stumbling over the shoelaces of reality. A quietly determined man of uncanny vision, single-minded determination, and utter ruthlessness, he expanded Pan American Airways explosively in the late 1920s and early 1930s, aware that the first airline in the field won the mail routes, the passengers, and the airfields. Once he made up his mind to go into a country, he would not be stopped, would not be turned aside. He might compromise, if it could be turned to his advantage elsewhere. In a single decade he expanded Pan Am westwards across the Pacific to the Philippines and New Zealand, and eastwards across the Atlantic to Spain and England with his famous "Clippers," giant Sikorsky, Martin, and Boeing flying boats. He also expanded into China and into Central and South America, either by buying up existing airlines or by setting up his own.

1928

In 1928, Trippe made three quick and decisive moves. He bought outright the competition on the east coast of South America. This was NYRBA, the New York-Rio de Janeiro-Buenos Aires Line. Trippe also bought SCADTA in Colombia, *sub-rosa*, by secretly buying controlling stock, but leaving the management in place to vote their stock

Right: Juan Terry Trippe, the man who built Pan American up from a tiny mail-carrier and who encouranged Panagra's establishment, only later to restrain its growth.

Below: Joseph P. Grace, Chairman and CEO of W. R. Grace & Co., 1907-1929.

for him. This arrangement also made the most of the Colombian enthusiasm for the Germans by retaining their managers. Lastly, he set up an assortment of airlines, mostly of the paper variety, along the western coast of South America, airlines that would quickly unite to form Panagra.

Peruvian Airways Corporation, PAC, was first. It attracted immediate attention, both good and bad. President-elect Hoover liked the idea when Harris briefed him, on board an American battleship anchored in the harbor of Callao, Peru, during Hoover's pre-inauguration tour of South America. Harris reported the conversation to New York and enthusiastic plans were made. Five more Fairchilds were purchased, these of six-passenger, 400-hp capacity, the FC2-W2 models, and plans were made to expand into Ecuador to the north and into Chile to the south.

One commercial entity was not so pleased, and was not to be easily brushed aside, either. The W. R. Grace Company, owners of everything from a steamship line to phosphate mines to port facilities to South American politicians, had plans for an airline themselves, one that would complement their steamship routes along the South American coast. Aside from the Guggenheim mining interests in Chile, Grace was perhaps the most powerful business entity on South America's west coast. Grace executives saw no reason why they should let an upstart like Trippe into their private domain, especially to compete with them for mail service and passengers.

Trippe realized that he was still a corporate lightweight compared to Grace, but he had one advantage. He had already locked up the mail routes from the United States to Central America; Grace's airline, if formed, would have to limp along without that advantage. Trippe proposed a compromise. Pan Am and Grace would split, fifty-fifty, the costs and profits of a western South American airline.

The cost aspect concerned everyone the most. The principals expected the airline to lose money. Pan Am and its investors were willing to subsidize it so as to stave off any competition on their other routes. Grace envisioned it as a logical extension of their overall transportation operation and was willing to view the expense of running their own airline as a cost of doing business. The structure which emerged from mutual discussions provided for a full sharing of responsibilities.

The new airline would have both company names incorporated into it, would represent both their interests, and would have no president; Pan Am and Grace would each appoint three board members, and there would be a managing director—a Pan Am man named John MacGregor—to handle the day-to-day operations. Grace would represent this new aviation company wherever it had an agency. Pan Am would handle the operational aspects.

The Panagra office in the Grace building in Cristóbal, Panama Canal Zone. The Grace Company's facilities and reputation throughout the area offered great advantages for the new airline.

Grace's own aviation plans had not advanced far, and the company was amenable to this joint venture. Their offer of agency representation was to prove invaluable over the years. A Chilean purser, Noel Chaytor, remembered, "We used to have emergency landings in some of the most outlandish little places. There would be four houses, maybe, and it wouldn't look good for getting any gas. And some old Indian would walk up to me and say, '*Yo soy el representante de la Companía Grace.*' And I'd say, 'Oh, thank God you're here.' They had an agent every place you could think of."

Trippe forbore to mention, during these negotiations, that he saw this as a way to lock Grace—and anyone else—out of the market. He would devote his personal efforts to the newly-acquired NYRBA— now Pan Am—route down the other coast, and concentrate on making money on South America's east coast, where he didn't have to split the profits. He would give Panagra enough to keep his peace with Grace, and enough to keep any other competition at bay. But no more.

It did not apparently occur to Trippe until some years later, much too late, that competition might arise on the spot. Local governments came to feel that their national pride demanded a national airline. Trippe reflected the bias of the developed world toward the underdeveloped countries. He assumed that his only competition would come from fellow Americans or from Europe. It was one of his few mistakes.

Between Trippe's pro-Pan Am bias and his failure to anticipate rising South American nationalism (if, indeed, anything *could* have been done about the latter), Panagra started life with two strikes against it. That it survived for forty years before the third strike, the assignment of overlapping routes to Braniff Airways, was a tribute to the fact that the fledgling airline *did* earn money, from the first.

In December of 1928, the first of the bigger Fairchilds arrived in Callao by steamer. In early February of 1929, Harris took it from Lima up to Guayaquil, Ecuador, to talk to the Grace people about an Ecuadorian route. The airline was then still called PAC, and Grace representatives pointed out that getting an Ecuadorian government concession for an airline with the name of Peruvian Airways Corporation was highly unlikely. It was a point well-taken. Harris flew some round trip Guayaquil-Quito flights to show the potential, then on February 16 took the president of Ecuador and the president's wife and son up for a spin. When he landed, Harris wore, pinned to his chest, Ecuador's Calderón medal. More importantly, he had in his pocket the Ecuadorian concession, issued in his personal name, with the right to transfer it to a corporation.

1929

On February 21, 1929, a new airline was incorporated in the state of Delaware by the Grace Company and Pan American Airways Corporation. The corporate name was changed to Pan American-Grace Airways, Inc., with J. D. MacGregor elected vice president and general manager and Harris elected vice president and operations manager. MacGregor would work out of New York; Harris would be stationed at Panagra's headquarters in Lima. Harris duly signed his Ecuadorian concession over to the new corporation and ordered the initials, "P.A.G.A.I." painted on all the aircraft fuselages. He even had baggage tags made up before he learned that this was not to be the new name. The new name, the airline's final name, would be *Panagra*.

John MacGregor (l) and Harold R. Harris (r) in front of a Sikorsky-38. MacGregor, Panagra's first Managing Director, went on to become one of two co-equal vice-presidents in the years when the airline had no president.

CHAPTER 3

1929

Panagra's most pressing business was to build some routes. At first these were to be within Ecuador and within Peru with some connection between the two. Logistics at this time would allow no more; for its first few years Panagra was still dependent upon the technical expertise and maintenance shops of Huff Daland at Lima and at Guayaquil. The Guayaquil-Quito route, established by Harris in February of 1929 with South American Airways and P.A.G.A.I. logos still drying on the fuselages, continued under the new name of Panagra. By March of 1929, Panagra was flying a regular route between Lima and Arequipa, in southern Peru.

The last of the stretched Fairchilds arrived and was put into service in April. Harris, thinking ahead to his ultimate destination, the Río de la Plata, also bought a Loening Air Yacht amphibian to use to service an Uruguayan mail route from Montevideo to Buenos Aires–despite the fact that he was nowhere close to Uruguay yet.

Today, a float plane is an unusual sight and a true flying boat or amphibian a rarity in the extreme. A flying boat's fuselage is boat-shaped on the bottom, and it takes off from (or alights directly onto) the water. Amphibians are flying boats and are so called because they can take off and land either on land or water. If flying boats or amphibians land on water, they can move, either under their own power or with the aid of shore personnel, up a seaplane ramp onto dry land. Float planes, which alight on pontoons hung from struts below the normal aircraft fuselage and/or wings, are now found only in such remote places as Alaska and the Canadian northwest. But in the 1920's, float planes and amphibians were common. Pan American used flying boats exclusively in its early years and pioneered the use of the giant "Clippers" across the Atlantic and Pacific oceans.

There was a practical reason to use amphibians for carrying passengers. If his engine failed, a mail carrier could usually put his Jenny down on the nearest dirt road, or in a corn field if necessary. New passenger-carrying aircraft were larger and heavier and needed longer and

A floating dock at Tumaco, Colombia. Panagra's Sikorsky-38s and S-43s would stop here on their way north to Panama or south to Guayaquil, Ecuador, and Talara, Peru.

smoother landing sites. From the earliest days of aviation, the sea, a lake or a river could offer a reliably smooth landing site—on a good day.

Panagra started with land-based planes, some of the earliest in the Pan American Airways inventory, because it serviced cities that were inland, located on torrential rivers. But from the outset Panagra also had some over-water flying to do. At first it was only the Talara, Peru, to Guayaquil, Ecuador, leg that connected the Peruvian and Ecuadorian operations. Later the route would extend to Panama, and, by the end of its life span, Panagra was flying far longer over-water distances.

Harris had planned for the first over-water route by buying one set of pontoons when he ordered the additional Fairchilds. A landplane would fly up from Lima to Talara, where the load and passengers could be transferred to the pontoon-equipped aircraft for the 181-mile ride into Guayaquil.

Captain "Dinty" Moore flew the first over-water flight of this combination. Moore certainly knew his way around amphibians and float planes; he had been one of the pilots in the U.S. Navy's crossing of the Atlantic in 1919 using a small fleet of Navy Curtiss flying boats.

"Moore had been in aviation since 1911 and came to Peru as a member of a U.S. naval mission to the Peruvian Navy," Loyal Domning recalled. "Harris hired him in 1927. He had been a member of the crew of the NC-3, one of three Curtiss flying boats that set out from Newfoundland in 1919 to fly across the Atlantic. His plane had engine trouble, landed some 200 miles short of the Azores, and reached those islands only after taxiing through stormy seas. He served with great distinction as a line pilot and instrument flight instructor until the end of World War II."

The flight was 100% booked, which is to say that there were four passengers. Harris was one; the others were Shorty Hebard, head of the Foundation Company in South America, his assistant, a man named Burke, and the U.S. Vice-Consul to Peru, Ellis Briggs.

"I suppose the total weight of the passengers and the captain was about 1,200 pounds," Harris recalled. "And then we had some mail, too. The low horsepower for such a heavy load tested the skill of the pilot, but he successfully took the small plane with its burden through the ocean swells at Talara and into the air. But, about halfway to Guayaquil, the engine stopped. Out of fuel! Captain Moore had forgotten to switch the gasoline feed from one tank to the other.

"We were about 2,000 feet over the water. It was a perfectly calm, beautiful day, and there would have been no problem landing on the water. But Mr. Hebard had not had too much experience with forced landings."

Today everyone would be scrambling for their life vests. There were none on the Fairchild, and reactions in the tiny cabin were varied. It quickly became obvious why Hebard took his assistant with him when he traveled. "As soon as the engine stopped," said Harris, "Mr. Burke reached under his seat and pulled out a bottle of whiskey, which he handed to Hebard." Harris, who knew the engine stoppage was only temporary, was mildly amused, and Vice-Consul Briggs maintained a diplomatic silence. Moore, with some muttering to himself, switched over to the full tank, pumped some gas up into the carburetor, and restarted the engine. The Fairchild flew on to land uneventfully in the Guayas River at Guayaquil.

Harris had also outlined a connection between Panagra and Pan Am at the Canal Zone. This was a long over-water route. From the Canal Zone, Guayaquil was more than 745 miles due south over the Gulf of Panama, a distance far longer than the 600-mile legs Harris had planned for his land-based aircraft. Long-range amphibian aircraft were needed.

Captain Dinty Moore.

Fortunately, Pan Am had locked up the entire production capacity of the Sikorsky aircraft factory, and S-38B flying boats were already coming off the line. Panagra was able to borrow one S-38B and a Pan Am crew to fly it until it could take delivery of its own aircraft.

The S-38 had a boat-hull fuselage slung between two upper and lower wings. Passengers and crew

The Sikorsky-38 amphibian.

entered the cabin vertically, climbing down a staircase at the back of the fuselage. Two engines were hung between the wings on struts. There seemed to be an inordinate number of struts and wires, and the air drag restricted the airplane to a stately pace. One wag referred to the S-38 as, "a flock of spare parts flying in formation." Nevertheless, the S-38 was to prove a reliable aircraft in South America, and many of them found uses far from the sea.

Panagra's growth was to be explosive, at least if Harris had anything to say about it. This meant ordering aircraft for which there was no current need, while at the same time holding countless meetings with government officials all along the rocky spine of South America in an attempt to arrange landing rights. If the rights were granted but Panagra had no aircraft to service the routes, those rights might be quickly canceled and awarded elsewhere. If the aircraft were delivered before the rights were secured, Panagra would have to absorb the daily amortization without any offsetting revenue.

Harris and Trippe didn't hesitate. They ordered six Sikorsky S-38B flying boats and ten Ford Tri-Motor 5-AT land planes for Panagra's use. These early purchase orders, some of the largest aircraft orders of the time, and for a fledgling airline at that, ensured a good supply of aircraft for the near future.

Other airlines had to wait their turn. If Harris had anything at all in common with Juan Trippe, it was the ability to move quickly, and, perhaps even more importantly, the ability to *recognize* the need to move quickly. These traits, in the early years of aviation when a few tiny factories produced only a trickle of hand-built aircraft, often separated the people who only had good ideas from the people with good ideas, guts, and functioning airlines.

L-R: Captain Homer Farris, Captain Tom Kirkland, and aircraft designer Igor Sikorsky in front of a Sikorsky-38.

The gamble paid off almost at once. South American governments faced with poor transportation and lack of cash were eager to join the aviation revolution. The fact that aviation cost these governments next to nothing was not lost on them either, and, with the help of the Grace Company influence, Panagra was able to secure a lock on commercial aviation on the west coast of South America for several decades.

But first Panagra needed the mail route through Panama. This was to be the airline's bread and butter, at least in the early years. In March 1929 Panagra was awarded Foreign Air Mail Contract No. 9 (Canal Zone to Argentina) by the Post Office Department. Panagra did not even have permission from Chile and Argentina to fly in those countries, but the airline's task, so far as then United States Postmaster General Brown was concerned, was to extend service as far down the Andes *cordillera* as possible–and to do so as quickly as possible.

On May 4, 1929, the first air mail flew north from Lima to Cristóbal, in the American Canal Zone of Panama. The route from Lima to Talara, Peru, and from Talara, using the float-plane, to Guayaquil, Ecuador, was by now routine. At Guayaquil, the mail bags were transferred from float plane to sea plane, and a Pan Am S-38B thundered down the Guayas River, lifted, and began a long dogleg out to sea to round Cabo San Mateo. Amphibian pilots habitually flew over water rather than across land if there was any choice in the matter. From Guayaquil, the S-38B flew north along the coast to Tumaco, Colombia, then on to Buenaventura, Colombia, and finally to Cristóbal, Panama. On May 18 the process was reversed, and Air Mail Route No. 9 was in business. American Ambassador Moore and Peruvian President Leguía turned out again to receive the first bags of mail.

The early Cristóbal-Guayaquil flights were flown by Pan American aircraft and pilots. Pan Am had the equipment and the all-important landing rights in Colombia. By November of 1929 Panagra had Colombian landing rights in its own name, and when it received the first of its own S-38Bs in January of 1930, the route became entirely Panagra-operated.

Finding aircraft was almost easier than finding and keeping good pilots. Loyal Domning recalled: "There was a constant demand for pilots. They came from many sources and brought with them varying backgrounds. Turnover was a real problem. For every one who stayed, at least two went back to the States. A lot of them found the change in environment too much to handle along with the demands of the primitive flying conditions."

Robert Reeve, who flew some of the first S-38s for Panagra, went on to build his own small airline in rough-and-tumble boomtime Alaska. He described in his book, *Glacier Pilot,* how the pilots of the S-38s would sometimes open their side windows in heavy rainstorms so as to see out. Even if they kept buttoned up, the fuselage seams leaked anyway. "It rained about as hard inside the plane as outside," Reeve wrote. Pilots carried blowtorches with which to dry out the magnetos so they could restart the engines after each stop.

Reeve himself was a memorable character. He did things his way, not the company way, which meant that he was always in trouble with the management. One Sunday afternoon, for instance, flying a Fairchild back to Lima from Arequipa, Reeve decided to buzz the Lima racetrack to see how the horses were running. The horses bolted in all directions, which Reeve thought was quite funny.

Finally, they told Reeve that if he buzzed the racetrack one more time, he would be moved to greener pastures with some other company. Undaunted, he buzzed again . . . and then he did move on.

He went to Alaska, started his own airline, and sent for a woman he wanted to marry. When she arrived in town and learned that he owed money to everyone in Alaska, he told her, "Well, at least you understand that I have very good credit."

Panagra's route expansion continued rapidly. The air mail route was extended to Santiago, Chile, on July 12. Now came some of the most challenging scheduling, planning, and flying yet.

Harris had always intended that Panagra's route down the west coast should extend across the Andes, across the broad pampas of the Argentine, and into Buenos Aires. This fit well with Trippe's ambitions. With the acquisition of NYRBA's east coast routes, Trippe could now tie his Pan Am routes to those of Panagra at both Panama and Buenos Aires. This was especially important in securing air mail concessions because the route down the west coast and across the Andes was two days shorter in flying time than was the east coast route.

On October 5, the first air mail destined for Buenos Aires left New York. There was a problem; the Santiago-Buenos Aires leg of the trip was over Uspallata Pass, where aircraft had to fly at altitudes of at least 14,000 feet. It was all the Fairchilds could do to get themselves and their mail over the pass. Passengers were too heavy. This would have to be, for the time being, a mail-only route.

Tommy Jardine remembered flying a Fairchild from Arica, Chile, to Lima, Peru, on a make-up mail flight that had to be flown at night. Night flights were unusual and were only made between well-known points. Panagra would not have considered a night flight with passengers at this time, but the mail was something else.

Jardine had been hired away from the Ford Aeroplane Company in the 1930s by Andre Priester. He was to go on to be Panagra's senior pilot for nearly all of his 31-year career.

Captain Tommy Jardine.

"I had no weather reports or radio," Jardine recalled. "I took off from Arica at midnight, following the coast north underneath the overcast. The glow from the engine exhaust stack eliminated any forward visibility, so I looked over my right shoulder to see where I was.

"At Chala I had to go up on top of the overcast, to about 5,000 feet. My first gas tank ran dry just then. It must not have been full. I switched over to the second tank, but I now knew I didn't have enough gas to reach Lima. But I did have two 5-gallon tins of gas, which we always carried.

"I crossed the Nazca and Ica Deserts, and about abeam Pisco I decided I had to get down soon. Rather than descend through the fog, I headed for the mountains and landed uphill on an old trail. I was out of fuel; it was just getting daylight, and the fog was rolling in. I walked up the hill and took a nap.

"When I woke up, I looked over towards Lima and saw that the fog had lifted. I poured the gas from the two tins into the fuel tanks. I didn't have anything else on board except possibly ten kilos of international mail. I fired up, held the brake, lifted the tail and just got off.

"I figured that I had just about enough gas to get to Lima. I came into Lima, landed, and rolled up to the hangar, and the engine just stopped. I was out of gas. This was at 11 a.m., and I had been due in at 6:30."

Jardine later got the mail through during a revolution in Chile. Landing in a torrential rain at a farm about ten miles north of Santiago, he, his co-pilot, and the Chilean route officer borrowed horses to reach a highway, then hitch-hiked into Santiago.

"We must have been stopped at ten barricades," Jardine remembered. "They didn't show our route officer much courtesy, but being with us and with the international mail was better than a passport. Nobody stopped us, and we got into the Grace office about 1 a.m. If it hadn't been for the U.S. mail, we'd be out on that road yet."

If you flew mail all the way to Buenos Aires, it was only a short hop down the La Plata estuary to the Uruguayan capital of Montevideo. Harris called for his Loening Air Yacht, and starting on November 30, 1930, it went into service ferrying mail between Montevideo and Buenos Aires.

The Loening was an oddball aircraft. A single-engine biplane with a small cabin, it sported an upturned duck bill appendage on the front that increased its overall length in the water and provided some spray protection and additional seaworthiness when landing. This particular aircraft was to prove itself a mechanic's nightmare, the maintenance required being far out of proportion to the Loening's usefulness.

China National Aircraft Corporation (CNAC), a Pan Am subsidiary, used Loenings extensively, where the abundance of wide, slow rivers permitted a successful operation. Captain J. R. "Bugle Mouth" McCleskey, who flew for CNAC and was to take the last flight out of Shanghai in 1937, just thirty minutes ahead of the advancing Japanese army, once said of the Loening that, "It flew at 100 mph, climbed at 100 mph, and landed at 100 mph." After the remnants of CNAC's fleet went to work for the Air Transport Command, flying cargo over "the Hump" during WWII, McCleskey came to work for Panagra.

That Harris had authorized the purchase of a Loening at all was broad-minded of him. Grover Loening was an early aircraft designer and member of Pan Am's board who had fallen out with Trippe. The two were now mortal enemies, and Loening, who had his own strings to pull in Washington, was to be a thorn in Trippe's side for years to come. As for Harris, he had once bailed out of another Loening when the aircraft fell apart, but he seems not to have borne a grudge.

In any event, the aircraft, though designed to carry six passengers in addition to the pilot, carried only mail for Panagra. Passengers continued, as they always had, to take the night ferry from one city to the other.

In August, September, and December of 1929, while Panagra was still expanding its routes, the first three Ford Tri-Motors arrived. This workhorse model had first been built in 1924. The design proved to be a good one, second only in long-term durability to the famous DC-3 of later years. Fondly called the "Tin Goose," the Ford was a 12-passenger, single-wing aircraft. But its best feature, so far as Trippe and Harris were concerned, was not visible to the naked eye. The Ford Tri-Motor was the first land-based aircraft that could generate a reasonable rate of financial return by carrying mail and passengers. That fact

A Panagra Ford Tri-Motor over La Puntilla, Ecuador.

alone ensured that it was to become for a time the mainstay of airlines the world over.

Panagra's first Tri-Motors instituted a new tradition. Pan Am's early planes were often named after local dictators. Indeed, Pan Am's first aircraft was christened *General Machado*, in honor of the Cuban dictator. (Pan Am aircraft #2 was named *General New* in honor of then-U.S. Postmaster General Harry New. Trippe was a man who buttered his bread on both sides.)

But dictators and postmasters general were temporary phenomena. Dictators had the added liability of having enemies, both within their own countries and abroad. Privately, Harris could work politicians with the best of them, but publicly he wanted neutrality. One thing South American countries had in common was the Catholic church and a host of saints. So on August 11 Harris invited the Archbishop of Peru to christen the first Ford as the *Santa Rosa*. On September 2 the *San Cristóbal* was baptized in Santiago, Chile, and on December 8, it was Ecuador's turn, with the *Santa Mariana*. It was a tradition which was to prove useful over the years; the aircraft were interchangeable between nations and did not need repainting with every passing revolution.

That this was a wise policy became evident in Peru that very year, when Sanchez Cerro overthrew Peruvian President Augusto Leguía. Tommy Jardine knew something was up when a bunch of generals went to Arequipa on a Faucett aircraft. When that airplane made a forced landing at Chala, Jardine was sent to pick the generals up and take them to Arequipa.

"We'd never had planes into Chala, which hardly had an airport, but I'd looked at it from the air, and I had plenty of Ford experience," Jardine recalled. "I picked them all up and went on to Arequipa. When I came to a stop at Arequipa, there was a whole regiment of soldiers with guns trained on us.

"Sanchez Cerro took us over, after talking with our agent," Jardine continued. Now Panagra had a problem. Jardine's flight had the mail aboard, destined for points in Chile. Negotiations followed. The Americans explained to the revolutionaries that the mail must go through, revolution or no revolution. It was in no one's best interests for Panagra to lose its mail contract. Sanchez Cerro was adamant that the airplane could not leave Peruvian territory until his own problems were solved. Eventually, the two sides reached a working agreement.

"They put me under guard to fly to Tacna, Peru, where the mail was delivered to the Tacna agent," Jardine recalled. "From Tacna, I understand, it was taken by automobile to Arica, Chile.

"In Tacna, we all went to the plaza. They put me in a chair on a balcony, with the guy making the speech standing behind me. I figured they'd shoot, and he'd duck first.

"When I came back to Arequipa, it was after dark. They wouldn't let me put any more gas into the airplane. We went over to *Tía* (Aunt) Bates, a guest house Panagra crews favored. Sanchez Cerro had a German interpreter, and he bothered me three times that night to take the Ford and all of Sanchez Cerro's people back to Lima.

"Well, by this time I didn't trust any of them. I said that the airplane needed some service.

"'Where can you get service?' the interpreter asked.

"I said, 'Well, I have to go to Arica to get service.'

"Arica, of course, was not possible because it was in Chilean territory. Sanchez Cerro, when he heard this, insisted on taking off for Lima at once. I told him, 'Okay, if you insist on it. But if I lose an engine somewhere out over the desert or something like that, don't blame me for it. I'm going to warn you ahead of time.' I finally talked him out of it."

Sanchez Cerro decided to go to Lima via some safer route, and Jardine was free to leave the next morning. He continued his scheduled trip south.

"We went back to Tacna—it was the regular stop. One of my passengers turned out to be President Leguía's new prefect for Tacna, or some such. Since the town had been taken over by rebels, I knew we were in for some business. I didn't even shut the props off. I went back to the door and let these fellows out, and they had a duel right there, guys shooting at each other. I just slammed the door and ran up and jumped into the pilot's seat and took right off for Arica."

Farther south, at Antofagasta, Chile, Jardine picked up Harold Harris. Harris had been trying to reassure the New York office that the aircraft, personnel, and mail were all okay. He had come over from Buenos Aires to see for himself.

"Things seemed to be back to normal," Jardine recalled. "We got out of Arica and picked up gas at Arequipa. When it came time to take off for Lima, the agent and five, six, seven people were standing in the back. The aisles were full of luggage and every seat was taken.

"I wondered why there were so many people on the airplane. I forget the name of the agent, but I told him to get the excess people off.

"'They won't get off,' the agent said. 'I'm not getting off, either.'

"'Well, why not?' I asked.

"He pointed through the cockpit windows and said, 'Look down the road.' I looked, and several hundred drunken Indians were coming at us."

Harris was sitting right behind Jardine, who turned to him for advice.

"Captain," Jardine said (using Harris' military rank at the time), "we're in a hellava fix. Here we've got an overload with all those people, and they won't get off."

Harris stood to get a better view down the road. Then he sat back down and buckled himself in. "Well, let's go," he told Jardine.

"We had hard tires in that deep sand at Arequipa, but with my past experience, I was confident I could do it. We had 500 gallons of gas on board and 500 miles to Lima. With that load, it took us nearly five hours. We'd have been in trouble if we'd lost an engine, but the old Ford made the trip without incident."

By January of 1930 the routes that Panagra was to use for the next 37 years were essentially established, with the exception of a later extension into Bolivia and northern Argentina. The expansion of mail routes continued to bring in income, but passenger traffic was coming into its own at last.

Captain Don Beatty and H.R. Harris, Miami, June 2, 1936.

Two "HRHs:" His Royal Highness, Prince of Wales (center with straw hat), who later became King Edward VIII, and Harold R. Harris (second from left, behind the Duke's right shoulder).

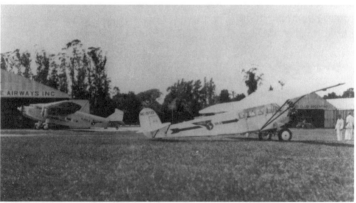

Fairchild and Ford Tri-Motor parked in front of the Morón airfield in Santiago, Chile.

CHAPTER 4

1930s

The fleet continued to build. By the end of the 1930s, Panagra had twenty-five aircraft on hand and the last two Fords on order. The fleet was a well-balanced one. The original Fairchild FC-2 and five subsequent FC-2-W2 models had been augmented by eight Ford Tri-Motors for overland work and six Sikorsky S-38Bs for the Panama-Guayaquil leg.

Pisco was a designated alternate for those times when Lima was fogged in. "I had a DC-3 trip from Panama to Lima one time," Chuck Schultz recalled. "At a stop in Guayaquil, Ecuador, some self-important American businessman asked me if the weather in Lima was good and how many times I'd had to deviate to Pisco. I assured him that the weather report was favorable and told him that, in seven years, I had never had to deviate to Pisco.

"He turned, and, in a loud voice, announced that our arrival in Lima was assured. The weather was good, and the pilot had never had to deviate to Pisco.

"Naturally, when we arrived at Lima, the fog had closed in. I could see the runway lights when I flew over, but there wasn't enough horizontal visibility to attempt a landing. So I went to Pisco. It was very embarrassing to go into the dining room that night and face those disappointed passengers."

One of the Fairchilds had been sold to the Runcie Photographic company in Lima. Panagra soon repented and bought it back, intending to make it into a two-seat hood trainer for Lloyd Aéreo Boliviano (LAB) in Bolivia. Alas, the act of selling, then buying back the aircraft had changed its status in the eyes of Peruvian authorities. It was now a Peruvian aircraft, not a North American one, and the government would not let Panagra fly it out of the country.

Frustrated in their original goal, Harris and Moore decided to use the Fairchild as a trainer for Panagra pilots.

"The company announced that all pilots had to fly it at least once," Chamberlin recalled. "When I was due to take a rating to fly safety

This Stinson SR-10F Reliant was used for route training at Limatambo Airport in the 1930s, and thereafter it saw service around Lima as an instrument trainer.

pilot in the Stinson, the Stinson was in the hangar for an overhaul. Floyd Nelson, who was going to give me the rating, told me to go practice a half hour in the Fairchild, and we would use it, since it had the same power.

"I objected, telling him that I had flown a Fairchild once, and once was enough. I lost the argument, and we had a fun ride. Shortly after that, on a Sunday morning, Jack Mitchell and I arrived at Lima's Limatambo Airport. Both of us had been told to fly the Stinson to test it when it came out of overhaul. The Stinson was still not ready, and we were about to go home when Nelson came along. I guess he decided to give us something to do, since we were there. He said, 'Bill, you like to fly the Fairchild, so you fly it, and Mitch can sit in the back with the chart, and check the height of every radio tower.'"

The Fairchilds stayed around for quite some time. Loyal Domning recalled flying one of them for training as late as 1943.

Harris often bought orphaned aircraft. In South America there was no shortage of oddball airplanes, brought there by equally odd pilot-entrepreneurs whose businesses then failed. There was a Fairchild 71, two Lockheed Vega 5Bs, the Loening Air Yacht for the Buenos Aires-Montevideo mail run, and in October of 1930 Panagra acquired a Curtiss Falcon from Charles Lindbergh, who no longer wanted it.

The Falcon, with a Cyclone 550-horsepower engine, was a "hot" air-craft; its single engine was slightly larger in diameter than the stubby fuselage. Intended solely for the mail run over the Uspallata Pass, it carried one pilot, the day's mail, and a lot of gasoline. The fuselage was painted, whimsically, to resemble an air-mail envelope, complete with *Correo Internacional* markings and oversize postage stamps. Put into service in December of 1930, the little plane made for great advertising as

Panagra mechanics at Santiago airport (at an early date). The Lockheed Vega at right rear was one of two that Panagra used for mail-carrying purposes only.

it buzzed into Santiago, Buenos Aires, and points in between. For Harris, it also freed his other aircraft for passenger duty over the high pass. The Falcon was sold to the Peruvian Air Force in 1939.

When Juan Trippe acquired NYRBA, he inherited a number of Consolidated Commodores, NYRBA's own amphibian aircraft. These were far larger than Pan Am's S-38Bs and had a range of 650 miles. They carried 24 passengers at more than 100 knots. The passengers sat on cloth seats; until then, wicker had been the standard. The Commodores were the most advanced aircraft of the day, and until Trippe took over NYRBA, Pan Am hadn't been able to acquire any; Ralph O'Neill, president of NYRBA and a man fully as visionary and dogged, but not quite as astute in business as Trippe, had locked up all of the Consolidated production line. Larger flying boats were on order from Sikorsky, and later from the Martin and Boeing factories, the style of aircraft which would become famous as the "China Clippers." In the meantime, Pam Am was happy to have the big Commodores, and they were quickly reassigned as needed to longer-legged, over-water routes.

Pan Am pioneered a Miami-Cristóbal route, using a Commodore, on January 4, 1931. Panagra's U.S. passengers had, until now, come down through Mexico and Central America, with some passengers flying from Key West into the Yucatán and then south. Now, with a big Commodore able to fly direct from Miami or Key West to Cristóbal, the U.S.-South American flight time was reduced by one-and-a-half days.

1931

The new Ford Tri-Motors were popular in South America, especially among national leaders and important businessmen, most of whom wanted a complimentary ride for themselves and their friends.

Harris didn't mind; gas and flying time were cheaper than bribes. He even arranged, on February 15, 1931, for the Prince of Wales and a party of ten to make a special trip from Lima to Arequipa aboard the *San José*.

The Prince (later to become King Edward VIII) and his party were not supposed to fly anywhere, ever. Harris had already been so informed by the British Embassy. But when they met at a reception, the prince exclaimed, cheerfully, "Oh, you're the fly boy, are you? I want you to see my equerry." Harris did so. The prince's equerry—or personal servant/arranger—explained to Harris that the entire party wanted to fly to Arequipa to catch the train up to Lake Titicaca. Harris pointed out that he had other instructions from the British Embassy. The equerry brushed that aside with, "When the Prince wants to go somewhere, he wants to go somewhere. Please lay this on."

Harris did, though privately he was worried. Airplanes weren't *that* safe, and Harris did not want Panagra to be responsible for the killing or injuring of the future king of England. But, aside from Pan Am's relations with England, he had to consider Panagra's relations with Peru. To refuse the Prince would be to embarrass the Peruvian government, which would surely retaliate.

To complicate matters, the Peruvian air force was upset because it had only a small 4-passenger Boeing, and could thus not carry so large a party. But it did offer to carry the luggage. The pilots and crew were a bit slap-dash about it and flew off to the south leaving a considerable pile of baggage behind. Harris waited until all the commotion had died away and the crowd had gone home. Then he rolled out one of the Fairchilds from its hangar, and he and one of the U.S. vice-consuls, whom he had quietly recruited to help, loaded up the baggage.

The vice-consul, who had never flown before, looked wistfully at the aircraft. Harris told him, "Well, you and I haven't got toothbrushes or shaving gear or anything at all. But if you want to come along with me, we'll fly back here tomorrow morning." The vice-consul climbed in, and he and Harris carried the last of the Prince's baggage down to Arequipa, managing to make it look as though it had been planned that way all along.

It was an exciting week for the southern Peruvian resort town. Just six days after the Prince's visit, Captain Byron "By" Rickards flew the *Santa Mariana* into Arequipa. Rickards, his aircraft, and his crew were seized and held captive by a company of rebel soldiers who were taking part in an attempted coup. President Leguía had been overthrown in 1930 by Sanchez Cerro, who was now facing his own first overthrow attempt. The coup leader, hedging his bets, had planned an escape route south to Arica, in Chile, just in case his revolution failed.

Arica was something of a staging area for disenchanted Peruvians. A dispute over the Atacama desert between Peru, Bolivia, and Chile started in 1879. Shooting had soon broken out in what became known as the Pacific War. The Chileans handily defeated their opponents. Bolivia lost its only water access and became a landlocked nation. Peru was also humiliated; Chile occupied Lima from 1881 until 1883, when a treaty was signed, granting most of the disputed area to Chile. Bad blood persisted until 1929 when the U.S. General "Black Jack" Pershing, hero of World War I, chaired a peace conference at Arica. Pershing, the leader of the American Expeditionary Force which turned the tide of battle against the Germans in Europe in 1917-1918, was no stranger to Latin America. He had pursued–to no avail–the Mexican revolutionary Pancho Villa from New Mexico into Mexico in 1916. At Pershing's suggestion, in 1929, Chile ceded back to Peru the town of Tacna and had also given Peru access rights to the port of Arica, on the new Chile-Peru border, but just inside Chile. Now the cafés of Arica were filled with the losers of Peruvian political battles, and the air was thick with intrigue.

"The Hotel Pacífico, built to accommodate Pershing and his neutral commission, became an important passenger accommodation," Frank Havelick recalled. "The Pacífico was famous for its odoriferous bath towels, the 'fragrance' of the nearby guano deposits, rancid butter, and delicious swordfish steaks."

The revolutionaries in Arequipa, while politely determined to have their way, did not seem likely to harm either their prisoners or the aircraft; Harris, in Lima, was more upset about the mail aboard the *Santa Mariana.*

"If we didn't fly the authorized mileage with U.S. mail aboard," Harris recalled, "we wouldn't get the subsidy payment for that part of the trip."

Harris called the U.S. Embassy and discovered that neither of the contesting forces had thought to cut the telephone link to Arequipa. Bill Burdette, the *chargé d'affaires* at the embassy, explained the problem to the revolutionaries in Arequipa and obtained permission for Panagra to send in a second aircraft, transfer the mail from the *Santa Mariana,* and fly it on to Chile, Argentina, and Uruguay. This was done, with a smaller Lockheed Vega taking the mail on to its destinations with only a one-day delay.

The revolution continued, going badly for the rebels, with Rickards and crew following its progress more and more intently as the sounds of gunfire crept ever closer. Rickards, who started his flying with Braniff between Tulsa and Oklahoma City, probably thought at this point that he had made a bad career move. On March 2, Rickards's tenth day of captivity, the coup leader gave up, and Rickards flew him to Arica. It was the first recorded hijacking of a commercial aircraft. It was not to be Rickards's last; he was hijacked a second time, some years later, while flying jets for Continental.

Panagra's hangar in Santiago, Chile. Aircraft (l-r) Ford Tri-Motor, Lockheed Vega, and Fairchild.

On the same day that Rickards was seized in southern Peru, Sanchez Cerro summoned Harris to the presidential palace. "You will turn over to the Peruvian air force all of Panagra's single-engined aircraft," he explained, "to be used in a war with Colombia."

Harris was horrified. Panagra was neutral, he protested. The company had to operate in Colombia, too. Sanchez Cerro was unmoved. The disputed territory was in the trans-Andean Amazon basin, in an area where Ecuador, Peru, and Colombia shared vague boundaries. The Peruvian air force needed more heavy transport capability to reach this remote region. Panagra would provide it. Now.

Harris had to make a quick decision, with no time to telephone his principals in New York, or even the American ambassador. He and Sanchez Cerro haggled and eventually compromised. Panagra would provide one of the six-passenger Fairchilds, and no more. The aircraft was never seen again, and later Harris learned that it had probably crashed in the jungle with six Peruvians aboard.

Harris, being no fool, had made sure that the Peruvians were "loaned" the use of the one Fairchild trainer which was no longer permitted to leave Peru. Apparently, it never did.

Sanchez Cerro pursued the war, fighting sporadically with Colombia until 1933, when he was assassinated. His replacement, General Benavides, terminated the hostilities at once.

Coups were common. In just six months in the 1930s, the governments of Argentina, Brazil, Chile, Bolivia, and Peru were all overthrown, largely as a result of economic upheaval caused by the worldwide depression. In 1933 shooting broke out between Bolivia and Paraguay over ownership of much of the Chaco desert. The Chaco War was of little consequence to Panagra, which serviced Paraguay not at all and served Bolivia only toward the end of the conflict.

Through revolutions and wars, Panagra's aircraft continued to fly largely without interruption. They even began to fly at night. On May

31, 1931, the first night passenger flight was made. It was a relatively simple and safe route, from Lima to Arica, where the pilot could follow the coastline most of the way, with no worries about mountains. On August 10 of that year, the first radio station was put into service.

As Panagra expanded down the spine of South America, land facilities were as important as the aircraft themselves. It was not enough to fly around in the glamorous aircraft. There had to be hangars for storage, machine shops for repairs, booking offices for the passengers, fuel supplies, hotel and restaurant accommodations, buses or limousines to shuttle passengers from hotels to airports, and radio stations.

Pan Am had pioneered the use of radio from the start. Hugo Leuteritz, an ex-Radio Corporation of America employee, had developed one of the first transmitters light enough to carry aboard an aircraft, sufficiently shielded to screen out the engine ignition noise, and sturdy enough not to be shaken apart by the engine vibration.

Although radio would eventually be used for voice transmission, in Panagra's early days wireless telegraph, or "continuous-wave" (CW) sets, were operated, employing Morse Code communication techniques. They were relatively impervious to background noise and had a longer range. Antennas were of two kinds, a long "trailing antenna" which had to be reeled out after take-off and then back in before landing, and a small loop antenna that could be mounted on the cabin roof. When operators realized that the ground stations came in stronger when the loop antenna was turned to face the signal, the idea of comparing the radio antenna's position to the pilot's compass bearing seemed obvious. To this day Radio Direction Finding, or RDF, is still used widely on aircraft. Most aircraft in later years took advantage of the best features of each antenna, and had both rotating loop antennas for RDF work and long trailing antennas for other transmissions. The trailing antenna was replaced in later models with a permanent antenna strung from the cabin roof just above the cockpit to the upper tip of the tail.

RDF was to prove a godsend to Panagra. When the weather closed down suddenly–which it did frequently in South America–the pilot was instantly lost. The standard trick in the United States was to drop to ground level, find a road or railroad track, and follow it until you saw a landmark. Railroad stations often had their names painted on the roofs as well as the sides for just this purpose. In South America, with a paucity of roads and railroads and a plethora of mountains, this was a last-ditch tactic.

The need for RDF was ironically demonstrated when Leuteritz himself almost perished with one of his early sets. He had been testing radio frequencies in August of 1928, flying as a passenger between Pan Am's Key West and Havana airfields in the land-based Fokker Tri-Motor *General Machado* when the aircraft was blown off course. Leuteritz

Panagra pioneered Radio Direction Finding (RDF) on its South American routes in the 1930s. The distinctive RDF "loop" antenna can be seen atop this DC-4 flying in the Peruvian Andes, and the system is still used on aircraft today.

was using a voice-transmission radio, but the receiver was broken that day. He could talk to the Key West station, but he could not hear them. Nor could he use the loop antenna as a directional aid.

Robert Fatt, the pilot, had once told Leuteritz that he, Fatt, had thrown better radio equipment out of his aircraft than Leuteritz had ever developed. His prejudice wasn't unusual; the last thing these resourceful, independent men wanted was to have someone on the radio telling them what to do. One of the best things about flying, after all, was the separation from the ground and from outside authority.

"One of the pilots," Leuteritz later recalled, "was not very enthusiastic at the idea of sending coded position reports at the same time he was flying the airplane. He said that since he always knew where he was, regardless of whether or not he told anyone else, that should be enough."

A later Panagra pilot, Thaddeus Young, once responded testily to repeated requests from his radio operator for a position report. "Tell them we're east of the moon," he snapped, "and slightly under it."

Now Andre Priester and others in the Key West radio shack listened in mounting horror as Leuteritz calmly described Fatt's attempts to locate Key West. Another pilot named Swinson took up a second aircraft in an unsuccessful attempt to spot the *General Machado* and lead it in.

The second aircraft had no radio whatsoever. Soon darkness fell, and Priester and his ground crew stood in the balmy tropical night listening. They lit gasoline fires, hoping that Swinson would see them. He did, and homed in on the flames, swooping out of the dark to land. When the aircraft rolled to a stop, Priester, the dour Dutchman, ran to hug Swinson.

Fatt, meanwhile, was now more than three hours out of Havana and closer to Tampa than to Key West. He had tried, futilely, to communicate with several ships by dropping messages to them, messages which invariably landed in the water and sank. Eventually, the gas ran out, and Fatt ditched the Fokker next to a tanker named the *American Legionnaire.*

The aircraft struck in five-foot seas, and Leuteritz was knocked unconscious. He was eventually rescued, and in turn saved one of the passengers. But the net result of Pan Am's first crash was the loss of one passenger and one aircraft, and there was much soul-searching about the advantages of radio.

When Panagra started flying just a month later, the only radio ground station was at the Canal Zone. Panagra had to install its own stations throughout its service area, a task made more difficult by the suspicion of local governments. In the paranoid political atmosphere of 1930s South America, about the only thing that each government had in common with its neighbor was a fear of foreigners with radios.

On August 15, 1931, Panagra's passenger route opened from Lima down to Santiago, using radio-equipped Ford Tri-Motors. By the middle of October, Panagra had passenger service, mail service, and even an express freight service established down to Chile. Passengers were flying across the mountains and into the Argentine, using Fords without radios, to save weight.

Every pound counted in the Uspallata Pass. The Andes, a massive wall of rock jutting four miles above sea level, had been an impenetrable barrier arresting the political, social, and economic development between Chile and Argentina. Uspallata Pass was one of several notches

Flying through Uspallata Pass en route from Santiago to Buenos Aires, Bill Krusen took this photo from the cockpit of a DC-3. Aconcagua, the western hemisphere's highest mountain (22,834 feet) is in the background. The blowing snow indicates high velocity winds.

in the wall. But it was not a deep notch; the air at the summit of the pass was too thin to breathe comfortably, and early aircraft did not have pressurized cabins. Stewards circulated portable oxygen bottles to ease the passengers' discomfort at the higher altitudes.

In January of 1818 General San Martín had led an Argentine army through Uspallata Pass to astound and defeat the Spanish viceroy in Chile. But few travelers of that time were willing to run the risks of avalanches, landslides, frostbite, and thin air. Instead, travelers from Santiago or Buenos Aires sailed around Cape Horn, a voyage that took more than a month and was subject to extremely bad weather.

More recently, a single-track railroad had been almost miraculously perched on the sides of the barren mountains to connect both capitals. The train took two days, but frequent snow storms and landslides made regular service impossible.

Now Panagra offered an alternative. The aircraft were more subject to the whims of bad weather than the train, but not dependent upon the easily-destroyed track. On some days the train was the only way, while on others, the best thing to do was to fly.

In late November, John MacGregor, Panagra's other vice-president, made one of his occasional trips from New York to the Panagra offices in Lima. Harris invited him along on a picnic. The two men in charge of Panagra flew an exploratory flight through the Monturaqui Pass, just north of the spectacular Llullaillaco volcano, on the first flight from Antofagasta, in northern Chile, into Salta, in the Andean foothills of northern Argentina.

"I was piloting the Fairchild P-4, with MacGregor as passenger," Harris recalled. "We were investigating the pass as an alternate to use when the Uspallata Pass, farther south, was closed on account of weather. This was the first flight made by anyone through the Monturaqui Pass. The only special equipment we took along were a few bottles of soda water and some sandwiches. Although the maximum altitude on the flight was probably 18,000 feet, the plane had no oxygen.

"Nor was there any radio or navigating device other than a compass. As we approached the top of the pass, I experienced something I had heard about from other pilots. The compass began to spin uselessly."

Harris was seeing a rare result of high-level non-pressurized flying: decompression of his compass. "A pinpoint leak in the case allowed air bubbles to leave the compass liquid," he explained. "As each bubble hit the compass card, it would give a little push.

"I was now in the middle of the crossing, and I had no way of knowing where I was going except by checking the sun. The Argentine side of the mountain was covered with clouds, but I found a small break, worked down through it, and flew until I came across a railroad. I followed the railroad north to Salta."

One problem Harris didn't mention on this trip was turbulence. The passes and canyons were notorious for their confused eddies of wind, particularly as they heated up during the day. A much heavier airplane, a Ford Tri-Motor, had once been flipped on its back for a few moments as it flew up the Humuhuaca canyon out of Jujuy, Argentina, just a few miles from Harris's destination of Salta.

Pilots flying through the "Corridor," the east-west route from Santiago, Chile, to Mendoza, Argentina, that included the notorious Uspallata Pass, often got bounced around, and occasionally had to give up the fight and return to their point of departure. One Chilean pilot, flying for LAN, was roughed up so badly in the pass that he thought his wings were going to fall off.

"How do you do it?" he later asked Panagra pilot Warren Smith. "You fly the Corridor all the time. How do you deal with the winds up there?"

"Well," said Smith, who had started his flying career in the 1920s as a stunt pilot and "wing walker" for the Gates Flying Circus, "I just pull the wheel back and warm up to it."

Not everyone shared this Zen approach to the Uspallata Pass.

1932

Throughout 1932, Panagra built up its service within its existing route system. In January "cabotage," or internal service, was inaugurated within Argentina. This penetration of a market almost totally dominated by the French and German companies required much political finesse. Although the influence of the Grace Line wasn't effective in Buenos Aires, Panagra was able to trade on both its status as the chief trans-Andean passenger and mail carrier, and on the fact that it was a partner of Pan Am, inheritor of the NYRBA route.

There was some expansion of routes into and through Colombia, and an express freight service was made available there. In Bolivia, also, attempts were made to establish airmail service. Panagra did not have landing rights in Bolivia at this time, and the route was set up in conjunction with Lloyd Aéreo Boliviano, the German-associated company operating in Bolivia. LAB aircraft would fly the mail from La Paz westward across the *altiplano*, then up and over the western *cordillera* and into the southern Peruvian town of Tacna. From Tacna, Panagra would take over. This method worked for only a month, May 27 to June 27, before LAB abandoned it.

On July 16, 1932, Panagra suffered its first fatal crash when a Ford Tri-Motor, with Captain C. J. Robinson at the controls, went down in the Uspallata Pass between Chile and Argentina. Robinson, his co-pilot, and eight passengers were killed. Uspallata had proved itself to be a treacherous place, with pilots frequently having to turn back as they approached the crest in lowering clouds. A railroad went through the pass, but no road, and sometimes the pilots almost skimmed the rails as they slipped over the pass under the weather and settled into the long downward glide into Mendoza, in the Argentine wine country, or into the Chilean capital of Santiago.

But there was never any guarantee of getting through, and the Santiago and Mendoza hotels as well as the Panagra guest house at Villa Mercedes in the center of the Argentine pampas were sometimes filled with frustrated businessmen who read the train schedules as they passed the time waiting for a break in the weather.

In August of 1932, Panagra achieved two new records: on August 7, the flight from Buenos Aires to Lima–some 2,500 miles total–took over 23 hours of flying time to complete. Harris seems to have been embarrassed by this slow performance and pointed out, defensively, that at least the aircraft involved made all of their regular stops despite extremely bad winter weather. But the fact is, that while this would have been a grueling flight for someone going the entire distance, it represents an average speed of 94 knots–not bad for the day, the equipment, and the head winds. Indeed, only a year later Harris was to boast of the swiftness of a 10-hour, forty-minute flight of 1,544 miles, for an average speed of 126 knots.

Panagra achieved the second record just a week later. When the railroad line across the Uspallata Pass was closed by avalanches, Panagra called in extra aircraft and flew thirteen flights that day to shuttle travelers across the Andes. It was a dramatic demonstration that aircraft had the capacity to do more than provide speedy travel for the wealthy and the few. Aircraft could actually move large numbers of people over otherwise impassable terrain.

In those days before weather stations, and with only primitive radios, pilots were often their own weathermen. Chilean purser Noel Chaytor described his early morning calls to the airfield outside of Santiago: "There was no operating manager at the airport, just a hangar mechanic named Stiles, whom I called Shoto."

Flights in those days almost always started at or before dawn; travelers had to be early risers, crew even more so. "I'd get up at three," Chaytor continued, "and I'd pick up the passengers to whom I'd sold tickets the day before. But before doing this, I'd call up the airport to find out what the weather was like. I'd say, 'Shoto, what do I do? Do I wake the passengers or not?' And he'd say, 'Wait a minute,' and I'd hear him shouting, 'Gerardo!' Sometimes Gerardo would say, 'No, no. Don't wake them up. Let them sleep at least another hour.' I'd call the captain and tell him that Gerardo at the airport says the fog is so thick that the birds are walking.

"In an hour I'd call again, and Shoto would call, 'Gerardo, *que pasa?*' and I'd hear Gerardo say, '*Dos están libre.* Call the passengers.' I was new, but I said to myself, this Gerardo, he must be high up. He was the man of the last word. He was the man who dispatched the airplanes, and I had never met him."

Chaytor was in for a surprise. "I went out to the hangar early one morning and ran into Stiles. There were some sheep grazing on the runway–in fact it was the best fairway in Chile–and I said, 'Hey, Shoto, I didn't know we had sheep.' He said, 'That's why it's cut so nicely. And that's Gerardo over there. You know, the fellow you used to call.'

"Well, Gerardo was a small man with a big hat and no shoes on his feet. He was the shepherd. 'How does he have such an influence on all this?' I asked Stiles. 'Oh,' he says, 'when it gets rainy or is going to rain, the sheep move towards the hangars. They always move towards the buildings. Gerardo counts his sheep, he has three hundred, you see, and if none is missing, this Ford's not moving. When they start moving out, he calculates how many move per hour or per minute and that's how he knows what the weather's doing.'"

Even after radio was installed, Gerardo's weather-consulting service worked equally well in the afternoons when he would start moving his sheep from outlying fields back toward the airport. The afternoon flights would usually arrive in Santiago right at "official" sunset; indeed, they weren't supposed to fly after that time, though they often did, and it was not unusual for the mechanic to have to put out fire pots to mark the runway in the gathering darkness.

"There was a ridge down there, called the San Ramón Ridge," said Chuck Curl, one of the pilots who flew into Santiago. "All the guys would time themselves. Fly over the ridge, dive to the ground, then turn to a 70-degree heading for three minutes. Fifty feet above the ground."

Curl, who was known as "Nimrod," not for his ability to locate landing fields but for his ability to locate women, lacked a radio but was able to land his plane without instructions from Santiago. Later flights got the benefit of Gerardo's advice. Someone would run to find Gerardo at about three in the afternoon for a weather update. The herdsman would commune with his sheep and arrive at a consensus opinion. "Captain By Rickards was flying in one afternoon," Chaytor recalled. "I ran up to Gerardo and said, 'Hey, Gerardo, what do I tell the captain?' He said, 'Better tell that plane to hurry.' And, bingo, just as Rickards touched down, it let go. Poured lightning. He had something with those sheep that they don't have now."

Sometimes even the sheep weren't enough. Chaytor recalled flying down to Santiago one day when the weather was bad. He had picked up a French pilot named Guillaumet at Antofagasta, Chile. Guillaumet had his own small air mail contract, which he flew with a tiny open two-seater Potez. Guillaumet would stuff the mail into the back seat, run around front to swing the prop, then scramble into the front seat and be off. To the pilots flying Panagra's Ford Tri-Motors, the tiny Potez looked like a kite. Guillaumet sometimes serviced his

Passengers embark on a Panagra Tri-Motor flight. The round window on the cabin door is barely visible in this photo, but the prominent "U.S. Mail" on the wing proudly proclaims the importance of Panagra's mail service.

route in marginal weather by hitching a ride on passing Panagra aircraft. He didn't need a ticket:

"I had just closed the cabin door and called over my shoulder to Captain Gardner, 'Ott, let's go,'" Chaytor recalled. "The cabin doors in those Tri-Motors had little round windows, and suddenly I saw a big hand that looked like a ham. The Frenchman was outside, knocking on the damn thing. I opened it, and Guillaumet just walked into the airplane. He had a sack on his back. The mail. No ticket.

"'The mail must go through,' he said, and took my seat.

I went up to the pilot and said, 'Captain, my load has been all reshuffled. I've got an extra 90 kilos at the back end.' He said, 'Who is it, Guillaumet?' I said yes. 'Well,' Gardner said, 'he may do us a favor too, someday,' and taxied out."

The day came soon. In fact, it came that same day. As the flight approached Santiago, the fog shut down totally. Gardner was blinded.

"Santiago was socked in from 500 meters right down to the ground," Chaytor recalled. "Guillaumet went up to the cockpit. He'd had the same problem, but with the smaller plane.

The Ford didn't fly very fast. We came down, down, down, and then hauled up again. Guillaumet took the "copilot seat."

Their first sight of Santiago was of San Cristóbal Hill, 1,200 feet high and topped with a huge statue of the Virgin Mary, a gift to Chile from France. A fine landmark–the Virgin is visible from everywhere in town.

In the Ford, the crew flinched as the statue appeared suddenly out of the fog and flashed past.

If she hadn't ducked, we'd have knocked her head off with our left wing," Chaytor said. Now, however, Gardner and Guillaumet knew where they were. Gardner bore grimly on through the fog with

Guillaumet navigating. Chaytor and the co-pilot stood just behind Gardner and Guillaumet, watching in fascination. Chaytor didn't want to go back to face his passengers. They were all gawking out the windows at the passing town, which was not nearly far enough below them.

"We went down the Plaza," Chaytor said. "And we went down the Julio Marcena. And the fog was low, low. Then the pilot saw a post that someone had painted red years before, and he turned right. We went down the Gran Avenida, and I swear that he was counting the lampposts. I could hear Guillaumet saying, 'One, two . . . .' Finally, we turned right, crossed, and landed at the airfield. You couldn't see thirty feet."

One of the earliest staff members and one who was to remain with the airline for many years was Douglas Campbell. Campbell was an accountant in W.R. Grace's South American division.

"In late 1932 or early 1933," Campbell recalled, "Grace put me to work assisting Harold Roig and Bill Cogswell, who were two of the Grace directors of Panagra."

There was a reason for this apparently odd appointment. Campbell had been a senior at Harvard in 1917, the year that all the Ivy League colleges closed down to send their students to war. Campbell wanted to fly:

"I had already made up my mind to go and drive an ambulance in France, as lots of my contemporaries were doing, only I wanted to finish school first. Then I read about, and was inspired by, the exploits of the guys in the Lafayette Escadrille. So I decided to join the Army Air Corps.

"One of the most difficult things, I learned, was just to *find* the Army Air Corps. That sounds silly today, but I went to the army recruiter in charge of Boston, who knew only that there were a handful of airplanes and a few officer pilots down on the Mexican border somewhere, flying unarmed airplanes. But he didn't have the faintest idea how to go about getting into that service.

"So a couple of other fellows and I went to Washington on a Thursday and spent all day Friday looking for the Army Air Corps. We didn't find it until Saturday morning. It was a one-room rented office in a downtown office building. It was called the Aviation Section of the Signal Corps of the U.S. Army and was populated by a captain and a secretary. They took our names and addresses, and within a month I got a telegram to report to MIT for ground school."

Campbell soon found himself in France, flying Nieuport 28s, as part of the 94th Aero Squadron, the first operational American fighter squadron. His first taste of combat was also the squadron's first encounter with the enemy.

"Two German airplanes came over to take a look at us," Campbell recalled, "and another guy and I shot them down in a fight over the airfield that lasted four-and-a-half minutes. That is to say, four-and-a-half minutes from take-off to landing." Campbell was, in other words, one of the first two pilots, in what was to someday be the U.S. Air Force, to make a combat kill. He went on to become America's first "ace," knocking down six German aircraft before receiving a minor wound and returning stateside. He was healed and en route back across the Atlantic when the Armistice was signed.

At the end of February, 1919, Campbell left the military. He found himself standing on the street in New York with a $60 discharge bonus, all the money to his name at the time. "I got a two-week job," he recalled, "the highest-paying job I was to have for the next five years. I was paid $250 for being at the first aircraft show in New York. I wore my uniform and showed visitors around, distinguished people, and introduced whoever was going to lecture. When I ran through that, I had no money."

On April 2, 1919, he started at Grace as an office boy in the mail room and began to work his way up. When his employers needed some expertise in aviation, they naturally turned to Campbell.

1933

One of Panagra's early tasks was to install some sort of weather-forecasting station in Uspallata Pass.

"Most of the weather was great for flying," Ernie Hummel recalled, "but when it got bad, it could be fierce." Nowhere was it fiercer than on the run between Mendoza, Argentina, and Santiago, Chile. "Severe turbulence and mountain waves at Mendoza frequently kept the aircraft and their passengers on the ground for days because the westward route over Uspallata Pass was unflyable. Either headwinds exceeding the speed of the aircraft, or turbulence resulting in the failure of more than ten percent of the total wing attachment bolts would result."

On May 8, 1933, Panagra succeeded in establishing a radio station at La Cumbre (The Summit), at the top of Uspallata Pass. Located just yards from the huge Christ statue, which was made of melted-down cannons and intended to symbolize everlasting peace between the two nations, it marked the border between Argentina and Chile. The antenna arrangement consisted of three radio towers with wires strung between them. A tiny hut contained a radio set, a six-month supply of food, and two Chilean volunteers hoping to start a family.

"The first radio was one of Leuteritz' telegraphs," Harris recalled. "Voice came later. Since the area was snowed in for weeks sometimes, we arranged for a Chilean radio operator who was married to a Chilean woman who was also a radio operator, to pass the winter in this isolated location. We gave them plenty of provisions and wished them farewell. The wife, coming down to Santiago in the late spring to have

The view from the radio shack on La Cumbre, between Chile and Argentina. Note snow on cables and the "Christ of the Andes" statue that can be seen through the cables to the left.

her first child, had been pleased with the arrangement, and she and her husband spent the next winter there as well. I hesitate to say how many children were the result of this situation."

The isolation of La Cumbre might have increased the local population, but not always in the way Harris thought. Hudson Strode, a travel writer, rode a Panagra flight over the Uspallata in 1936. Bob "Gimlet Eye" Disher was the pilot, and as he circled the statue to give all the passengers a better look, the purser, a man named Elliott, told Strode that the radio operator now was one Gregorio Nemsoff, an Argentine born in Russia. Nemsoff was a huge man, bearded. Elliott told Strode how the crews would sometimes throw down bundles of magazines and newspapers, then watch as Nemsoff bounded, goat-like, down the slopes in pursuit of these gifts.

Nemsoff lived alone on the roof of the world, surrounded by blinding whiteness, howling winds, incredible vistas, and prowling pumas. The latter, attracted by the meat Nemsoff hung up to store, were a constant problem. Nemsoff usually carried a rifle with him when he went out-of-doors, especially at night, and he shot a number of the big cats.

Nemsoff would climb his frozen towers in the early morning darkness to obtain a better feel for the strength and direction of the winds. With daylight he had a theodolite and some weather balloons to use to measure currents in the upper air. He would judge with his own eyes what the visibility was like far down the pass to both east and west. Then he would radio this information to the approaching pilots. After that, he had nothing to do but admire the scenery or read his magazines.

Iquitos, Peru. The Amphibian S-38, the San Blas, *had canvas covers over its engines for protection from salt spray. Note the mechanic's head and upper torso at the hatch in the "stern." A flight of stairs led down into the passenger compartment.*

For his first eighteen months of duty, Nemsoff lived entirely alone, without coming down off the mountains. Then he tried an experiment, bringing up not one but two Argentine women to keep him company. This *ménage a trois* at the very foot of the Redeemer didn't last. The women fought, Nemsoff claimed, and he threw them out in exasperation. Now, Elliott said, on those rare days when no flights were scheduled, Nemsoff would radio that he was going into the nearest village for a haircut, and would walk the two miles to the railroad line and flag down the daily train. The radio operators in Mendoza and Santiago would smile. They knew what a "haircut" was.

It's possible that some of Nemsoff's excursions were merely attempts to recover his belongings. "Panagra's weather station at La Cumbre was twice blown into Argentina by winds exceeding two hundred knots," Ernie Hummel recalled.

While Panagra's routes did not expand significantly in 1933, there was a substantial upgrade in equipment. The S-38s continued to fly from Panama to Talara, but south of that point, all traffic went by land-based aircraft, the Fords being large enough to carry the additional passenger load. The little Fairchilds were being retired, relegated to special flights or to back-up work.

Expansion continued also in the service mix, with air freight, called "express," taking on more importance as businessmen came to realize the advantages of overnight delivery of some goods.

In December of 1933, a Pan American Conference was held in Montevideo, Uruguay. Although arranged for diplomatic purposes, the conference was a one-shot opportunity for publicity for Pan Am and for Panagra, and both took full advantage of it.

It was the seventh such conference since 1889 and was expected to be yet another ho-hummer, with South American countries making bland promises to settle their differences, and the United States telling everyone what to do, while at the same time promising not to intervene in their internal affairs. Then everyone would go home and do just the opposite. Argentina, in fact, did not bother at first to send a delegation, although it had only to take the night boat across the river.

On December 19, Panagra flew a special flight from Lima to Montevideo to deliver U.S. Secretary of State Cordell Hull's wife to the conference. Other flights were fully booked as hundreds of government officials, dignitaries, and journalists flocked to Montevideo. As the conference warmed up, it was obviously not to be the usual set of easy promises, and more journalists wanted to get there quickly. The Argentines finally broke down and sent a hastily-prepared delegation across the river.

The outcome of the conference, aside from a temporary boost in passenger traffic, was of long-term benefit to Pan Am and Panagra. There was progress in ending the Chaco War. There was movement to implement U.S. President Roosevelt's Good Neighbor policies by lowering trade barriers between the participating nations. All of these decisions took more time and effort to realize, but the 1933 Pan American Conference was one of the most successful ever.

The lowering of trade barriers and reduction of travel documentation were of immense help to Panagra's rapid expansion in passenger traffic and the newly-developing air freight trade. This improvement in relations between South American countries, and between them and the United States, could not have come at a better time. Panagra was about to increase the stakes in the South American air travel contest by bringing on line much larger aircraft and much more sophisticated equipment, passenger routing, and freight operations. The first of the new generation of passenger aircraft, the Douglas DC-2, were starting to roll off the huge (by the standards of the time) Douglas Aircraft production line in Santa Monica, California. Panagra was among the first customers waiting.

A DC-2 flies through Uspallata Pass en route from Santiago to Buenos Aires. Mt. Aconcagua is in the background.

Captain Bob Disher with lobsters. Ford Tri-Motors continued to be important for passengers and cargo, as shown in this 1934 photo.

CHAPTER 5

1934

The first of Panagra's DC-2s was built late in August, 1934. On September 5 Tommy Jardine and Bob Disher flew the new aircraft from Santa Monica, California, to Brownsville, Texas, where it was painted and fitted with radio equipment. On the 13th, the two men took off for South America. They followed a leisurely route at first, flying from Brownsville to Cristóbal in the Canal Zone with one overnight stop. On the 17th, the aircraft lifted off the tarmac at Cristóbal and headed south for Talara, Peru, where it refueled and then continued on to Lima, arriving that same day after 9 hours, 35 minutes total flying time. Harris and two more passengers were on board. The 1,573-mile trip, flown at an average speed of 175 mph, set several records for South American aviation. It was the fastest flight, to be sure, but more importantly, it was the first time that Cristóbal and Lima had been connected in one day.

The record stood for only three days. On September 20, Warren B. Smith, who had come to Panagra from the old NYRBA airline, flew Panagra's second DC-2 from Cristóbal to Lima in just 8 hours, 45 minutes, at an average speed of 185 mph.

By the end of September Panagra had three DC-2s operating between Lima and Cristóbal. From September through year's end the usual round of courtesy flights was conducted in Peru, Chile, and Argentina. V.I.P. passengers included the daughter of the president of Peru, the minister of justice for Chile, and a 28-day-old infant named Elizabeth Garrison, carried aboard by her enthusiastic mother.

On October 6 Warren Smith took the first DC-2 flight over the Andes, flying empty from Santiago to Buenos Aires. En route, Smith conducted a required one-engine check, and he reported everything normal and in operating order. Arriving in Buenos Aires, Smith flew a courtesy flight around the capital; guests included the primate of Poland, Monsignor A. Lord. It was the first time a cardinal had flown in South America without the use of feathers. The next day, Smith brought back a full passenger load from Argentina, up the pass to the Christ statue, then down into Santiago.

Smith's flights did more than set speed and load records for that route. They were a milestone in South American aviation. The longer ranges, greater speeds, larger pay-loads, and better radios all meant more scheduling flex-ibility. Some intermediate stops for fuel, or those forced by oncoming darkness, could be eliminated. Now, because of its faster turnaround time, one Douglas could replace two Tri-Motors on the same route.

The Douglas was a dra-matically different type of air-craft. While the Tri-Motors had pioneered passenger air trans-port, the Douglas was twice as comfortable. No longer was an air trip an adventure of noise, vibration, hardships, and pri-vations. Now it was becoming comfortable and convenient.

Captain Warren B. Smith (at top), with Harold Harris's children, Alta Mae (l) and Harold, Jr. (r). Mrs. Harris looks on.

The DC-2s did have one unpleasant feature that passengers never knew about: "Coming down through clouds on long descents from high altitudes, we would usually pick up ice on the propellers," Ernie Hummel recalled. "Of course, the ice came off, and lots of it would get slammed into the side of the aircraft exactly where the radio op-erator was sitting. The FRO (flight radio officer) would practically break his seat belt jumping as these loud slaps hit the side of the fuse-lage."

The DC-2s, like the Fords, were quickly named after saints. Within a few short years, Panagra was to acquire seven of the new aircraft. They soon earned a reputation of another sort: they were prone to ground-looping. Multi-engine aircraft whose engines are running at different power settings can suddenly spin around on the ground. On the DC-2s, the throttles weren't all that precise; when the pilot thought he had them lined up properly, one engine would be delivering more power than the other. That, combined with poor brakes and a non-locking, fully-rotational tail wheel, could throw the aircraft into an ever-tightening loop.

The brakes were operated by a very long lever. "I remember Glen Carrol, coming in to Lima," says Paul Willey. "He was a copilot, but for some reason he was sitting in the left seat. He rolled right past the terminal, waving that brake lever out the window. He'd pulled it right out. Naturally, when he ran out of field, he had to ground-loop the plane in order to stop."

The Tri-Motors were by no means obsolete yet. Aside from their continued use for passenger hauling, a use which would continue for several years, they, and the newer Douglas DC-2s, proved quite adaptable to freight traffic and to special charters. Two such charters occurred towards the end of 1934 when Dr. Serge A. Korff, of the California Institute of Technology, had himself and his instruments flown to high altitudes to study cosmic rays. On November 11, the Tri-Motor *San Fernando* carried Dr. Korff to 26,100 feet over Lima, breaking all South American altitude records in the process. On December 9, the DC-2 *Santa Lucia* reached an altitude of 30,300 feet over the same city.

About this time, Panagra faced a fleet-wide repair problem with its Ford Tri-Motors:

"On Frank Achilles's first day with Panagra, he showed up in civilian clothes and was told he was now a copilot," Ernie Hummel recalled. "Someone handed him a Panagra cap, and he climbed up onto the wing of a Ford that was out on the ramp, to check the fuel levels.

"He measured the fuel in one tank and was walking across to the tank on the opposite side when the top of the tank caved in. Achilles ended up with one foot down through the wing and inside a full gas tank. This was an early instance of micro-biological corrosion, and we found that more than one Ford had heavy corrosion in the wing fuel tank area."

1935

Panagra started 1935 briskly, with a special charter on January 5 from Mendoza, Argentina, to a nearby power plant which had been isolated and damaged by heavy seasonal rains. As it had when avalanches blocked Uspallata Pass, Panagra was showing that aircraft were not just a travel solution for the wealthy. At times an airplane was the *only* solution.

In 1935 Panagra once more entered the Bolivian market. This time there was to be no "cooperation" with L.A.B. (Lloyd Aéreo Boliviano). Such cooperation had faltered in 1932. Now Panagra would fly the routes itself.

The government concession came with a deadline. (The airports were actually to be phased in throughout 1936.) All infrastructure, fields, radio networks, passenger stations, and the rest (if none existed) were to be built by Panagra. The runway construction sometimes was as simple as arbitrarily marking off a runway on the hard salt pans, then clearing away the larger rocks.

H. R. Harris, in the *Journal of the American Aviation Historical*

Society, recalled that:

> The field at Uyuni and the station and radio had to be built and operational before the deadline. The Chaco War was in progress between Bolivia and Paraguay and no manpower was available; however, one of our airport engineers was assigned the job.
>
> Nerves were getting a bit frayed as we heard nothing from him until the day before the deadline. Then his radio station went on the air advising us to proceed with the planned flight schedule for the next day.
>
> When he returned to Lima, I asked how much the Uyuni job had cost. "Two bottles of scotch," he replied. When he arrived he had sought out the chief of police, handed him a bottle of Scotch, and outlined his airport problem. The chief got out his truck and started across the pampas, lassoing every Indian man he saw. He brought them back to a barbed-wire enclosure—the site of the new airport. Indian women followed their men with all necessary cooking gear. The women parked outside the wire and fed their men through the wire. All day the men picked up rocks from the airport surface, piled them into the truck, and picked up more rocks as an empty truck arrived. Within a few days the field was cleared and the Indians turned loose. Whereupon the chief of police received the second bottle of scotch! Try that for an airport construction job today.

Harris didn't mention that the Bolivians sometimes piled up the excess rocks in the wrong place. For years after, some Bolivian fields had mounds of rocks piled across the *ends* of the runways, not *beside* the runways, causing pilots no little aggravation.

On May 18 a decree was signed opening Bolivian air express to Panagra for the first time. And on May 31 a Tacna, Peru, to La Paz, Bolivia, mail and passenger service began. The Grace Company manager in La Paz, known as "the Black Tulip," had pilots smuggle live lobsters to him. This was not at all difficult; Panagra routinely carried lobsters from Santiago, Chile, to Mendoza, Argentina. Sometimes the pilots flying the Black Tulip's lobsters would conveniently forget to unload the smuggled lobsters at La Paz, carrying them on to the overnight stop at Uyuni. As the lobsters wouldn't keep, there was nothing for it but to share them that night with the small British railroad contingent at Uyuni, who did so many favors for the Panagra pilots.

Frank Havelick, who came to Panagra from China National Airlines and went on to become chief pilot, remembered the La Paz, Bolivia, airport as having a canyon at one end and a rock pile at the other. "The runway was nothing but loose gravel, with a drop-off at the east

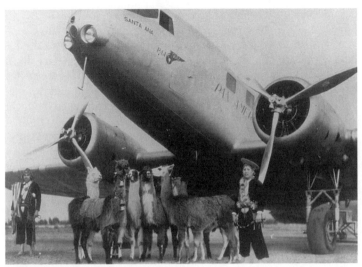

The DC-2 Santa Ana *in La Paz, Bolivia.*

end of about 1,000 feet. If you got off and then had engine trouble, you could end up going down into that canyon. We always kept our fingers crossed until we managed to make a turn out of there and get back over the table-land where, if something happened, we'd have a fighting chance to get the plane down and not hurt anybody.

"The Indians who maintained the runway were always pulling oversized rocks, some of them as big as boulders, out of the runway area and piling them at the west end. They didn't realize that if something happened to you on a take-off in that direction to prevent the plane from lifting off the ground, you would go straight into that great pile of rocks. In addition to that, there were herds of llamas and burros which would run across the runway, and what we called 'dust feathers,' small whirlwinds which obscured visibility on takeoff and affected our controls as well."

A common complaint Havelick also heard was the lack of oxygen at La Paz. The town was higher than most mountaintops in the U.S. But more important to pilots flying across the Andes, it had no medicinal-oxygen plant. This meant that air crews could not get their oxygen bottles refilled there. The Bolivians didn't care. They were used to the altitude and had developed oversized lungs to compensate. The American air crews, who had to fly *higher* than the *altiplano*, with no oxygen if refills weren't available, sometimes felt as though their eyeballs were about to pop out.

The usefulness as well as the prestige inherent in the employment of Panagra aircraft to fly diplomats to conferences, proven so well in December of 1933 with the Pan American Conference in Uruguay, became an aid to Panagra in its penetration of the Bolivian market. In June of 1935, a conference met at Buenos Aires to settle the Chaco War between Bolivia and Paraguay. On June 9, Panagra took the Peruvian minister of foreign relations, his wife, and his secretary down to Santiago and across to Argentina. On the 12th, the DC-2 *Santa Ana* left Santiago for the conference with Chilean diplomats and newspaper correspondents aboard. The newspapermen christened the flight the "Ministerial Special."

On June 13, the *San Felipe*, a Ford, left Buenos Aires on an inspection tour of Paraguay. It carried the American and Chilean military attachés, both on assignment from their respective Buenos Aires embassies. They stopped at Monte Caseros, Asunción, Pinasco, and Camacho, Paraguay, before arriving at Paraguayan military headquarters in Ivamirante. Two days later, the aircraft and passengers retraced their steps.

On that same day, June 15, the *Santa Mariana* lifted off from Santiago with a combined American/Chilean military mission en route to Bolivia. It is doubtful if any of the passengers remembered that this was the same Ford which had been hijacked at the end of the abortive coup attempt in 1931 in southern Peru. Harris knew it and derived some satisfaction from the knowledge that the military was paying its own way this time.

After stops at Ovalle and Antofagasta in Chile, the aircraft headed into Bolivian territory to Tarija. From Tarija, the delegation continued by auto while the Ford returned to Santiago, flying south and then west through Argentine territory and arriving on June 18th. En route the Ford stopped at La Paz, where courtesy flights were conducted. The wife and daughter of the Bolivian president were among the passengers taken up for a spin. Harris had long perfected this technique of reaching the influential men in government by giving their wives and children free rides. The combination of cheerful assistance to a nation just ending a war and a willingness to deal with the peculiarities of South American politics was to pay off handsomely.

Meanwhile, Panagra's first Consolidated Commodore—its own amphibian—left Cristóbal for Guayaquil on July 16. It had taken a long time for the factory to fill all of Pan Am's orders. By the time Panagra finally had a Commodore of its own, the DC-2s were on the verge of taking up the slack on the long-legged Cristóbal-Guayaquil run. But the Commodore, despite being of older technology, still carried a few more passengers. The Commodore, like the S-38s, stopped for refueling at Buenaventura, Colombia. It might have had a longer range, but it was not *that* much longer.

The Douglases were making courtesy flights in Ecuador in July. By August 24, a DC-2 service was available from Guayaquil to Lima and through to Santiago and Buenos Aires. By November 1, a new "fast schedule" was in effect. Passengers now could traverse the Panagra route in just four days, leaving Cristóbal on Sundays or Thursdays. A once-per-week passenger flight had been inaugurated from Buenos Aires to Montevideo. If the passenger caught the Sunday flight from Cristóbal, the timing worked out at the other end to take him or her down the Río Plata and into Uruguay on Wednesday afternoon.

The faster schedules and greater passenger capacities were putting a strain on Panagra's operations and reservations people. The radio capabilities of the DC-2s, while in themselves a great step forward, emphasized the need to install more radio stations and relay posts along the Panagra route. Progress completing these stations was still slow at this time, and to satisfy suspicious governments, local operators had to be trained. In April, 1935, a new station opened at Pisco, Peru. The first Bolivian station opened at Charana on May 30, the day before the first passenger flight clawed its way up onto the *altiplano* from the Peruvian lowlands. Another radio station opened at Junín, Argentina in September. In December a station was opened at La Paz, Bolivia.

The Bolivian radio beacons were especially important. The higher elevations (in some cases near the operating limit of the aircraft), the narrow, twisting canyons, and the strong, shifting winds all added to the normal problems of navigation. The stations were also useful for aircraft flying certain freight operations up into mountainous eastern Peru, and to passenger aircraft operating along the Lima-Arequipa-Antofagasta-Santiago corridor. They served as well to convince the Bolivian government that Panagra was indeed serious about serving their mountain-locked nation.

"I remember flying up to Santa Cruz (Bolivia) with a DC-3 full of radio gear for the stations being established in theBolivian jungle east of Santa Cruz." Paul Willey said. "I was with Frank Achilles. There was a German Junker that someone had parked in the treetops east of Santa Cruz. It became something of a checkpoint for us to look for. I think it was a LAB plane."

Willey also recalled the day the station cook was along on one of these cargo flights, sleeping in the last seat. The weather turned bad, and Willey and Achilles were forced to nearly 20,000 feet. The aircraft cabin was unpressurized, and the cook was feeling a bit woozy. Achilles, by manipulating the rudder and elevators, tried to see if he could flip the cook from one side of the aisle to the other.

The cook, known to all as "the Russian," must not have taken this treatment personally, for he always had pitchers of cool lemonade and fresh hamburgers waiting for the air crews when they came in after a long, hot day of flying a roundabout Bolivian milk run that came to be known as "the Sawtooth."

Other problems were being addressed, too. Passenger needs were better met by establishing a central reservations control at Panagra's SAGO (South American General Operations) in Lima. SAGO controlled all spaces on Panagra planes between Cristóbal and Montevideo. A through airway bill was put into use for freight transiting country "B" en route from "A" to "C". Air express insurance was offered for the first time in the Canal Zone, Colombia, Chile, Uruguay, Argentina, and Ecuador, and separate air express manifests for Montevideo only were eliminated. Paperwork was being simplified and at the same time becoming more useful as a control measure.

A continuing problem was the distrust the governments had for one another along Panagra's route. Chile and Peru, in particular, still did not get along, half a century and more after the 1879 War of the Pacific. The American General John Pershing had mediated a "solution" in 1929, by which Chile returned Tacna to Peru, but old hatreds still festered. The Chilean government insisted that Panagra air crews flying into Chile had to be either from the U.S., in the case of the pilots and copilots, or Chilean, in the case of everyone else. This made staffing the flights difficult, and permanent assignments nearly impossible.

Antofagasta, Chile, was a hardship post by any definition. "Even the avid golfers avoided the local course," Chuck Schultz recalled. "The trees, fairway, roughs and greens, even the traps, were all the same sand. The only delineation they had was whitewashed lines. At least there were no water holes."

Although located right on the edge of the Chilean desert, which helped explain the amount of sand on the golf course, Antofagasta was a seaport on the Pacific Ocean, and Schultz and several other pilots bought a small cat-rigged sailboat to use on days off. They were not very good at it and almost swamped the thing in the Pacific swells. When their schedule was changed to make Antofagasta only an overnight stop, the neglected boat developed a hole in the bottom, and the sails, stored in the Grace Company warehouse, were lost in a warehouse fire.

Panagra employees overnighting at Antofagasta stayed at a Grace Company guest house adjacent to the field. "All four crew members bedded down in the same room," Chuck Schultz recalled. "If Warren B. Smith was with us, the other three of us would lie awake all night listening to him snore, wondering if he would, hoping and praying he would, take another breath."

If Smith was not present, servants were supposed to wake the pilots up in time to make their flights. One time they forgot, and the pilot, Robert Reeve, awakened just in time to sprint for his airplane, still wearing his pajamas. The next day, all the Chilean pilots at the local air force base arrived in their pajamas to do their flying. A precedent had been set.

The DC-2s proved their worth immediately. On July 27 the *Santa*

The new civilian airport known as Limatambo was the frequent place of arrival for important dignitaries. One such occasion is shown here. A portion of the landscaping is also visible in this photo.

Lucia and *San Martín* took 28 tourists from Santiago over the pass into the Argentina. Three days later the *Santa Elena, Santa Silvia,* and *Santa Ana* flew the same way carrying 42 passengers in total, the largest number of aircraft passengers to cross the Andes in a single day.

On November 3, 1935, the Panagra offices in Lima packed up their belongings and moved from the Peruvian air force base at Las Palmas to the civilian airport, just finished, known thereafter as "Limatambo" ("Lima" plus "*tambo,*" the Spanish word describing an inn or place where travelers could rest. That "*tambo*" was also slang in some parts of South America for "brothel" never seems to have become an issue.).

Limatambo had something new: landscaping. Charles Schultz recalled that the median between the inbound and outbound roads to the terminal was planted with calla lilies, whose big flowers were a common sight around the Lima area.

Limatambo was just south and a trifle east of Lima, while Las Palmas, which continued to function as a Peruvian air force base, was more southeast. They were too close together for comfort, and at first the pilots, and later both pilots and air traffic controllers at the two airports would keep a wary eye on one another's operations.

The end of 1935 and early 1936 saw Panagra's first reaction to an increasing nationalism on the part of the South American countries. The whole world was taking to the air, and, outside the United States, most major airlines were national lines, operated as much for the prestige of the governments funding them as for profit. Small South American countries, and especially the rulers of small South American countries, wanted their own airlines, too. The utter lack of trained personnel, or of facilities, hampered this nationalistic goal. (Most air facilities to date, had been built by Panagra or by one of the few other airlines

Panagra's Limatambo office at Lima, Peru. Limatambo was the first decent passenger terminal, succeded by a larger international terminal.

on the continent; the era of publicly-owned and -operated airports was yet to come in South America.)

Panagra dealt with this problem as best it could by creating spin-off or associated airlines. On December 18, 1935, the first Panagra subsidiary went into service. Aerovias Peruanas S.A. (AVP) took over the Lima-Arequipa and Lima-Chiclayo runs, both inside Peruvian territory. On January 17, 1936, AVP began service from Lima to Huancayo. The flight ran only every other week and was among the more arduous, despite being only some 130 miles direct-line. It was not unusual for an aircraft to take an hour and forty minutes to weave up the canyons of the Río Rimac and through the first of the *cordilleras*. Then came a right turn and still more climbing, this time up the Mantaro River valley to Huancayo. The altitude and the tortuous route through the passes and valleys, as compared to the straight-line distance, created the illusion that the aircraft had flown all the way at nearly stalling speed. Flying "downhill" was faster, usually around one hour and five minutes in this case. The route was just as byzantine, but the aircraft made better time on the way down.

1936

As newer airports were being built, some of the older, smaller stops were being phased out. On January 1, 1936, Villa Mercedes, Argentina, was made into a "flag stop." It had once been an important refueling point midway between Buenos Aires and Mendoza. Panagra had even maintained a guest house at Villa Mercedes for its passengers to use when Uspallata Pass was closed by weather. "Flag stops" were the flying equivalent of railroad secondary stations. Instead of placing small flares on the tracks to tell the engineers to stop for a passenger, the station managers would run up a flag on an outside pole. Pilots flying overhead would look at the flagpoles at each flag stop, circling and landing if they saw the flag. In short order, of course, radio rendered the flagpole unnecessary.

On April 25 a new airport, Chachani Field, opened for business at Arequipa, Peru. As passenger aircraft grew in size, they also increased in weight. Soon the old military airfields, used for smaller aircraft and usually made of well-rolled dirt–perhaps with grass, perhaps not–became inadequate. Even a DC-2 smacked the runway with the force of a heavy dump truck taking a bounce. Later aircraft were to challenge paving and surfacing engineers even more. Ordinary asphalt suitable for highway construction "flowed" too much for these stresses. Macadam, a road-building technique of crushing small stones into a level surface, could take the weight without "flowing," but what was to keep the stones from splattering in all directions when the wheels hit? So a mixture of crushed stone, with asphalt filling in the cracks to act as glue, came into use. This tarmacadam mixture became known as tarmac, which then became a generic name for airport runways. The term is sometimes used today, erroneously, to describe modern runways made of concrete.

Sometimes pilots preferred dirt strips. They were softer if you landed on the plane's belly. "I'm not a technical man," the Chilean purser, Noel Chaytor, said, "but those engines on the DC-2, they gave us a lot of problems. Up in the *cordillera* something would freeze up, or in the heat they would quit."

Chaytor was purser on a flight from Santiago, Chile to Buenos Aires, Argentina on just such a hot day. At the Mendoza, Argentina stop, the manager of the Argentine Railways and his wife climbed aboard, very nervous. They were accompanied by the station chief, a very large man named Alluralde. Alluralde's entertainment was to read books on how to beat the casino, although no one at Panagra had ever actually seen him putting any of this knowledge to use at the roulette tables. Alluralde was sweating, both from the heat and from nervousness. He pointed out to Chaytor that these were VIPs indeed and that it was their first flight in an airplane.

"Nothing's going to go wrong," Chaytor assured Alluralde. "They're going to have the finest flight in the world."

Alluralde left the aircraft, heading for his cooler office. Captain Warren Smith fired up the engines, and the DC-2 lumbered into the air after what seemed to Chaytor like an awfully long take-off roll. Just as they left the ground, Smith lost power in both engines.

"I was in the back," Chaytor recalled. "They had sold my seat, and I was standing up, holding onto a coat rack. Anything the captain does in the front is exaggerated back there, and the tail was going this way and that, and so was I. Smitty was fighting this thing to keep it straight and try to put it back on the ground.

"Next thing, the landing gear goes, and we hit the ground. There was nothing he could do. He just belly-landed it, and we walloped in there. I opened the door and stepped onto the ground. I didn't have to step down much, and I didn't need a stair. I said, 'Ladies and gentlemen, in a quiet and orderly fashion will you all kindly get out.'"

The far end of the airfield was adjacent to an Argentine army post, and Chaytor bundled his passengers into some borrowed army trucks. He also convinced the army troops that he was the captain and got them to chase some news photographers from the site. He busied himself helping the rest of the crew and only got back to the Panagra office at the terminal later. To his surprise, there were no passengers there.

"What happened to your passengers?" he asked Alluralde, who was sitting at his desk, holding his large head in both hands.

"They all went by train," Alluralde said.

"The same thing happened to Smith and me in Mendoza two months later," Chaytor recalled. "And to Pop Colliver and me in Arequipa. Something would happen to those goddamn engines, heat problems. You'd get just a meter off the ground, and then the engine would quit. The DC-2 didn't have a single-engine take-off."

On May 26, 1936, Captains Jack Miller, Jack Squire, and Craig Brown each received the Abdón Calderón medal from a grateful Ecuadorean government. They had searched for, found, and assisted in the rescue of two downed Ecuadorean military pilots whose plane had crashed on March 3 while ferrying mail between Quito and Guayaquil. Fortunately, such air searches were rarely needed, and Panagra itself enjoyed an exemplary safety record. Panagra never failed to provide all available aircraft to look for a downed flyer, to assist in medical evacuations, to fly in emergency supplies and medicines to stricken communities, and even to airlift out earthquake victims.

Aside from satisfying a purely humanitarian urge, such selfless service went far towards helping Panagra overcome an inbred antipathy towards things *norte americano*. This commitment to help out was one of the reasons for Panagra's early acceptance by South Americans and for its continued success in the face of rising nationalism.

The Commodore making the Cristóbal to Guayaquil run was returned to Pan Am, and, on June 4, a Sikorsky S-43, the newest long-range amphibian, was put in its place. The S-43s could stay aloft more than 17 hours, and fly more than 2500 miles, but the tradeoff was low payload; the S-43s could seat just 15 passengers, fewer than the Commodore. It had range; it was the first aircraft specifically designed for low fuel consumption, with engines tuned to pull immense propellers so strongly, and so slowly, that flight engineers shining their flashlights out the cockpit windows at night swore they could almost count the blades as they turned.

Apparently, the 15-passenger limitation was tolerable, for this aircraft flew the water route until such time as Panagra dispensed entirely with amphibians.

Every shortening of routes, every lengthening of flight time to eliminate intermediate stops, every increase in speed had its effect upon Panagra's bread-and-butter business, air mail. By July 15, 1936, Pan Am and Panagra could fly a letter or small package from Miami to Montevideo, Uruguay, in five days.

Ironically, this speed sometimes caused problems. The need to move the mail from certain contracted points with the greatest speed occasionally conflicted with Harris's desire to expand his passenger service to more cities. The usual trade-off between speed and more stops was complicated by the overriding need to fulfill the federal air mail contracts that provided Panagra with its base income. Sometimes schedules were juggled so that the number of stops an aircraft made during the flight depended on the day of the week. It was just one of the many complexities of Panagra operations.

In August, with the new mail schedule scarcely inaugurated, a goodwill mission composed of the attorney general for the U.S. Post Office, various Pan Am representatives, and the press visited South America. The mission flew down the Pan Am, or eastern, side of South America, to Buenos Aires. Harris flew to meet them and accompanied the group across to Chile and up the west coast to Cristóbal.

On September 22, Panagra flew the president of Peru and ten others from Zorritos, a small government petroleum field near the Ecuadorean border, back to Lima. It was the first time in his life, *El presidente* assured Harris, that he had flown. Harris said nothing. He was already aware that one side effect of Panagra's policy of giving "courtesy" rides to South American dictators was that you had to give a *lot* of rides. Given the frequency of revolutions in South America, sometimes the first airplane ride a dictator got was his flight into exile.

By late 1936, as mentioned earlier, Panagra had expanded its foothold in Bolivia. On October 9 service to La Paz was extended south to Oruro, and then to Uyuni, both cities on the *altiplano*. On October 16 a radio station went into service at Uyuni. Another, at Oruro, was established just three days later.

"Two delightful British railroad veterans, Messrs. Payne and Hopwood, spent the better part of their lives maintaining and repairing rolling-stock at the Uyuni repair yards of the Antofagasta-La Paz Railways," Frank Havelick recalled. "They also offered their homes to passengers and crews of flights that couldn't go on because of the late hour or bad weather.

"After one such overnight, Mr. Payne took the crew to the field for the pre-flight procedures. This was before dawn, and, as was usually the case, the temperature was sub-freezing. After a while, the crew became aware of a native Bolivian standing some distance off, dressed

First Officer Charles Beatley at Oruro, Bolivia, 1942. The boarding steps also announce the altitude, 3705 meters or 12,155 feet. Beatley and his airplane, sitting on the Oruro runway, were already at a higher altitude than most pilots in the U.S. had ever flown.

in his homespun finery with a wide-brimmed hat, silver ornaments, knee-length pants, bare feet and legs. He had been waiting since the previous nightfall, Payne said, to see this big bird lay an egg."

Payne and Hopwood, another pilot, Ernie Hummel recalled, sometimes took the overnighting air crews up to the mines. "The Pulucayo mine was located at 17,000 feet, and the Payne daughter and the daughters of the British and American mining engineers and geologists all wanted to dance the whole night away. Many a Panagra crew member was fagged out to the point of exhaustion, trying to keep up some semblance of a dance step at 17,000 feet." A more sedate activity for bored air crews was to borrow one of the rail yard switch engines and run it up and down the track. Panagra crews made sure that they kept Payne and Hopwood well-supplied with hams from Buenos Aires, lobster from the west coast, and other amenities they could not get in Uyuni.

Simultaneously with the expansion into Bolivia and the establishment of the *Diagonal* route, those flights between Buenos Aires and Santiago which did not carry mail (the air mail contract was flown only on certain flights, not every day), began to stop off en route at Córdoba. This was 180 miles north of the Buenos Aires/Mendoza flight path, but Harris wanted to start servicing that important city. He hoped soon to link Córdoba to the southward-reaching Bolivian connection.

Flying from Buenos Aires across the vast Argentine plains to Mendoza or Córdoba might seem to the mountain-weary Panagra pilot like a vacation, but even the Argentine plains held their hazards. The *pampero*, a hurricane-strength wind, could sweep across the plains in long line-squalls. The primitive weather reporting of the day was barely capable of informing en route pilots of the storms. There was no capability of predicting them in time to avoid the flight entirely.

"One memorable DC-2 flight out of Buenos Aires for Córdoba encountered, with no warning, a *pampero* crossing its course," Frank Havelick recalled. "The crew learned from the radio that the Morón airport at Buenos Aires was closed and that the winds were tearing the Panagra hangar apart."

Ernie Hummel remembered a later *pampero* that hit the same hangar and also a DC-3 which had to be left outside but which was tied down and weighted with filled oil drums. The wind picked up the airplane and dropped it on top of the hangar, breaking the DC-3's back. It took Douglas Aircraft engineers nearly a year to rebuild the airplane.)

"Ahead was a sharp squall line on the left, sunshine on the right," Havelick continued. "but the squall line was crossing, forcing them more and more off course. Not knowing how far ahead the front extended, the crew throttled the engines back to idle and rode the tremendous updraft in front of the roll cloud. They found that they could maintain altitude with little fuel being consumed.

"Riding the top of the cloud, carried swiftly north by the winds, the crew watched as, in full view below, the *pampero* uprooted trees and damaged buildings. Finally, almost a hundred miles north–well beyond

Ernie Hummel in the cockpit of a DC-3

their intended destination–the DC-2 finally managed to circumvent the *pampero* and descend to a lower altitude. The crew applied normal engine power and flew back to Córdoba, landing there almost on schedule, and with most of their fuel still on board."

On October 21, John MacGregor, who had flown in from the New York office, took off with Harris in an S-38 from Chiclayo, on the Peruvian coast, for Iquitos, in the eastern Peruvian jungle. Don Beatty, who had joined Panagra in 1931, was the pilot as the amphibian threaded its way through the Chamaya and Marañón River valleys and deep into the Andean *cordilleras*. They flew over the Pongo Manserichi falls, where the Marañón tumbles down out of the Cerros Campanquiz and onto the broad, flat Amazon basin. At Iquitos, where the Amazon begins, they circled around and then splashed down onto the river.

Waiting for them was M.J. Rice, Pan Am's Brazilian director, who had made a similar survey flight upriver from Manaus, the capital of Brazil's Amazon basin, located at the juncture of the Río Negro and the Amazon. The object of this exercise was to see if a route could be established connecting Pan Am and Panagra across the widest part of the continent. It was not a successful idea, for, at the time, there was none of the boom-town atmosphere in the Amazon basin that we see today. The few towns, no matter how eager they might be to have the service, simply could not generate enough traffic and income to support the effort.

1937

Panagra started the tourist season of 1937 with a novel idea suggested by a Santiago company called Chile Cruises. For $650 U.S. dollars, a U.S. citizen could enjoy an all-expense-paid vacation. Trips originated either in Miami, Florida or Brownsville, Texas, and the tourist could leave from either point of origin and return to either, so that he could, for example, leave Miami on a vacation in South America that returned him to Brownsville, Texas. The total time required was 17 days, of which eight would be spent flying.

Harris, in Lima, and MacGregor, in New York, watched this program with some interest, and soon Panagra was offering its own vacation packages on a more-or-less regular, if varied, fashion.

As part of Panagra's shift away from amphibian aircraft to land-based planes, Douglas Campbell went to Colombia in 1937 to begin arrangements for an inland route for Panagra.

"I really had no experience in air transportation," he said. "All I knew was flying airplanes. At any rate, the route we had been flying was Panama to Guayaquil, Ecuador, with seaplanes along the coast. Our amphibians would make stops an Buenaventura, which was a port but which was miles from anywhere. We thought that Cali, Colombia's third largest city, would be a good traffic port, so I spent three or four months in Colombia arranging that. In 1938 I went to Colombia again to arrange for the DC-3s to land there. Until the DC-3s, you didn't really have enough range to fly the distance . . . certain distances you had to fly with seaplanes because your next airport was too far away. It wasn't really a safe operation to do with land planes."

On March 12 Panagra extended the Bolivian route one step further, to Villazón, in the south, near the Argentine border. And on April 16 service was provided for the first time between La Paz, Bolivia, and Córdoba, Argentina. The route, which became known as the *Diagonal* was one of the most difficult to date. The DC-2s labored at near their operational ceilings over much of the route. This was an era when, in the United States, flights were usually flown at around 5,000 feet. The *altiplano* was at more than twice that altitude, and pilots reporting for duty in La Paz, Bolivia, were thus at twice their normal cruising altitude while still sitting on the runway. Bolivian cruising altitudes were at 16,000 feet to ensure clearance of the mountainous terrain. Not surprisingly, payloads were low, and made lower still by use of a safety practice that required that each flight carry more fuel than was necessary for the trip.

"Our one-in-a-million airport engineer, William Pepper, hacked out most of the landing areas on the *altiplano* by inveigling bands of natives to work from sunrise to sunset for little compensation," Frank Havelick recalled.

"During the first days of building the Villazón field, at more than 13,000 feet above sea level, Pepper heard that the Bolivian national boxing champion was due in town, but his challenger had not shown up. Thirty minutes before starting time, with ringside and the entire building filled up, the promoter announced that he would welcome anyone willing to go a few rounds with the champ.

"Well, Bill, a one-time swimmer who had represented Holland in the Olympics, decided to give it a try. He stripped to his trousers, donned boxing gloves, and, despite his fatigue from the day's work at the landing field and the rarified atmosphere, knocked out the champion in three rounds and was carried back to his hotel on the backs of a mob of cheering Guaraní natives."

Loyal Domning recalled a new safety feature of the DC-2, which was to prove useful on the *altiplano*: "The DC-2 was able to jettison excess fuel to lighten the airplane in the event of engine failure," he said. "This made possible the carrying of somewhat improved payloads, since the weight of the airplane at takeoff could be increased by a predetermined proportion of the dumpable fuel weight. Thus, in the event of an engine failure, the pilot could dump enough fuel to allow him to continue on to the nearest airfield."

Panagra continued its penetration of the Argentine market. The

Diagonal route was beefed up to two flights each way each week. On August 10, a Panagra DC-2 carried President Justo and the Argentine war minister from Buenos Aires to Córdoba for the opening of the Argentine air force aviation school. It might have been the same DC-2 which crashed at San Luis, Argentina, just 13 days later, killing pilot Joe Pursley and his copilot, Frank deCesare. This was the first crash of a DC-2 for Panagra. There would be others.

In early June 1937 two Panagra pilots participated in a huge land and sea search for a missing Chilean aircraft. "LAN-Chile operated a service from Puerto Montt to Punta Arenas, using two Sikorsky S-43s amphibians," Fritz Sterling recalled. "These usually flew under the clouds and just above the water. In May, one of the planes had been forced down, slid up a beach and into a tree, and had a wing tip damaged. Now the other was missing.

"I picked up P-25, our Sikorsky S-38, in Buenos Aires and flew it to Santiago, having to huff and puff to get it up to 14,000 feet to cross over *El Cristo* (Uspallata Pass)," Sterling recalled. Sterling spent several days searching, helping to recover one body. Another body and some bits of debris were all that turned up. "An officer of LAN told me that the Chilean government had wanted to decorate the two Panagra pilots who had helped," Sterling recalled. "but the decoration had been taken over by an official in New York."

Nineteen thirty-seven was a year of flux, with Panagra changing parts or all of its schedule ten times, as longer-range aircraft came on line and as new stops were added and old stops discontinued. Because Panagra's was such a linear route, a change of one stop could throw the entire system off, and small discrepancies in timing or passenger load at one end could multiply into large problems at the other.

Christ the Redeemer statue, Cordillera de los Andes.

Panagra's Santiago to Buenos Aires flight map highlights the Christ of the Andes (Christ the Redeemer) statue in its insert.

On July 23, 1937, Panagra began to carry U.S. mail on the *Diagonal* route across Bolivia and northern Argentina to Córdoba, for Buenos Aires.

Competition along the high route was heating up as major powers sought to tap the rich mineral and agricultural interiors of Bolivia and northern Argentina. A U.S. Government report from 1935 states that:

> . . . French and German companies were strong and offering stiff competition to Pan American Airways on the west coast [of South America]. In the latent industrial wealth of Bolivia and the agricultural resources of northern Argentina there was a lucrative reward for the first venturers. German interests planned an enlargement of their services into this interior section of South America. Also, a service westward from Brazil to Bolivia was considered. This threat from foreign sources gave added incentive to Panagra's diagonal route.
>
> When the Interdepartmental Committee on Aviation at Washington considered a United States air mail service which would branch to Buenos Aires, Panagra then proposed an extension of the Arica-Uyuni route to Buenos Aires by way of Córdoba. The new route was granted a mail contract . . .

Considering this document in light of what was happening in Europe, we see that, while still officially neutral towards the rise of Hitler, behind the scenes American officials were already taking steps to block fascist and other European expansion into South America, and they were using North American companies as front-line troops. Note, too, the U.S. Government's reference to the French and Germans as "foreigners" in South America. The philosophy of the Monroe Doctrine was still prevalent. South America was reserved for United States companies and interests. The governments of South America, as we shall see, had very different ideas about this.

Meanwhile Harris, in Lima, and his associates in Miami and New York, were facing new difficulties. Gone were the problems of securing landing rights, of finding qualified pilots, of buying enough equipment.

Now they had to learn to control their creation, which was growing faster than anyone had expected. New problems—large passenger loads, complex schedules, great quantities of baggage, the burgeoning air freight business—all these needed solutions. Gone, even, was the trepidation of the average first-time passenger. Flying was glamorous; flying was what the movie stars and government officials did. Even the rudest *campesino*, boarding a Panagra DC-2 at La Paz, knew *something* about aircraft, having seen them in the movies, and he probably knew something about Panagra! In fact the word *Panagra* became such a synonym for *high* that Peruvians called the balcony seats at the theater "the Panagra seats."

On December 13, 1937, the first of the new breed of DC-3s went into service, flying the Lima-Buenos Aires air mail schedule. It is doubtful if anyone at the time had any idea of what the DC-3 was to mean to Panagra, to Douglas Aircraft, or to the world. A DC-3 looked like a slightly larger version of a DC-2. It seated two passengers on the right side and one on the left, as opposed to the DC-2's single seating on each side of the aisle. Thus, with seven rows of seats, it carried 21 passengers, seven more than the DC-2. Later versions, with other airlines, carried even more passengers, with two seats on each side.

It also had greater range, higher operating ceilings (though this depended quite a bit on which engines the particular aircraft was fitted with; Panagra was to use three configurations), and it flew faster. Despite its similar appearance, the DC-3 was more than a bigger version of the DC-2. It was the first universally popular commercial aircraft, flying more people, for more airlines, in more countries than ever before. The DC-3 never seemed to run out of miles; it is the oldest commercial aircraft still in use for commercial flights today, flown by pilots who are the sons and grandsons of the first DC-3 pilots. It has never been grounded by any certificating authority for any mechanical or constructional defect or shortcoming. With a full load, with all of the passengers paying full fare, it could, for the first time in the history of air transportation aircraft, make a profit without subsidy.

"Panagra was always in the forefront in terms of pushing for bigger, faster, and more reliable airplanes," Loyal Domning recalled. "Its association with Pan American was an important factor, as Pan Am was one of the most demanding customers of airplane and engine manufacturers. The flagship of Panagra's fleet until late 1946 was the DC-3A, twenty-six of them, powered by twin Pratt & Whitney R-1830-92 engines developing 1,200 horsepower. The airframe and engines combined to produce an efficient and reliable airplane."

The DC-3 was both the solution of Panagra's passenger-load and scheduling problems, and by raising the stakes in the game, the source of further problems. The next few years would determine whether Panagra could keep up with South America's demand for air transport. New routes, more airports, more personnel, and more operations and planning capability would be part of it. However, the good mix of aircraft that Panagra had always maintained would also give it the flexibility to meet any challenge. The DC-3 would play a large part in that flexibility.

A Panagra DC-3 at Arequipa, Peru. Mt. Misti, an active volcano, dominates the landscape in the background. Also in the background is a smaller plane belonging to Faucett Airlines. Faucett still operates in Peru today.

A Pratt & Whitney R-2800 engine being loaded for shipment to a maintenance facility.

CHAPTER 6

AIR FREIGHT

Aviation was probably no more than a week old when the idea of using aircraft to haul freight first occurred to someone. Indeed, if you consider the mail as freight, then hauling goods, not people, was the early economic backbone of the aviation industry.

Air freight created whole new industries. Perishable fruit and plants could be rushed to new markets. Drugs, antibiotics, and vaccines could be rushed to regions suffering from disease outbreaks. Panagra once flew over a million wasps from Peru to Louisiana to fight an infestation of the cane borer. The wasp shipment was especially satisfying for an airline which had originated as a crop-dusting outfit with a former Louisiana parish agent for a chief entomologist.

There were four kinds of air freight: First were shipments of low-weight, high-value goods. Mail was thus the first air freight commonly transported. (We're taking liberties with our definitions here; mail was always considered, by the airlines, as a separate category from freight and passengers.) Second came emergency shipments which would normally be moved by cheaper means, but which, because of some urgency, needed to reach their destinations as quickly as possible. Typical examples of this were medications, or heavy machinery and spare parts sent to relieve some plant breakdown. Panagra sometimes carried such shipments on its regularly-scheduled passenger flights. Third were loads of heavy, low-value, bulk goods where no other way existed to transport them. Such shipments often had little to do with economics. LAB, in Bolivia, for years carried salt, beef, rubber, etc. Although such shipments could sometimes be carried as "stand-by" or "fill-in" cargo on flights already scheduled, the low value of the material usually did not justify the high freight costs. Most of such traffic was subsidized by local governments for reasons of their own. The fourth type of air freight was the occasional shipment of bulk cargo to remote points inaccessible by other means of transportation, or which could be reached by other means of transportation only with great difficulty. This type of air freight sometimes required extensive modification of aircraft and different procedures for loading, flying, and maintenance.

Starting in 1933, Panagra carried out a number of these special flights. These jobs were handled under separate contract, using case-by-case aviation technology. Sometimes the areas served were so remote that Panagra personnel would first have to go in and build airstrips. In the course of these early contracts, Panagra learned how to set up the logistics for an operation, how to load and unload aircraft swiftly so as to fly the most flights per day, and even how to modify aircraft structurally to suit the current need. Along the way, the pilots became experienced in rough-field landings and nasty weather surprises.

Harris first saw the possibility of heavy equipment transport in 1932, when he spoke to representatives of the A&F Wiese, S.A. mining company. Wiese had a subsidiary, *Compañía Explotadora Cotabamas, S.A.*, whose mission was to rework some old gold mines and tailings in the Huanacopampa, Peru region. The mines had been known from Inca times, but had been "worked out" by humans with pickaxes. *Compañía Explotadora Cotabamas* now proposed to resume mining by using modern machinery.

The mine site was near Cochasayhuas, deep in the Andes, about 300 miles southeast of Lima. The site was extremely remote. As Fritz Sterling recalled: "There was a railroad from Arequipa to Cuzco, but between Cuzco and the mine lay the Apurimac Canyon, 10,000 feet deep with only a switchback trail going up and down. Transport of heavy machinery would have been impossible, and building a railroad from Arequipa, 250 miles away, so as to avoid the canyon, was too costly. The only answer was to carry the freight by air."

In June of 1933, Panagra carried out an airlift of fifty-five tons of hydroelectric power-generating machinery, water wheels, generators, switchboards, and transformers. A Ford Tri-Motor, the *Santa Rosa* (P-8), did this work, with Tommy Jardine flying it from the 10,900-foot-high airfield at Cuzco to Huanacopampa, the nearest small town to the mining site at Cochasayhuas. The Ford had to fly over a 15,000-foot mountain range to make the deliveries, and all parcels had to be cut down to two tons or less.

A problem with larger-sized pieces still remained, and when Panagra contracted with the mine owners for further, more extensive, air transportation of mining machinery, Harris decided to modify one of the Fords by cutting away much of its roof.

"The Ford Airplane Company said that it could not be done," Sterling recalled, "but Ken Hawkins, Panagra's chief engineer, maintained that it was possible.

"Panagra bought a used Ford from TWA, which was phasing them out," Sterling continued. "I understand the price was $5,000."

The aircraft, newly-named the *San Fernando* (P-27), was rebuilt as a freighter by Panagra mechanics from the Lima machine shops. On this project Hawkins was advised by Brad Young, an aeronautical engineer hired by Panagra. In the process, the aircraft lost its U.S. licenses and was registered under Peruvian laws as aircraft number OA-AAA.

"An opening nine and a half feet long by four feet wide was cut into the cabin roof above where the passengers would normally have sat," Harris recalled. "This required considerable engineering skill in redesigning the longitudinal strength of the fuselage because of the unusual length of the open area and the important problem of balance in flight

Loading a Ford Tri-Motor for its first freight contract (Cuzco-Huanacopampa, Peru). The manufacturer said cutting the roof away would ruin the aircraft, but Panagra engineers reinforced the top to allow for the 4' by 9' removable panel. As a result, the San Fernando *(P-27) had a stronger airframe than the original design.*

with the concentrated loads that were planned." Hawkins and Young also had to take into account some unusual flight stresses caused by the high swirling winds at the minimum 15,000-foot-plus altitudes at which the aircraft would be flying.

"As it turned out," Sterling recalled, "the work actually strengthened the back, which had been a weak point with Fords."

Tommy Jardine, who had flown the earlier flights and who was familiar with the terrain and the route, was assigned the job as pilot, with C.H. Pursley, another pilot, as radio operator. Harris paid special attention to his choice of mechanics; this aircraft would have to be babied throughout the performance of the contract—it wasn't as though he could send in a replacement and take the *San Fernando* down for some leisurely maintenance—and services and conditions on the ground at Huanacopampa were minimal. Senior mechanic was to be

Richard Ewing. Two Peruvians, M. Vargas and J. Sosa, were assigned as junior mechanics.

Harris was also concerned about the weather. The pilots would be flying off the usual routes and into an area where rapidly-changing weather could mean trouble. Some of Panagra's precious few radio sets were sent along to Cuzco and to Huanacopampa. This arrangement worked out very well, and weather never proved too much of a problem.

There was an additional benefit. "The radio permitted the pilot to be in continual contact about the weather conditions, thus insuring the success of each flight," Harris recalled. "It also allowed him to stay in contact with the Lima headquarters and with other planes flying on scheduled routes. I anticipated that the plane crew would feel rather isolated, flying above the center of the mighty Andes, so far from the regular airways, but thanks to the radio, such was not the case."

Or so Harris thought.

Although radio had already begun to be a standard item in directing passenger flights, this was, as far as Harris knew, the first use of radio for overseeing freight operations.

Jardine started the special flights on August 4, 1934, with Fritz Sterling and Haynesworth Lesesne taking over from him on August 17 and continuing to the end of the project on October 31, 1934.

Wishing to complete the flights before the start of the rainy season, Harris asked Byron "By" Rickards to assist. Flying a second, unmodified Ford (P-22), Rickards joined Sterling on September 25 and carried whatever machinery parts which could be passed through the passenger door.

Total machinery lifted, both for the mining site itself and for the associated hydraulic power plant, amounted to over 815 metric tons. The average flight was about one hour in duration, an air distance of 85 miles, but loading and unloading took so long that Jardine and Sterling were lucky to do four flights a day.

With careful planning this was extended to five or six trips a day. Sterling recalled that on September 18 he flew seven. Harris described the set-up:

"Marks were made on the ground, at which the plane would stop upon arrival. Additional marks were placed under the loading boom in such a position that, when the wheels of the plane were on these marks, the opening in the back of the plane would be directly under the suspended cargo already slung in the tackle from the boom.

"The plane was pulled into the designated position, working platforms were placed on either side, and the hatch cover removed, after which the cargo would be lowered into the plane or taken out. The loading usually consisted of at least two large pieces and a number of smaller ones. While the load was being secured inside the plane, the top was replaced and secured, and the loading platforms removed. When loaded, the plane was pushed clear of the hoist, guy wires, etc., before the engines were started.

"On landing at Huanacopampa a similar procedure for placing the plane under the hoist was followed. While some men were placing the working platforms in position and removing the top cover, others were removing the chains that secured the cargo."

In addition to the cargo, nearly fifty employees of the mining company traveled as passengers. The trip would have taken a week on the ground.

The pilots were evidently more ambitious than even Harris knew. "In order to cut down the plane weight so as to carry more cargo," Sterling admitted later, "the radio was removed, and we flew without co-pilots. The routine was a real bruiser; it meant getting up well before dawn and working twelve to fourteen hours a day, seven days a week. When By Rickards came up, he said, 'Captain Harris sent word to take it a little easier.' We then held it down to four or five trips each day."

"These flights were loaded to the hilt, and an engine failure might have been a disaster," Sterling added. Jardine had tested the Fords a year earlier on this route, determining that with a full load, and with one of the three engines shut down, he could still operate safely over the entire route.

Sterling's experience was far different, perhaps because of the added weight, perhaps because of the modified aircraft. "I once tried throttling back the center engine on a fully-loaded plane," he recalled, "and found that I had a steady rate of descent of 400 feet per minute. Fortunately, during my 243 round trips, I had engine trouble on only one flight, and that was on the return to Cuzco with an empty plane."

At the end of the contract, Harris recalled, the local indian population was so delighted that they put on a fiesta for the Panagra crews, complete with gifts of coca, slingshots, ponchos, pottery, and one large black ram, which flew back to Lima with everyone else.

There were other, smaller jobs that Jardine recalled only as brief logbook notes. Even his brief notes reveal some of the difficulties of air freight operations in the hinterlands:

> Nov. 16-27, 1934. In three trips, flew the heavy cargo Ford with five and a half tons of machinery from Cajamarca to Chachapoyas. Had to go to 14,000 feet to get over the tops of the two mountain ranges that encircled the valley of the Marañón River. Flew the first trip before the field was completed. One-way, into the mountains.

> Jan 17, 1935. Special, Ford OA-AAD. Lima to Huancayo and return. Chris Evans of IPECO was on return trip. Earthquake that A.M. and Evans got to British American Hospital and walked

through hole in hospital room to see wife and new baby about one hour after leaving Huancayo.

March 11, 1937. Ford OA-AAD. Arequipa to Alpacay and return. Landing area for gold field on side of mountain. Made a number of trips early as could operate only in early A.M. due winds.

Sept 1-7, 1937. La Paz to Tipuani. Aramayo Mining Co. As weather permits. La Paz at 13,000 feet, Tipuani at 3,000 feet in jungle.

Loyal Domning had vivid memories of the Tipuani "airport":

Tipuani was the one reasonably convenient access to a gold mine owned by the Aramayo Mining Company of La Paz, Bolivia. The mine lay at the bottom of a narrow gorge less than 100 miles north of La Paz. To reach it by land took about a week in good weather, but an airplane could make it in less than an hour, weather permitting.

First, there was the takeoff, a long slowly accelerating roll down the sloping two-and-a-half-mile La Paz runway perched on the edge of the *altiplano* at 13,434 feet above sea level. Then came the climb to 17,000 feet and threading the pass along the southeast side of 21,000 foot Huayna Potosí. Once in the clear on the north side of the *cordillera*, the pilot reduced power to descend at 150 miles per hour for exactly twelve minutes. This would put him in sight of his destination if there were not too many clouds.

The Tipuani Canyon and its river ran in a roughly southeasterly direction between two ridges some 1,000 higher. About a mile to the northwest another canyon paralleled it. The approach to land began by flying northwesterly along the second canyon until reaching a low saddle which permitted a left turn to enter Tipuani Canyon. Here the pilot lowered his landing gear and began to extend the flaps. He could still not see the landing strip. In a minute or so the plane crossed a ridge and the field was in sight, but well below. The pilot then extended full flaps and reduced power to a near glide. Yet he could still not see the entire "runway" as it had a dog-leg bend to the right a few hundred yards from the threshold. A firm touchdown and equally firm application of the brakes completed the arrival.

The departure was nearly as interesting. Not until full power had been applied and quite a bit of speed built up could the pilot see around the big rocks at the bend. Then the necessary turn was made. As a precaution, a signalman was sent down to warn of stray animals or people on the runway. Safety margins were tight; the pilots were alert, and few chances were taken.

In spite of its absolute non-conformity to any criteria for airport suitability, few accidents occurred at Tipuani. However, one was fatal. Brake failure of a Ford Tri-Motor (not one of Panagra's planes) caused the landing plane to swerve into the rocks at the dog-leg and the cargo of pipe ripped through the cockpit.

From June 28 to August 26 of 1936, Panagra carried 350 metric tons of heavy mining equipment to northern Peru for the Sindicato Minero Parcoy. This required 76 hours of flying between August 30 and September 13 from Huamachuco, where the equipment was staged, to Piaz, where the flight was unloaded, then back. Even Huamachuco was pretty remote; its sole claim to fame was that it was at the end of the hard road, and as far into the mountains as a heavy truck could be driven.

Charles Haynesworth Lesesne and Frederick "Fritz" Thorne Sterling were both hired in 1934. Lesesne was just two years out of Air Corps flying school and had just completed his duty with the government. Lesesne rejoined the Air Corps for World War II and left flying at the end of the war.

Frederick T. "Fritz" Sterling had been a pilot for Isthmian Airways (which flew between Cristóbal and Panama City—a distance of 50 miles—and claimed to be the fastest transcontinental airline in the Americas) when Harris talked him into joining Panagra. After taking part in the air freight mining operation, Sterling moved to Santiago, Chile, and made hundreds of crossings of the Andean *cordillera* between Santiago and Buenos Aires. Moving back to Lima, Peru, in the early forties, he acted as operations manager for a time before moving permanently to Miami in 1947.

The newcomers were assigned to relieve Tommy Jardine and By Rickards on the Ford Tri-Motor freight operation to the gold mines in the high Andes.

"Living at Huamachuco was bare bones camping," Lesesne recalled. "Our only shower was a 10-quart bucket with nail holes in the bottom and cold water. I don't have a record of the number of showers, but we didn't shave...."

The landing field at Piaz was nothing more than an ancient river bed, at about 6,000 feet altitude. Lesesne flew the assignment in the *San Fernando* (P-27).

"The trip east was over an intervening ridge at some 12,000 feet altitude, then down to the 6,000-foot elevation dry river bed designated the 'Piaz Terminal,'" Lesesne noted in his log.

For this contract, too, portable radio stations were installed, one each at Huamachuco and Piaz, to keep pilots apprised of current weather conditions.

"It was usually calm early in the day, but later, severe turbulence and wind shifts would force a halt to flying," Lesesne recalled. "We

Captain C. H. Lesesne photographed the landing field at Huamachuco, Peru in August 1936. The field, on the sand bar in the middle distance, was the pickup point for heavy mining equipment bound for Piaz, Peru.

didn't use the term 'wind shear' then, but we knew what it was, all right. At Piaz the wind would sometimes seem to come in from the left valley, impinge against the steep slope on the right, and divide up and down the river. You could come in with power, have it drop out, and finish the landing roll with a tail wind." Lesesne doesn't mention it, but his logbook indicates that on at least one occasion he simply couldn't land at Piaz and returned to Huamachuco loaded. Even on that day, however, he made five successful round-trips; on better days he made as many as nine.

One advantage of the confusing wind at Piaz was that it took the pilot's mind off the landing surface itself: "It was all rock and gravel," Lesesne recalled. "Some of which was inevitably kicked back against the tail section."

Lesesne had had an earlier experience with a Peruvian gold shipment. The previous year he had casually signed for a 6-inch by 6-inch by 12-inch wooden box at the airport in Nazca. "Here was this little wooden box with a heavy manila rope for a handle," he recalled. "I went to snatch it up like a shoe box and it nearly flipped me on my duff." This is hardly surprising; a quarter of a cubic foot of gold would weigh more than 300 pounds.

The gold shipments came from the Aramayo Mining Company. "After Panagra completed its freight contract with Aramayo," Frank Havelick recalled, "they organized their own flight operations division. The hired a pilot, Bill Wincapaw, who was known as 'the flying Santa

Claus of New England,' to operate a company-owned Ford Tri-Motor, which Aramayo had bought from Panagra."

By 1937, when the DC-3s began to arrive, Panagra had solid experience in heavy freight hauling. Other contracts, other adventures lay in the future, especially the effort at Shell Mera in 1942. But no longer did anyone wonder if heavy machinery hauling was *possible* in these mountains. The only questions now would be which aircraft to use, how to juggle other schedules to accommodate the temporary contracts, how to fit the extra flights into the personnel roster, and how to improvise a host of other unorthodox procedures.

A Panagra DC-3 at La Paz, Bolivia, in the early 1940s. The fact that the door opens on the right side identifies this as an aircraft that came to us from American Airlines.

CHAPTER 7

THE DC-3s: 1938-1940

1938

In Argentina the new aircraft ironically resulted in temporarily re-duced service. The DC-3 could carry more passengers, but it had to *have* more passengers to carry or it would not be operating at maximum fis-cal efficiency. Starting in April, 1938, Harris ordered the Monday, Tues-day, and Thursday flights between Buenos Aires and Santiago to be changed to one flight, on Sunday, from Buenos Aires to Santiago, with the return flight, Santiago-Buenos Aires, the next day. On June 15 the Montevideo passenger service was discontinued because Pan Am man-agement felt it was competing too directly with its own operations.

The Montevideo route had been flown with an S-38 since the day, a few years earlier, when the Buenos Aires chief mechanic, a man named Sibbetts, had been told to "survey" the old Loening amphibian with which Panagra used to take mail across the Río de la Plata. Sibbetts, the story goes, was an old Navy man, and to him a "survey" meant to remove the engine and anything else usable, and burn the rest. This he did, before anyone could stop him. Another version of the story has Sibbetts complaining so frequently to New York about the maintenance problems with the Loening and the lack of parts that some wag in New York finally sent a telegram ordering Sibbetts to burn the damn thing, little realizing that Sibbetts would take the order seriously.

On June 19 Captain Don Sheets, copilot Bob Supple, and a radio operator took off from Santiago in P-30, a DC-2. They were bound for Lima with an empty plane, and as they climbed to cruising altitude a heavy cloud layer built up. They climbed higher, until they had reached the operational limit of the aircraft, without breaking out of the clouds. They reported all this in radio transmissions back to Santiago, and also noted that, as their route took them along the coast-line, well away from the mountains, they would continue on toward Arica, where clear weather was reported. They never transmitted again and never arrived in Arica. Search planes combed the Atacama desert; amphibians searched the offshore waters, to no avail.

Some three years later the aircraft was found by an Indian sheepherder, high on the slope of Cerro Amarillo, a 23,000-foot peak on the Chilean-Argentine border north of Santiago. The sheepherder had driven his flock into the Andes from the Argentine side. When he came down on the Chilean side he was wearing a blue pilot's jacket. Suspicious police questioned him, but he refused to talk. So they followed him when he left town, and located the DC-2 just emerging from the base of a glacier.

Experts who compared the aircraft's actual flight path to the planned one determined that the weather front must have contained southwesterly winds in excess of 250 mph, winds which blew the DC-2 sideways and far off the safe course. Sheets and Supple, of course, had no way of knowing, given the primitive state of navigation of the time, that they were drifting so far sideways.

Frank Havelick remembered Sheets well. The two men had been in the same military "pursuit squadron" in earlier years. Havelick went to China, and Sheets went to Panagra. The two didn't meet again until Havelick came to Panagra after the operations of China National Airlines were severely curtailed by the Japanese.

"Sheets was tall and gangly," Havelick recalled. "He was a great lover of things Argentine. He bought himself a whole gaucho outfit. It had to be made especially for him; I mean he couldn't buy anything off the rack.

"Now the gaucho attire consists of a shirt, a bandana, loose jacket, wide leather belt studded with silver ornaments, and the knife which they use during their meals. Then there were the pants, the *bombachas*, which looked like plus-fours. They were very loose, very voluminous, designed to give complete freedom in the saddle or squatting by a campfire. Then came the "accordion" boots of leather soft as a glove, with creases from the top to the ankles. Then there were silver spurs for the boots.

"Don loved his outfit so much that he would bring it with him, wear it off-duty wherever he was, be it Buenos Aires, or Santiago, or Lima. He would dress up and go walking in the streets with his baggy pants, jacket, and boots. If there was any wind up, he looked like a ship under full sail."

On July 10 the northern route switched over completely from the amphibians to the DC-2s and DC-3s, and the route was changed to pass again through Cali, Colombia. Buenaventura and Tumaco, the seaport towns on the Pacific coast that had sheltered passing S-38 and S-43s amphibians for so long, were discontinued as stops.

When H. R. Harris was transferred to corporate headquarters in New York in 1938, a balancing appointment from W. R. Grace was needed to replace him. Doug Campbell, who had recently arranged the Colombian landing rights for Panagra, was appointed vice president for operations, with offices in Lima.

Expansion into the interior, and up onto the *altiplano*, continued. By October there was twice-weekly shuttle service between La Paz, Bolivia, and Arequipa, Peru. By December, the *Diagonal* route terminus had switched to Arica, as Harris continued to re-arrange schedules to provide more frequent La Paz-west coast service with the DC-2s.

The switch to land-based aircraft brought Quito, Ecuador, back into the picture. When the big S-43s used to bank left around the western terminus of La Puntilla, float in over Puná island, and alight in the estuary at Guayaquil, poor Quito, national capital or not, had been serviced by feeder flights. Now it was on the main route, and weekly service into Quito was inaugurated on November 19, 1938.

1939

On January 25, 1939, an earthquake smashed Bío-Bío province, in south-central Chile, killing 30,000 people. For the next two weeks Panagra aircraft flew victims out of the inland city of Chillán and the coastal city of Concepción to hospitals in Santiago. In all, some 700 casualties were transported by Douglas and Ford aircraft.

"I flew a DC-2 with injured from Chillán to Santiago," Fritz Sterling recalled. "On the way back I brought supplies. Concepción had no airport, so we used a farm field that a Ford could get into and out of. I switched from the DC-2 to P-9, a Ford Tri-Motor and flew to Concepción. The next several days, until February 8th, we carried injured out of Concepción and ferried in emergency supplies. I would make two trips to Chillán, where a DC-2 would take the people on to Santiago. Warren B. Smith flew the DC-2, and he had stripped the seats out of it. He took 22 people at a time, eight more than the normal 14-passenger load."

On March 18 Tommy Kirkland, the Panagra operations manager, and eight Panagra pilots were decorated by a grateful Chilean government. Among the pilots honored were Chief Pilot Charles Robert Disher, Harry Colliver, Warren B. Smith, and Fritz Sterling. The pilots were made officers of Chile's Orden de Mérito. Kirkland was made a commander of the order.

"Thomas Jefferson Kirkland, a graduate of the Naval Academy and a naval aviator, joined Panagra in 1931 as a pi-

Thomas J. Kirkland. As an early pilot with Panagra, Kirkland flew S-38s from Panama to Buenaventura, Colombia.

lot," Loyal Domning recalled. "His managerial talents took him out of the airplanes and into operational management in a short time. He was made a vice-president in 1942, and shortly thereafter returned to the Navy for the duration of the war. Coming back to Panagra after the war, he continued to supervise its operational growth until the Braniff merger.

"Bob Disher came to Panagra in 1932 and became chief pilot in 1937," Domning recalled. In fact, Charles Robert Disher had been an Army Air Corps pilot in Panama who watched wistfully as the Panagra flying boats lifted off and headed south. He quit the service to join Panagra.

"Disher succeeded Tom Kirkland as operations manager when Kirkland was

Chief Pilot Charles Robert Disher.

appointed vice-president in 1942," Domning recalled. "When Panagra began a military cargo service from Miami, Bob transferred there from Lima to manage that operation. He retired in 1950 for medical reasons."

Harry "Pop" Colliver also came to Panagra in 1931, in company with Red Smalling and Ken Hawkins. He was more than a hero to the Chileans; his abilities to eat and sleep were legendary among the Panagra copilots.

Frank Achilles, in particular, hated it when Colliver first ate his meal back in the passenger cabin, then went straight to sleep. Since regulations required one pilot to be "on duty" if the other was either eating or sleeping, and since those same regulations forbade eating and flying at the same time, Achilles had a hard time getting anything to eat.

Achilles waited until the perfect flight, and it soon came. There was only a single passenger aboard, a regular courier who was well-known to the pilots. Achilles waited until Colliver was fast asleep in a seat in the cabin, then switched the engines over to run off a gas tank which was nearly empty. Then he put the aircraft on autopilot, tiptoed to the rear to explain things to the courier, sat in a seat across the aisle from Colliver, and feigned sleep. There was no danger, Achilles explained to the courier, who agreed to the game.

In a few minutes the engines began to sputter and complain. Colliver, who like any long-time pilot slept with one ear cocked to the sound of his engines, woke with a start, saw Achilles apparently fast asleep next to him and stampeded to the cockpit to take charge.

The joke backfired when Colliver took to eating and then sleeping in the cockpit, without moving from his seat. He was a large man, well-known to pilots who had to share hotel rooms with him as "old thunder-guts." Achilles began quietly switching on the autopilot, then slowly turning the nose up more and more with the trim tabs. Of course, the autopilot would compensate to keep the aircraft flying straight and level. Eventually, Colliver would wake up, take over from Achilles, notice that the autopilot was on, and reach to switch it off. When he did so, he would release all of that pent-up energy, and the yoke would slam back into his belly.

One reason Panagra was able to maintain its stature and reputation as long as it did in the face of pressure for national airlines in South America was the enormous good will engendered among the populace by actions such as the swift aid to the earthquake victims of Bio-Bio. In any emergency the governments and people alike knew that Panagra would be there as soon as it was possible for pilots like Colliver and Achilles to make a landing. Panagra aircraft and pilots would work non-stop as long as their help was needed. There wasn't even a hint that anyone should pay for it. In a remote town in proud and sensitive South America, the sight of a *gringo* pilot, with a week's stubble on his chin, throwing himself flat on the ground under his wing to catch a few winks of sleep, and then climbing wearily into the cockpit to haul out yet another plane load of injured, was worth a thousand pious pronouncements from Washington.

While overnighting in La Serena, Chile, Ernie Hummel remembers being awakened in his hotel room by a violent earthquake. Hummel and his roommate, Dick Witt, flipped over face-down on their beds and grabbed the sides as the beds waltzed around the hotel room. Then they went to the airport to check on their DC-3. George Porter, the flight radio officer, had drawn the short straw and had slept in the airplane. Company policy required that one crew member stay with the aircraft in out-of-the-way places.

Porter was covered from head to toe in fine white powder. He had awakened to feel the DC-3 actually rolling around the airport. Thinking someone was trying to tow it somewhere, he opened the cabin door and leaped out, landing in a pile of fine white sea shell aggregate that the airport used to surface the runways.

On February 16, 1939, John MacGregor resigned (effective February 28) as Panagra vice president and general manager. MacGregor had been honored with the Chilean Orden de Mérito the previous October. Panagra had been run jointly, by MacGregor working in New York, and by Harris, as vice president and operations manager in Lima. This was the result of the informal agreement between Pan American World Airways and the W. R. Grace Company, the two co-owners of Panagra. Neither company wanted to see a president at Panagra who was the other company's "man." For its first ten years (February 21, 1929, to February 28, 1939), Panagra had operated without a president.

With MacGregor's resignation this position needed to be reconsidered. Pan Am, perhaps because its expansion down South America's east coast had been so successful, perhaps because ten years of reasonably amicable relations with W. R. Grace had given Juan Trippe more confidence, relented on the point. Harold J. Roig, a vice president at W. R. Grace, was named Panagra president.

Harold Harris might have been expected to bristle somewhat at this. After all, Panagra wasn't Roig's idea. But Harris was quick to credit Roig with the upcoming rapid expansion of the airline and specifically mentioned Roig's management success. The only thing Harris objected to was that the new arrangement required that he transfer to Panagra's New York office, which he did on March 1, 1939.

Panagra's new DC-3s were only a part of Pan Am's overall expansion and upgrading. The increased ranges of the land-based aircraft freed Pan Am's amphibians for other duties, one of which was the long over-water Florida-Panama connection between the two airlines. By April 4, Pan Am had a second weekly direct service between Miami and Cristóbal. Panagra's second Cristóbal-Quito weekly service started the very next day.

Meanwhile, Guayaquil, once home to those amphibians and the hub of air traffic in Ecuador, was languishing. Not only were the amphibians no longer calling at Ecuador's second city, but the airfield there was too short for DC-3s. On July 22, 1939, Panagra instituted shuttle service between Guayaquil and Quito, using a DC-2. By September the airfield had been lengthened and DC-3s were used thereafter. Indeed, for a short period (December 9, 1939, to January 31, 1940) the second weekly flight from Panama to Ecuador flew direct to Guayaquil, instead of Quito.

"In those days we operated three Wright Cyclone-powered DC-3s and four DC-2s," Loyal Domning recalled. Domning came to Lima by steamer in October, 1939, just in time to see the last Panagra S-38 amphibian sold to Gordon Barber of La Paz, Bolivia, and the last Ford Tri-Motor sold to the Aramayo Mines, also in Bolivia.

In this, the tenth year of Panagra's existence, Pan Am's Juan Trippe and Panagra's Harold Roig continued to look carefully at their precious mail contracts. On May 17 and 18 messages from President Roosevelt, commemorating the tenth anniversary of air mail service between the United States and South America, were delivered to the presidents of Colombia, Ecuador, Peru, and Chile.

Yet another public relations and marketing tool was a sales conference held in Lima in late July. Harold Roig flew down to preside, and Panagra representatives from almost all the South American offices attended. So, too, did officials of United Air Lines, Eastern Airlines, and American Airlines. Because of the importance of the conference, and because it was attended by representatives of so many airlines, this meeting went down in history as the first International Air Travel Conference, at least in the western hemisphere.

By the end of 1939, DC-3s were standard equipment on most routes, with the DC-2s filling in as needed and finding a good use in cargo operations. The last of Panagra's Ford Tri-Motors were sold in 1939.The amphibians had been turned over to Pan Am. Almost all of Panagra's routes were now predominantly over land, and all landing sites were land-based airports. The airline had shaken the "bugs" out of its routing and scheduling, had learned to work with the larger cockpit crews and the enhanced radio communications, and had done a good job of upgrading its people-and baggage-handling procedures to deal with the larger numbers of passengers.

Panagra had pretty much locked in the routes on the west coast of South America, parallelling Pan Am's near-monopoly along the east coast. Only the interior, and some Río-Buenos Aires-Europe routes remained significantly in the hands of other airlines. That the Pan Am and Panagra routes tended to connect towns along the coastline was a phenomenon reflective of the two airlines' original amphibian equipment, although in Panagra's case, only from Peru northward. Now that they had sorted out the internal difficulties caused by an almost explosive expansion program, Trippe, Roig, and Harris cast their eyes more and more to the continent's interior, where the use of radio equipment had proved valuable in the past. Now Panagra focused still more on safety equipment.

Enhancements to safety included better meteorological data and forecasting and increased use of "aerophares," today called radio beacons. These transmitted a coded signal in all directions. An aircraft could, with a loop antenna attached to a compass rose, determine the

A DC-3 parked at the airport of Santa Cruz, Bolivia.

direction, relative to its own flight path, of the RDF transmitter. Panagra pioneered the use of aerophares in South America. The airborne RDF receivers could also be set to any commercial radio station. They also, unfortunately, tended to home in on thunderstorms.

I was climbing up out of Panama one morning, and there were two tremendous build-ups, clouds that must have been 50,000-60,000 feet high. There was a clear spot between them and we just sailed right down in between them. I watched the two RDFs–we had duals–one needle turned to point at the cloud on the right, and the other slowly turned to point at the cloud on the left.

There were other problems with RDFs, not the least of which was that the commercial radio stations could decide to go off the air, or to start operating from another location but on the same frequency. A third possibility had not occurred to Panagra pilots until it nearly killed some of them: a DC-2 approaching Buenos Aires ran into dense fog just at the outskirts of town. The pilot and copilot tried to use their RDF receiver, but soon lost the signal from the airport. They changed the receiving coils in the machine and picked up a Buenos Aires radio station.

What the crew did not know was that this station also broadcast, on the same frequency, from a "repeater" antenna in Montevideo, Uruguay, 160 miles away. While the RDF tried to average out the signals to some central location, the pilot and copilot wasted considerable time trying to make sense of the erratic behavior of their equipment.

"When their gas ran low," Frank Havelick related, "the pilot elected to descend to sea-level over what he hoped was the sea. He had calculated that he was now somewhere out over the Río de la Plata estuary.

"The flight finally broke out of the fog just above the coffee-colored waves of the estuary, narrowly missing a steamer outbound from Buenos Aires. The engines were coughing from carburetor ice caused by the crew's attempts to 'run lean' in order to save gas.

"They headed west under a 100-foot ceiling, looking for land. The ceiling gradually rose to 500 feet and dead ahead appeared the lights of a large city. The crew was jubilant as they crossed the coastline, even though it soon became obvious that they were looking, not at Buenos Aires, but at the town of La Plata, just southwest of the Argentine capital.

"One minute after crossing the coastline, the engines coughed one last time and died. The pilot instantly turned the airplane completely around and headed back to a cornfield they had just passed. The copilot shot off two distress flares just before the pilot hopped the DC-2 over a fence and down onto the field, which turned out to be full of standing water. The main wheels sank to their axles instantly and the faithful DC-2 almost went up on its nose.

"Soon two-wheeled *carromatos* appeared from the surrounding farms, and their astonished drivers gladly transported the passengers and crew to the nearest highway where taxis were hired for the one-hour drive into Buenos Aires. The crew even remembered to bring along the precious mailbags. By the following day, the cornfield had drained, forming a reasonably solid base. The same crew pumped two drums of gas aboard the plane and took off from that field with no problem."

1940

"In 1939 and 1940," Douglas Campbell recalls, "we hired Jim Scholtz to establish our own meteorological forecasting, headquartered in Lima. We began in Santiago, then added observation stations as the routes expanded. We especially wanted to know, at first, what the weather was going to be like 'over the hill,' i.e., on the other side of the Andes mountains on the Santiago-Buenos Aires run. That was our main problem."

Another problem was Lima and its notorious fogs. "July and August are the worst months for those fogs," Campbell recalls. "We often had airplanes overnighting, unable to continue on. Or we'd have an airplane coming from the north that would have to overnight at Chiclayo or Trujillo. Planes coming from the south would sometimes have to stop at a place near Pisco, an emergency field where there was a hotel of sorts.

"At Lima, the radio beacon gave guidance in marginal weather. A pointer on the pilot's radio compass indicated the direction of the beacon from the aircraft. As the plane approached the station, the pointer wiggled straight ahead. As the plane passed overhead, the pointer swung around to point to the tail."

Cy Collins, who came to Panagra after years in various executive positions with W. R. Grace, was sometimes bemused by the Panagra pilots. The latter were far more casual than the sea-going people Collins had been accustomed to. On his first flight in an airplane, Collins was asked by Bill Sindo, the pilot, to take the wheel. Collins thought at the time that this flying business was all very easy. He admitted that later, when he found out how complicated flying really was. He admired the pilots the more, knowing by then that, even when they seemed most relaxed, most playful, a great many calculations and considerations were still going on in their heads. A good pilot in those days had an instinctive feeling for his position and for the status of his aircraft.

It was a good thing. The first DC-3s didn't fare very well in the high passes and over the *altiplano*. The engines were just not powerful enough to handle the altitude and still permit the aircraft to carry an economic load.

"The first of what was eventually a fleet of 26 DC-3A airplanes was put into service in May, 1940," Loyal Domning recalled. "The Wright-powered DC-3s were phased out as rapidly as they could be replaced with the new airplanes. The new DC-3A had much more powerful Pratt & Whitney engines, which resulted in higher speed and improved high performance, to say nothing of superior reliability. The older DC-3s were delivered to the Compañía Mexicana de Aviación."

Panagra bought a Stinson Reliant SR-10-F twin-cockpit trainer, equipped with a Pratt & Whitney R985 engine. Everyone had to qualify for an instrument rating, which they did on the Reliant or, later, on other equipment.

W. B. "Bill" Chamberlin recalled his instrument training first in a Link trainer that Panagra owned, then flying the Stinson with Lloyd R. "Dinty" Moore.

"Later, during our upgrading as copilots, we were required to qualify to fly the Stinson as safety pilot while Dinty had a trainee under the hood," Chamberlin said. "There was a full panel and set of controls behind the safety pilot, and Dinty sat in the back beside the trainee. For a period of several months while we were at that stage, Dick Witt and I were Dinty's favorite safety pilots, and if either of us was in Lima, Dinty wouldn't fly with any other. I probably had more time in the Stinson than any other pilot.

"Once during that period, all the radios failed in Pisco, Peru, and I had to take Ken Albright and Carol Busby down to Pisco in the Stinson to fix them. We had to stay under the overcast because there was no radio for a let-down, and about 30 miles south of Lima the clouds were on the ground, and we had to go out to sea. In 1947, the Stinson was sold to somebody in the Chiclayo area."

Charts were rudimentary. The Aeronautical Chart and Information Center in St. Louis, Missouri, had charts for some of the northern half of South America by 1938, but emphasized that the charts were being updated as fast as "newer and more adequate" information became available. The Center also implored pilots to supply such data. Even today, nautical and aeronautical charts carry such a standard message, but in 1938 one wondered if the chart was supplied to advise the pilot, or for the pilot to revise as he flew, for the benefit of those who would come after.

For most of South America in the early days, pilots relied upon their wits and whatever maps they could personally find. "In 1934," Fritz Sterling recalled, "I was told to 'obtain' a coastal chart of the northwest coast of South America, printed by the U.S. government and available in the Canal Zone. I got one, and then filled in the prominent inland landmarks with a pen.

"The situation farther south was better. The Argentine air force printed some very good maps, which I bought in Buenos Aires. Also, each of us had an Argentine railroad map. These showed all the railroads in the country and had an alphabetical list of all the stations with coordinates. Each station had a large lettered sign on the building, which could be read while passing over at 200 or 300 feet. There was quite a lot of flying with undercast conditions. All you needed to do, if you felt you were lost, was to drop down through a hole in the cloud cover, locate a railroad—and you couldn't go very far in Argentina without seeing one—then follow it to the next station.

Later things became more organized. "Topo" maps were obtained from various sources by SAGO and compiled into a fairly standardized form. But no aeronautical charts of the day had compass roses around the bigger airports, and all of them relied, ultimately, upon mapping techniques which were primitive by today's standards, even when carefully and properly carried out by skilled surveyors. In South America, the latter situation was, at best, improbable. A 1938 chart showing part of Peru just north of Lima blithely informs the user that a huge area of the Andes *cordillera* has, "Relief Data Incomplete." Many mountain peaks were marked as "position indefinite," or "height indefinite." This did not inconvenience a truck driver much; he had to follow the road anyway. But to an aircraft pilot, such areas could be a definite challenge of life-or-death proportions.

The pilot also had to have both an encyclopedic knowledge of the terrain over which he flew and the ability to acquire this knowledge quickly. Pilots could not only name every geographic feature they passed, but they *knew* that if they held to such-and-such a course for so many minutes, they would see a lake under the left wing, or a *hacienda,* or a road intersection.

"I remember flying with Dick Witt one time," Collins recalls. "It was a freight plane, and we were going from Lima to Santiago. I was sitting in the copilot's seat, looking out at the scenery, and I asked Dick the name of something down there, some little dried-up river-bed or something.

"It turned out that he could name absolutely every peak, every river bed, everything. I asked him where we would go if we lost both engines. He answered right away, 'We'd glide down and get into that little place over there.' Then I found out that this was only his second trip on this route, and his first as captain."

On another flight Collins himself did not do so well as acting captain.

"I was in Arequipa one day, and coming back to Lima, the captain, knowing that I could fly a DC-3 in the air, said to me, 'After we get up in the air, you come up and sit in the left seat, and I'll take a nap.' We took off from Arequipa, and he got us down over the mountains and over the ocean, and he said, 'You know what to do, and when the Lima aerophare comes on, you just call me, and I'll come up and we'll land it.'

"I was flying along in the left seat, with a young fellow I'd never met before sitting in the right seat.

"'Who are you?' I said.

"He introduced himself and added, 'This is my first flight.'

"I told him I'd been around for several years. We flew along, and after a while we turned on the RDF, and soon the little needle started to turn ever so slightly around. It seemed to be going very slowly, so we called the captain, and he came up rubbing his eyes, and said, 'Jesus Christ, where are you guys?'

"I said, 'I think we're over Lima because the little needle just went around, went around sort of slowly.' He looked out and said, 'Well, you guys are thirty miles out to sea.' Whereupon he called Limatambo and said that he had been looking at an emergency landing field that we had designated just south of Lima before we came on in. The tower said, 'O.K.,' and we went straight in to Lima, arriving only three or four minutes late."

Collins reports that another pilot liked to take brief side trips for sightseeing.

"We had a pilot, on loan from another airline, who was a tourist at heart. One day, coming into Arequipa, he decided to take a look at Misti, the volcano near Arequipa."

Arequipa is dominated by Misti, a volcano which is the center of three mountains just east of the resort city, the others being Mt. Chachani, to the north, and Mt. Pichu-Pichu, to the south. Misti was not active in those days, but another volcano just to the east, named Ubinas, was. The pilot headed for Ubinas.

"The captain went up to altitude and then over the rim and flew around *inside* the volcano. They were looking at a live volcano, spewing flames and smoke. His copilot, Panagra-trained, realized that they were over the single-engine ceiling of the DC-3, and he was nervous as hell. An engine failure just then would mean the aircraft would be unable to climb back out of the volcano.

"But the passengers just thought it was the greatest thing in the world. It was only when they wrote us letters, thanking us for the novel experience, that somebody interviewed the copilot and found out what had happened. Shortly after, that pilot was dispatched back to North America where, as far as I know, he never got into any trouble whatsoever."

Collins adds a disclaimer: "Although I believe my source for this story is impeccable, he is no longer alive to confirm it, and (then Chief Pilot) Frank Havelick insists the event never occurred."

War clouded the horizon at the start of 1940. The Germans had invaded Poland on September 1, 1939, and within weeks the conflict reached South America when British ships attacked the German battleship *Graf Spee*. It fled into the Río de la Plata, and into neutral Uruguayan waters, was bottled up by the British, and eventually scuttled by her crew. Clearly, the conflict was going to be worldwide and, clearly, South America was going to play some role in it.

In Washington, officials were especially upset by two additional factors, one an accident of geography, the other a fact of social history. First, Recife and Natal, Brazil, at the eastern tip of South America, were just 1,600 miles from the cities of Freetown and Dakar in French West Africa, just within the flying range of modern aircraft. Second, the Germans struck at France early in 1940 and Marshal Pétain, rejecting an offered union with England, established the Vichy government. Suddenly, French colonies in Africa were, administratively at least, in the hands of the Axis powers. The Germans could, in theory, ferry heavy aircraft to West Africa, and thence across the Atlantic to Brazil. From Brazil, of course, the aircraft could be sent up to Colombia, threatening the Panama Canal. The German and Italian air forces had maintained close ties with the South American air forces. Germany, in particular, supplied pilots for airlines in Bolivia and Colombia. It even had a subsidiary based in Peru and supplied aircraft to Bolivia's LAB and Argentina's Aeropostal. Condor introduced the first four-engined aircraft, the Focke Wulf Fw 200 Condor, into South America, late in 1939. Germany's airline Deutsche Lufthansa, also ran SEDTA in Ecuador and the Condor airline in Brazil, and Condor was already operating across the Atlantic.

Suddenly Billy Mitchell's old fears about German influence over the Panama Canal had resurfaced. Pan Am had originally been encouraged, even abetted, with generous mail contracts, to move into South America precisely to avoid this scenario.

To add to the danger, German equipment, in some instances, was far superior to that used by the Americans. "All trans-Andean flights at the time were made under visual conditions by both Panagra and Air France," Fritz Sterling recalled. But the German airline, Condor, which was a branch of Lufthansa, had sophisticated direction-finding equipment on Junkers-Ju 52/3m planes, and they carried out instrument operations over the Andes.

Even in the 1930s the Germans were much more advanced in the technique of instrument flying than we were. In both Santiago and Buenos Aires, their 'minimums' (the vertical clearance a pilot needed between the runway and any cloud cover) were 160 feet. Twenty years later, with ILS (Instrument Landing System) and other aids, we were still only at 400 feet.

"Flying westbound from Buenos Aires to Santiago, upon arrival in Mendoza, if either Air France or Panagra found that the other had canceled the flight across the Uspallata Pass to Santiago because of bad weather, they would do the same. Not so with one German pilot, whose name was Feuer. I don't believe he ever canceled, although on one flight he ran out of gas while on instruments and descended to land in a potato field near Valparaíso."

While planners in Washington mulled this over, Harris and Roig continued to work on Panagra's basic structure. On July 1 a third weekly service from Panama, down the length of the South American spine and across to the Río de la Plata and Buenos Aires, was established. That schedule was speeded up as part of an overall Pan Am rescheduling on September 1, 1940. Pan Am began operating "Strato Clippers" (Boeing 307 Stratoliners) over the Miami-Cristóbal run, reducing traveling time on that leg alone by six hours. Now a passenger could fly from New York to Buenos Aires in three and one-half days. Santiago was a three-day flight from New York; Lima two; and Cali, Colombia, just twenty-four hours.

Smaller towns now had airfields, making commercial stops possible as additional aircraft made more equipment available. On November 8 a fourth Guayaquil-Cristóbal service was instituted. This "milk-run" flew first to Salinas, just eighty miles away on La Puntilla, then up to Manta, about ninety miles and also on the coast, on to Esmeraldas, 150 miles, then inland to Cali, Colombia, about 330 miles, taking into account the jog needed to line up with the Cauca valley. From Cali it was another 520 miles to Cristóbal, on up the Cauca valley to the pass near Manizales, and thence northwest up the Panama coast.

The airstrip at Manta slanted away from the beach, and aircraft landing from offshore had to do a last-minute hop over the high dunes, then drop down onto the runway. At least, pilots didn't need to worry about rolling too long and going into the drink, when landing from the other direction. "That berm would stop you pretty quick," Charles Schultz recalled dryly.

In those days Guayaquil was typical of a medium-use airport, with a small terminal building that sported on its roof a one-man control tower hardly bigger than a telephone booth.

Something of a grudge-match once developed between the station agent at Guayaquil and a Panagra pilot. Thaddeus Luther Henry Young, known to one and all as "Ty," was approaching Guayaquil from Quito and was still about 50 miles out and at 10,000 feet when he heard an angry squawk on his CW radio. A DC-2 piloted by Don MacArthur had taken off, northbound, from Guayaquil just moments earlier. Each pilot had been assured that there was no conflicting traffic in the area.

Ty Young collared, literally, the station manager in the cafeteria, and the two had a serious discussion about air-traffic control.

But Young still wasn't satisfied. There was a flimsy barrier, no more than a 1x8-inch board painted white, across one end of the field, but a short distance away. Young, who liked to fly in low anyway, took to knocking the barrier down with his landing gear every time he flew into Guayaquil. "Young would do just about anything to get the manager's goat," one pilot recalled.

Panagra was adding more runs to existing routes to increase frequency of service. On December 2 a fourth weekly service was added between Santiago and Buenos Aires.

Two days after Christmas, Thomas Kirkland, operations manager, was elected a vice president of the airline at a board of directors meeting in New York. He was to play a role in Panagra's fastest expansion yet; in the United States, defense planners had finally decided what to do about the German influence in South America.

"When I arrived in 1939," Loyal Domning recalled, "the pilot staff consisted of 16 captains and nine copilots. Now Panagra was declared a strategic airline by the War Department and asked to help oust the Germans from western hemisphere aviation, and to pursue the overall objectives of the war.

"Tom Kirkland visited my squadron at Norfolk to see my skipper, who was an old Navy buddy, and to recruit pilots. The result was the first wave of what eventually were more than one hundred Navy, Air Corps, and civilian pilot-trained crew members who came as fast as they could be absorbed by new routes and equipment."

Ernie Hummel was recruited in September, 1940, from the Army Air Corps' 9th Bombardment Group, stationed on Long Island, New York. Floyd Nelson came to fetch Hummel and another pilot, Pat Trees. Hummel, after a short vacation, met Trees again at the Washington Hotel in Cristóbal, Panama, where they spent ten days waiting for seats on a southbound Panagra flight.

"We had been told to present ourselves to the captain of the layover crew from Lima," Hummel recalled. "So on the first day Pat and I got dressed up and waited in the hotel lobby for the captain and copilot who, we were told, had gone out shopping.

"We waited all afternoon, more and more annoyed by this crummy-looking pair, dressed in shorts and thongs, who were playing a riotous game of cribbage in the hotel bar.

"These two were taking on plenty of food and drink, and the game got louder and louder, despite the efforts of the bar boys to get them to quiet down. Suddenly we heard one of them say that the other couldn't play cribbage any better than he could fly a DC-3. Could these two guys be the Panagra crew?

"We went over and introduced ourselves. They were, indeed, the Panagra crew. We explained who we were and so forth, while the captain gave us a bleary-eyed stare. Finally, he offered a cold-fish handshake and said, 'Lots of luck. You'll sure need it.'"

Hummel and Trees did eventually get out of Panama. Approaching Quito, Ecuador, the new hires were told by the purser to go up to the cockpit. There the pilot pointed to the right side of the airfield, where Jack Scheidel's wrecked DC-2 lay.

"That's yesterday's flight," the pilot said.

"The implication was clear," Hummel recalled. "This was not an infrequent occurrence. The accident had happened on a local Ecuadorean run. An engine had failed on take-off and the aircraft, attempting to return to the field, had run out of speed and altitude."

Jack Scheidel had indeed lost an engine just at takeoff, and the airport runway was already above the single-engine ceiling for a DC-2. Scheidel didn't have a chance to make it to a nearby river gorge, where he could have controlled the airplane with one engine while descending to sea level near Esmeraldas. Instead, he crashed just beyond the end of the runway and slid into some trees. While no passengers were hurt, Scheidel, his copilot, and the radio operator were all injured, and Schiedel's ankles were so badly broken that he had to move into a desk job. The aircraft remained at the end of the runway for some time afterwards, a grim reminder to other pilots of the hazards of high-altitude flying.

With some arm-twisting by the United States State Department, Panagra was allocated some new routes, parallelling the old LAB, SCADTA, SEDTA, Lufthansa, and Condor routes. "SCADTA, in Colombia, was transformed into Avianca," Domning recalled. The majority stockholder of SCADTA was none other than Juan Terry Trippe. Trippe had secretly acquired control of SCADTA in 1931 to eliminate SCADTA's objections to Pan Am's penetration of the South American air market. Sensitive to Colombian sentiments about their beloved airline, he had just never advertised the fact.

"SEDTA of Ecuador and Lufthansa-Peru ceased operations entirely," Domning continued. "Lloyd Aéreo Boliviano (LAB) was nationalized, continuing operations under a five-year technical advisory contract with Panagra, during which our personnel trained and supervised LAB personnel in all departments."

The LAB transition was personally supervised by Harold Harris, and it was during this period that Domning first met the airline's founder. It was to be the climax of a very rough week: "Half of the engine failures I was to suffer during 40 years of flying happened on one round trip," Domning said. His week started on November 18, 1940, when he, as copilot, and Frank Achilles, pilot, took off from Lima, Peru, for Arequipa, and thence to Arica, Peru, the first leg of the *Diagonal* route. They were in a DC-3, number P-38, with the older Wright Cyclone engines. At Arica the two men would switch to a DC-2, brought up from Santiago, Chile, by another crew, and continue on to Buenos Aires, Argentina, by way of Bolivia and the *altiplano.*

"On the flight from Lima," Domning recalled, "we noticed a tendency for the right engine oil pressure to drop. I rotated a cleaner brush inside the oil filter, using a handle in the cockpit, and corrected the problem several times.

"At Arequipa it was time for a command decision. There was evidence enough to ground the airplane, but to do so would inconvenience the passengers who were expecting their connection at Arica, where the DC-2 waited. Frank decided to continue to Arica.

"The sick engine had other ideas. Immediately after take-off, the oil pressure dropped drastically and this time the temperature shot up to the limit of the gauge. No amount of filter cleaning made any difference, and when I looked out my window I saw a plume of black smoke coming from the right-hand propeller dome."

Achilles immediately turned back to Arequipa, ordering Domning to feather the bad engine. Because Arequipa's runway was already very near the single-engine operating ceiling for the DC-3, he also ordered Domning to dump fuel. The fuel dump chute deployed and a stream of fuel now joined the black smoke pouring from the aircraft. The propeller, however, would not feather properly because of the low oil pressure.

"The combination of high altitude and prop drag was too much," Domning said. "The plane continued to descend." There was worse to come. Achilles was attempting the usual up-wind landing, but things happened so quickly that he couldn't get into position. He was forced to fly around the field, hedge-hopping, and make a down-wind landing at the other end.

"A railroad track ran a few yards from the end of the field," Domning recalled. "Fortunately, the morning train was not passing, as the plane would not have cleared it. The airplane arrived at the station platform after some tricky single-engine taxiing. For once, the normal protocol of having the passengers remain seated until the captain strode down the aisle was disregarded."

Naturally, Achilles received all manner of advice as to what he should have done. "On one point," Domning noted, "there was com-

plete agreement. This was a very
close call, and only superb flying
brought it to a successful finish."

The DC-2, number P-26, was
brought from Arica to Arequipa, and
Achilles and Domning, after switching planes, went on to Buenos Aires
via the *Diagonal* route. After a two-
day layover they returned, Buenos
Aires to Córdoba and Tucumán, an
overnight at Salta, Argentina, then on
to Uyuni, Bolivia, on the 22nd. It was
here that they picked up Harris.

Achilles must have felt a bit de-
fensive. He had nearly splashed an
aircraft just days earlier, and now

Captain Loyal Domning

here was the airline's founder in his cockpit. If Achilles thought he was
going to be in for an uncomfortable day, he was right.

"Twenty minutes after leaving Uyuni," Domning recalled, "near
Río Mulatos, the right engine oil overheated, and the oil pressure
headed for the basement."

Though he must not have believed his bad luck, Achilles was getting used to the scenario. He instantly ordered Domning to dump fuel
and to feather the bad engine.

"For the second time in four days," Domning said, "we had a propeller that would not feather. And this engine didn't have the kind of
oil filter you could clean from the cockpit. But this time the fuel dump
valve jammed, too." Domning even wrapped a cloth around the dump
valve toggle and pulled on it with both hands, to no avail.

And so for the second time in four days, Domning and Achilles
were in a fix, with only one engine, operating at too high an altitude,
with a windmilling prop causing additional drag on the bad engine.
They also had an interested observer standing right behind them.
Harold Harris, the Panagra founder and one-time Army Air Corps
chief of test pilots, seemed mildly fascinated, though he did not say
much.

"Frank elected to return to Uyuni because the salt lake there provided a giant emergency landing field," Domning said. Uyuni's "field,"
in fact, was simply part of the salt bed, marked off at the corners by
four rock cairns. Oruro's field was the same.

It was quickly obvious that they were going to run out of air before
they ran out of distance. In a desperate move, Achilles ordered
Domning to restart the bad engine, though it was anyone's guess how
long an engine with no lubricating oil could pull before flying apart
from the strain, making the situation even worse.

"The extra bit of power from the right engine did the trick," Domning recalled. "We nursed the DC-2 to a downwind, upright landing at Uyuni. The local manager of the Bolivian railroad provided an *autocarril,* or automobile on railroad wheels, so that Harris could continue to La Paz. Frank and I stayed in Uyuni for three memorable days awaiting a replacement engine.

"The working conditions for the three mechanics, who removed the sick engine and installed the one they had brought, typified the hardships of a company pioneering civil aviation in remote places. Uyuni is situated at more than 13,000 feet above sea level. The terrain is always cold, windswept, and inhospitable. Heat was not regarded locally as a necessity, largely because of an almost complete lack of fuel. The one hotel was primitive to an extreme. Fortunately, there was beer, which we stood in the sun for a while to bring it up to drinking temperature.

"The replacement engine arrived with four cylinders removed in order to get it through the cabin door (of another DC-2). Standing in the cold wind with a tarpaulin for a shield, the mechanics re-assembled the engine and hung it on the airplane. Then they took the old engine apart and loaded it on board. It was a real test of endurance and fortitude."

Panagra and LAB aircraft at La Paz, Bolivia.

CHAPTER 8

THE WAR YEARS, 1941-1945

1941

If Panagra hoped not only to hold its own in South America in the coming war, but to expand its service, taking over routes held by airlines affiliated with the Axis powers, it had to do several things and do them quickly. First, the weather problem had to be addressed and controlled. Fortunately, new equipment and techniques were coming on line. Second, the airline had to be able to obtain equipment, and everyone knew that equipment, maintenance supplies, and fuel were going to be scarce in the years to come. Third, it had to restructure its administration and ground operations to keep up with a rapid expansion. Finally, Panagra had to negotiate the delicate political sensibilities of Latin American governments, some of whom had close ties with the Axis powers.

Panagra executives did not waste time. In January of 1941, a million-dollar expansion and modernization program began to improve communications between ground stations and aircraft. Weather predicting went hand-in-hand with improved communications.

"We had the first continental network of stations," Cy Collins recalled. "It was a tremendous accomplishment, even if the results were a little irregular. We were able to predict fairly well the frontal activity in the southern part of the route in Argentina and Chile, but we had less luck in predicting the fogs in Lima. We never totally succeeded at that in the days when I was involved in Lima, 1941 to 1948."

Collins had come to South America with the Grace Company, worked in the Grace office in Lima in 1940, and met some of Panagra's meteorological people then. He actually joined Panagra in 1941.

"Jimmy Scholtz and his meteorologists were proceeding in almost primitive conditions to advance the great cause of meteorology in South America," Collins recalled. "I remember talking to Scholtz about the successes of the meteorological program further south, and the questionable successes when it came to predicting fog in Lima. We actually looked it up and found that the meteorologists, when it came to predicting fog in Lima, were right about 50% of the time. I suggested to Jim Scholtz that we could have saved hundreds of thousands of dollars by just flipping a coin. He said, 'No, this is a science, and it's on the march. It's better to do as well as you can do if you use the state-of-the-art knowledge.' He was quite correct, and he accomplished a tremendous feat, eventually creating a totally private continent-wide network of stations with refined meteorological predictions."

Safety, and the greater difficulty of ensuring safety in the challenging conditions of western South America, had been a Panagra priority from the start. In 1941, when the Civil Aeronautics Board (CAB) stepped in, things became tighter still.

"Flight operating standards enforced by any government agency were practically non-existent before 1941," Loyal Domning recalled. "But in 1941, the CAB decided to impose jurisdiction over Panagra (which, like Pan Am, was a U.S. company), even though none of Panagra's routes was within the U.S.A.

"In the early 1940s Panagra's resources were severely taxed by the demands of its rapid expansion to satisfy the pressures of political, commercial, and military needs. The CAB became impatient with the progress being made and imposed severe operating limitations. No night flying was permitted, and a one-thousand-foot ceiling and five miles of visibility were required for all takeoffs and landings.

"In response, Panagra strengthened its operating and training staff as well as its maintenance and communications departments. Manuals were written and programs established to standardize all aspects of flight and ground activity. As fast as it could be procured under wartime conditions, radio communication and navigation equipment was bought and installed. A radio servicing facility was set up in each country for the prompt handling of communication and navigation problems. By 1946 the CAB recognized the adequacy of our efforts and permitted the use of normal operating limitations."

In July Harris arrived in Bolivia to supervise the takeover of Lloyd Aéro Boliviano (LAB) on behalf of the Bolivian Government. This arrangement, structured by the U.S. Department of Commerce, effectively took LAB out of German hands. German pilots went home to Germany, and Americans began to supervise LAB's flight operations. In August Panagra became the official "administrator" of LAB for a period of five years.

"The U.S. wanted the German airlines kicked out of South America," Douglas Campbell explained. "Those governments agreed to kick the Germans out, but they insisted that Panagra replace all the services that the Germans were performing in their countries. We had to do that in Ecuador and in Bolivia.

"In Bolivia, the government got rid of Lloyd Aéreo Boliviano by expropriating all of the stock in the company, in effect nationalizing it," Campbell noted. "A large part of the stock was already owned by Bolivians, and I think we had to buy some, too, in order to make it work. After the German pilots left, we had a management contract to run the company."

Payment was the problem. Bolivian currency was worthless. Chuck Schultz once wrote a check for some small purchase in Santa Cruz and wondered why it never cleared his bank. More than a year later, a Bolivian approached him at the same airport. The Bolivian had the check. It had been circulating around Santa Cruz all that time, serving as currency. Now it was reduced to tatters from having changed hands so often. Schultz reached for his wallet and offered to buy back the check. No, said the Bolivian. He didn't want money; he wanted Schultz to make out a new replacement check.

Nor was the U.S. government in any position to pay for the outright purchase of LAB routes. What the U.S. government wanted and what it was willing to pay to get it were not always the same. "The problem, which I guess fell on Harold Roig's shoulders, was how to persuade the U.S. government to pay us enough so we wouldn't go broke doing it," Campbell recalled.

Partly as a result of these actions and partly as a result of previous expansion plans now bearing fruit, Panagra's route mileage increased enormously. In March internal service within Ecuador became more frequent, and a new twice-weekly Guayaquil-Loja service began.

Loja was approached through a narrow canyon that opened suddenly into a small plain. Pilots had to make a fairly sudden left turn to line up with the sloping, grassy field that doubled as a runway. Landings were made uphill and takeoffs downhill, regardless of the direction of the wind.

"We had to time our flights into Loja carefully," Chuck Schultz recalled. "By ten in the morning the winds were too tricky to land there."

In April Arequipa replaced Arica as the juncture point for the North-South route and the *Diagonal* route. In Ecuador, service was inaugurated to Cuenca, with Panagra, represented by Douglas Campbell, presenting the airport to the Ecuadorean people in a ceremony on April 25. As was by now usual with these affairs, local officials were given a big part. In this case, the President of Ecuador, Sr. Arroyo del Río, made the first flight, accompanied by his minister of defense and other high government officials. Loyal Domning and Howard Caldwell were the flight crew.

On June 10 the Bolivian route was extended as far as Puerto Suarez by means of a fourth weekly service to La Paz. Puerto Suarez was still within Bolivia, but only a few miles from the Brazilian city of Corumbá served by Pan Am. On July 29 Panagra extended service to Corumbá, and Panagra and Pan Am had their third juncture, in addition to those already in place in Panama and Buenos Aires. On August 6, the same day that Panagra became administrator of LAB, a *Transcontinental* service was inaugurated–an echo of the one started by the German-affiliated airlines, from Rio de Janeiro to Lima, in 1938.

"We didn't even bother to put our landing gear up," Paul Willey recalled of the flight from Puerto Suarez to Corumbá. "There just wasn't time, the two airfields were so close to one another." Pilots could fly straight down the center of Lake Cáceres, or at treetop level along the lake's southern shore. The lake emptied into the Río Paraguay at Corumbá.

The Bolivian run quickly developed into the "Sawtooth" route, a sort of internal roundabout. By September, flights flew from La Paz to Santa Cruz. From Santa Cruz, the flight went to Concepción, San Ignacio, San José de Chiquitos, Roboré, Puerto Suarez and Corumbá. From Corumbá, the aircraft returned direct to Santa Cruz, and then back to La Paz.

"It soon became apparent that something was wrong with the Concepción flight," Frank Havelick recalled. "Many pilots couldn't even find the place and had to go on to the next stop with passengers ticketed for Concepción still aboard, along with their personal baggage and their live chickens and ducks, which they held in their arms.

"Finally, we installed an aerophare at Concepción, and with the aid of the RDF, the pilots were able to find the town. After about a year, we figured out, with the help of celestial sightings, that Concepción was misplaced on the charts."

Chuck Schultz had his own memories of Concepción, memories which might explain why the place was so hard to find:

"Whenever we arrived, we were met by two missionaries, Hammon and Pencil, and their families. The youngsters always wanted handouts of chiclets. On one occasion, Pencil brought along two natives with whom they had managed to make contact out in the field. They had asked him to bring them to see this huge bird they'd been shooting arrows at. He had stopped them at the edge of the clearing to get them into some pants and shirts.

"These two had their teeth filed, and Pencil said they were from a tribe that was cannibalistic. The chief had a beautiful headdress made of ocelot fur and bright bird feathers. He also had a pigtail wrapped with a rope made from vines.

"They looked the airplane over thoroughly, and Pencil took them inside to show them the accommodations. They smiled a lot, which was not pleasant to look at.

"When they got out, the chief took the rope from around his pigtail, laid it on the ground and measured the plane, nose to tail and wing tip to wing tip. Pencil explained that the length of the rope around the chief's pigtail was the basis of measurement for the tribe. With this, he

The Santa Cruz, Bolivia, air terminal, built by Lloyd Aéreo Boliviano, a German airline which Panagra took over and ran during WW II. The German engineers designed the terminal to look like a miniature of the Tempelhof Terminal in Berlin.

would be able to go back and tell the other members of his clan just how big that bird was."

The Santa Cruz terminal, built by the Germans for Lloyd Aéreo Boliviano, was far more comfortable than most. It was self-contained, with its own dining hall and passenger hotel. Rumor had it that, when first built, it was fortified as well against Indian attacks.

Captain Paul Willey remembers taking a day off in Santa Cruz to go jaguar hunting with the station manager, Tom Elder. "We spent the day in the jungle in a jeep and on foot and never saw a jaguar," Willey recalls, "but we *did* discover that we had both attended Colby College, in Waterville, Maine. He had graduated a year or two ahead of me, and we'd never met, to our knowledge, while we were at school."

One of the less-enviable jobs in the Bolivian highlands was to carry raw rubber out of the plantation areas. Chuck Schultz recalled getting up early each morning to fly an empty aircraft from Santa Cruz to Concepción. At Concepción, workers would carefully drape cloths over the passenger seats, then pile big cylinders of uncured rubber on top. Schultz would fly back to Santa Cruz, unload the rubber, remove the tarpaulins, and be ready by 8:30 or 9 a.m. to resume his morning "Sawtooth" run, with passengers.

Less easy to get rid of than the rubber was the rubber's powerful smell. Airline personnel usually sprayed the interior of the plane with some kind of deodorant to conceal an odor Schultz described as being "worse than raw onions."

But Schultz also recalls how he loved to fly at treetop level on the

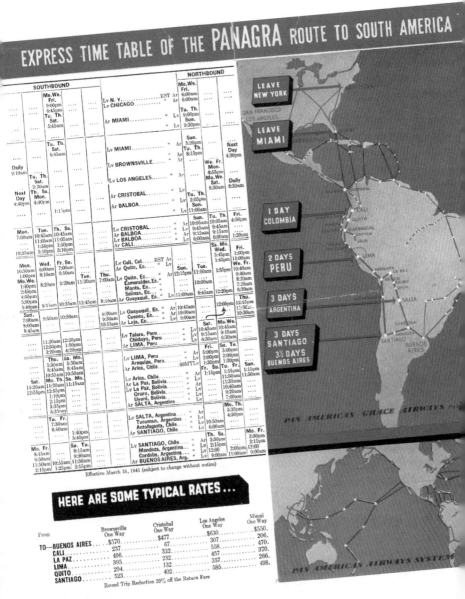

This 1941 time table shows flight times, typical fares, and some of the Panagra route connections.

rubber run—with no passengers, he could get away with it—and watch hundreds of red macaws flying up out of the light green jungle canopy. "It was a beautiful sight, right at dawn," he said.

In August fighting broke out between Peru and Ecuador over an ancient border dispute. Frank McGann and Loyal Domning flew a number of trips to Loja, carrying in medical supplies and carrying out wounded soldiers. All the while, machine guns covered every approach, until the defenders were satisfied that this was a friendly airplane.

And speaking of bullets, I helped start the Panagra flight that became known as "The Bullet." For years Panagra had operated between Lima and Panama by overnighting at Cali, Colombia. You flew from Lima to Cali, overnighted in Cali, flew on to Panama, and did the reverse on the way back. One day in Lima the flight was delayed by 24 hours for some reason. I suggested, "Give me an early start, and I'll go all the way to Panama today."

"'That's impossible,' they said.

"'Well, let's skip Chiclayo," I said. "Let the regular flight that's going to stop in Cali catch Chiclayo. I'll skip it, go non-stop to Talara to refuel, stop in Guayaquil and Cali, and keep going on to Panama." And that's what I did. The next day I turned around and came back, showing that it could be done. They called it "The Bullet" run, and it eventually operated once a week.

On August 26 the "Bullet" service was formally established from Panama to Lima. This schedule, which stopped at Guayaquil but not Quito, connected with the *Transcontinental* route through Bolivia, and with one of the Lima-Santiago runs. To accommodate this particular flight, a weekly Quito-Panama service had been inaugurated in June 1941, and changes were made to the schedule within Ecuador. The net result was that there were four weekly services between Quito and Guayaquil.

The busiest leg of the Panagra route was always the Lima to Balboa, Panama, route, where Panagra fed into the Pan Am network. Pilots often waved to one another in the passes, or over the high valleys of southern Colombia. Sometimes they did more.

"Jack Miller must have flown that Lima-Balboa run forever," Bill Chamberlin recalled. "I flew it quite a lot, too, when I was senior enough to get it. I was coming out of Lima one day when Jack was coming south out of Balboa. Somewhere in Colombia or Ecuador we were about to cross paths, and there was a little vacant field not too far from Cali. It wasn't in the Cauca Valley, but just over the ridge to the east.

"Jack called me on the radio—by this time we had voice communication—and said, 'Have you got *La Prensa*, the Lima morning newspaper?' I said, 'Yes, I do,' and he said, 'Do you have another copy, so that I can have one?' I said, 'Sure.' He said, 'Why don't we land at Dos Ríos, and I'll give you the paper from Balboa.'

"I didn't know a darn thing about that field. There could have been holes in the thing, and it hadn't been used in years. But Jack said he had buzzed the field once and that it looked okay. Now, he had 21 passen-

A DC-3 at Cuenca, Ecuador.

gers aboard, and so did I. But we landed, taxied up beside one another, exchanged our newspapers, took off, and were on our way again."

Miller had been an instructor at the Great Lakes Naval Air Station before coming to Panama to fly with Isthmian Airways. After joining Panagra in 1931, he did most of his flying north of Lima, through Ecuador and Colombia to the Panama Canal. A full-blooded North American Indian, Miller was greeted by swarms of natives at every landing. Loyal Domning recalls that Miller "was loved by all who knew him, and he could be relied upon to do favors for the most humble as well as for presidents. The requests were many, but Jack felt privileged to be able to help with purchases of medicines and newspapers. As time went on, Jack flew all the routes of Panagra until poor health grounded him in 1954."

Service within Ecuador continued to fluctuate throughout 1941. On September 21 the Quito-Guayaquil route was increased to six weekly round trips, while service to Cuenca and Loja increased to three. However, on October 3, and again on November 15, Quito was eliminated from other international flights, and after that only one international round trip per week stopped at Quito. On December 3 Quito was dropped entirely from direct international service. Northbound and southbound international routes now all went into Guayaquil.

"Local service in Ecuador frequently meant flying around and through cloud canyons which obscured the Andes," Frank Havelick recalled. "Pilots always had to keep foremost in mind a 'way out' should one of the two engines fail. Finding a small airport in mountainous terrain under these conditions kept everyone awake and lent a certain excitement to flying which has now vanished."

Adding to the excitement were the unpredictable updrafts and eddies that swirled through the Ecuadorean passes and canyons. "One time we came into Quito," Ernie Hummel recalled. "Jack Miller was pilot, and I was copilot, and we were trying to land to the south at the old field in a big wind storm. The valley was filled with blowing dust, but we actually got into the airport on our fourth approach. On the first three approaches, with power off, gear and flaps down, we were unable to descend enough, due to the tremendous updraft. Jack had the airplane almost standing on its nose, and we still couldn't get down."

Taking off could be a bigger problem. A DC-2 could not fly on one engine at the altitude of Quito's airport, so there was no safety margin. Pilots taking off to the north always held their breath until they had passed over the gorge of the Río Guaillabamba, a tributary of the Río Esmeraldas, which ran all the way down to Esmeraldas on the coast. Even on one engine, you could always fly down the gorge to sea level, but you had to make it to the gorge. Pilots taking off to the south had no such escape route, and Jack Schiedel, just a year earlier, had not even made it to the gorge.

On March 15 the Inter-American Safety Council recognized Panagra for having transported 14,600 passengers in 1940, over a total of 15,259,891 miles, without a fatality. This was just one of a regular stream of annual safety records.

No one gave awards for in-flight food service in those days, but Panagra might have won that, too. These early aircraft had no galleys. Instead, Mike Clavarino, head of Panagra's commissary department, or one of his helpers, would prepare meals ahead of time and store them in glass-lined, aluminum Thermos bottles.

Clavarino had been an Italian merchant seaman at the end of World War I and volunteered to serve on the ship taking Woodrow Wilson to Europe for the Versailles Peace Conference. There was concern at the time that some German U-boat captains who hadn't heard about the armistice yet might try to sink Wilson, so a volunteer crew was assembled. For his service, Clavarino was awarded instant American citizenship.

His meals, pilots agreed, were usually pretty good, although Clavarino did love duck *á l'orange* to a fault. What Clavarino liked, everyone ate, even people hundreds of miles away. It would be nearly forty years before pilot Dick Witt could bring himself to eat duck again.

In some instances Clavarino would go out of his way to satisfy particular tastes. On a flight up the *Diagonal,* Clavarino so admired the spectacular view that the pilot, Chuck Schultz, got out his camera and photographed whichever views Clavarino especially liked. "From then on," Schultz recalled, "whenever I was scheduled out on a freighter, the crew got a large thermos full of vanilla ice cream and a quart jar of chocolate sauce."

There were two other notable events in mid-1941: on April 22 cigarette smoking was permitted on Panagra planes for the first time. And on August 16 and 17 the airline established a new trans-Andean record, hauling 422 passengers, including fifty members of the American Ballet troupe and tons of mail and express freight across the "hump" between Santiago, Chile, and Mendoza, Argentina. The backlog had been caused by several days of bad weather in Uspallata Pass, but as soon as Panagra's new meteorological organization could predict improved weather, an extra plane was sent south from Lima to be ready when the clouds finally lifted. With the regular route re-established, and with the help of the extra plane, twenty-five trips were flown in two days to move all the backlogged passengers and cargo.

The trans-Andean service improved markedly with the advent of better meteorological data. On October 8 a fifth weekly round-trip service was established between Santiago and Buenos Aires. By November 25 there was daily service.

Administrative upgrades in 1941 included the promotions of Charles Disher to operations manager, and Floyd Nelson to chief pilot, both effective on November 28. Two weeks earlier, in New York, John T. Shannon had been promoted to vice president.

Shannon was a former U.S. Navy flier who had just become involved with the New York-Rio-Buenos Aires airline (NYRBA) when Pan Am scooped it up. On a business trip to Santiago, he met Dan Tobin, who had flown Panagra's first flight from Lima to Talara. Tobin told Shannon about Panagra, and Shannon came to Lima at the end of the 1930s. His administrative talents took him into management, and he headed the Panagra maintenance department for several years before becoming a vice president and moving to New York to take charge of the passengers and sales department. In 1950 he went over to Pan Am as vice president in charge of the Atlantic division.

In the lower ranks, the rapid expansion and the war were fast creating a specialization within the flight crews that had not been seen before.

"Until late in 1939," Loyal Domning explained, "copilots had to operate the radio using Morse Code. They also were trained to qualify as airplane and engine mechanics, but the training load for the large numbers of flight crews Panagra now needed brought about two major changes. A radio operator was added to the flight crew, eliminating the requirement that pilots obtain a second-class radio-telegraph license. Next, mechanics at all bases were trained for the U.S. CAA airplane and engine licenses, thus relieving the operations department of this large training burden."

In Panama, on December 11, three days after the United States declared war on Japan and Germany, Panagra moved its operations from France Field, Cristóbal, to Albrook Field, in Balboa, in order to participate more fully in the war effort.

1942

Panagra started 1942 with a minor war of its own. Shell Oil company employees, exploring for oil deep within the Ecuadorean jungle, were attacked and then besieged by Aushiri indians.

Shell Mera was a forward camp established by Shell Oil on the Mera River. It was at the terminus of a very bad road, and served the actual oil exploration camp of Arajuno, thirty miles farther into the jungle by river.

When the Indians attacked the camp, three white men were killed and one wounded. The remaining 200 sent radio messages pleading for aid. A Panagra aircraft, piloted by Captain R. G. Fussell, circled low over the camp and dropped twenty rifles and some ammunition, in ten well-padded canvas bundles. With these weapons, the oil company workers were able to break the siege and escape.

I joined Panagra in 1942 and lived for a time in Lima. In many ways, my experience was typical of the new pilots Panagra picked up at the start of the war. I had been flying DC-2s for Braniff and living in Houston when Pearl Harbor happened. I assumed we would be drafted immediately, but the Army Air Corps didn't seem to touch the DC-2s or their crews.

I still tried to go to the Army Air Corps as a pilot, but was turned down due to dental work, of all things. Then I thought, "I'm not going to stay here, flying DC-2s all my life. There's a war going on. Pan Am is flying all around the world and will probably be directly involved with war support. I want to fly, and I want to be involved in the war effort." So I wrote to Pan Am, and in due course I was hired to go to their

Bill Krusen smiles, from a Panagra cockpit shortly before take-off.

When I first landed at Albrook Field in Panama, they already had barrage balloons up, and I could see the strategic importance they placed on the Panama Canal. I knew I had made the right choice.

They housed me in a little hotel that was infested with roaches. I was rooming with Lee McBride, who had come down from Delta. We had to wait several days for room on a flight to go on to Lima, and Lee said, "I don't like living here. I'm going back to Atlanta. Why don't you come with me? You can get checked out as quickly with Delta as with Panagra." I said, "No, I've come this far, and I'm going to see it through all the way." That was another crossroad that shaped my future.

Lima was a different world. It was primitive, and yet the people were friendly. I ended up sharing a rented house with Dick Witt, Chuck Beatley, and Eustis Hetzel. We bought some beds, a few basic items, and hired a maid.

We always had a full house, including a young man named Jamie, who was from Argentina. His parents were American, and Jamie was completely bilingual. He was also an expert with radios, working with the radio sector of Panagra. He built us a small transmitter station at the house, which allowed us to play records in one room and tune in our radio to the transmitter in another room. This impressed the local folks, who came over to hear our old records."

Unfortunately, we had only old big-band records, the music we had listened to in college, for our miniature radio station. Any time we went any place on a trip, we would look for records to add to our collection. Panagra only flew as far north as the Canal Zone. We had no real access to buy U.S. products, other than what filtered to us through the Canal Zone post exchange. If somebody was making a trip to the U.S., he might bring back things for us. That's how I got my first Ray-Ban glasses. We quickly came to think of ourselves as part of Panagra, sharing an interest and pride in its history and confident that we would be able to contribute to its future.

Panagra aircraft, between January 10 and January 30, aided in the movement of 200 delegates, staff, and press people to the Pan American Conference in Rio de Janeiro. This effort was the largest mass movement to date in South American air traffic.

On May 31 Peruvian President Manuel Prado, returning to Lima from a visit to the United States, addressed his nation from the cockpit of a Panagra aircraft, the signal then being relayed from the ground station to *Radio Nacional*. President Prado thus became the first chief of state to deliver a speech from an aircraft in flight.

On June 1 Harold R. Harris was "borrowed" by the U.S. Army Air Transport Command as a civilian consultant. On September 15 Harris resigned as a Panagra vice president to accept a commission as a colonel on the staff of the commanding general of the Air Transport Command. After fifteen years, Harris was back in uniform, having

jumped three ranks in the process. It was not long before he was promoted to the rank of brigadier general. Although Harris would join
the management teams of several airlines after the war, he never returned to Panagra.

The war caused an immediate shortage of pilots, especially men
with enough experience to be captains. Not only was the need for pilots suddenly greater, but many pilots were Army Air Corps and Naval
Aviation reservists who wanted to get into the war theaters. Among
Panagra pilots and operations men who either took temporary leave or
resigned outright to join the fight were Tommy Kirkland and Ott
Gardner.

As a strategically important airline, Panagra remained vital to U.S.
military interests and was able to recruit some just-graduating military
pilots assigned to it. Three of the most experienced pilots around, Frank
Havelick, James McCleskey and Floyd Nelson, came from another Pan
Am subsidiary, China National Aircraft Corporation (CNAC). Havelick,
McCleskey and Nelson became known as "The China Gang."

These well-seasoned pilots joined some of Panagra's most senior
imports: Warren Smith, from NYRBA; By Rickards and Pancho
Ramsey, from Braniff; Tommy Jardine, Bob Disher, Ott Gardner, Fritz
Sterling, Kelly Achilles, and others from the military; and Jack Miller
from Isthmian Airways in Panama. Pancho Ramsey actually checked
out as a captain in a matter of days, as he was already familiar with the
aircraft that Panagra used.

Havelick recalled meeting some initial hostility during his first days
in Lima. "I was billeted at the historic Maury Hotel, which, along with
the Bolívar, was the accepted place to stay. I spent a week there, being
consumed by fleas and gradually realizing that I was *persona non grata*
among the Panagra pilots."

The copilots hoping for promotions to captain were quite naturally
resentful at first of these "transplants" from another Pan Am subsidiary, but the rapid expansion of routes soon required even more people
than Panagra could hire, and quarrels over seniority were forgotten.

One of the oldest of the old-timers, Dinty Moore, had been on the
original crossing of the Atlantic aboard U.S. Navy NC-4s. Moore had
retired from passenger flying by this time and was in charge of
Panagra's training program. He had an assortment of tools, leftover
airplanes that he had converted to "hood" trainers, one Link Trainer
(invented by Edwin Link, the Link Trainer was a standardized cock-
pit-in-a-classroom, the forerunner to today's aircraft simulators), and a
lot of imagination.

Dinty checked me out in a DC-2, and that was a very full check-
out. He insisted we do a steep turn under the hood, a 720-degree turn,
and hit our slipstream twice around. To do that you had to make the
turn without losing any altitude, not even twenty feet. I didn't think

that was possible, but after a few trips with him, and after his showing us how to fly the airplane, we learned the techniques that carried us through the day-to-day routine of blind flying. He also taught us how to land and take off on a short field. He was a tough instructor, but very fair and extremely patient.

I must have practiced the 720-degree turn trick a hundred times or more, and it was a good thing. I was flying up the Mera River one day, having just left the Shell Mera oil exploration base with a Pan Am engineer and Dinty, who had come to observe the freight-hauling procedures Panagra used.

There was low cloud cover overhead so we were flying in a sort of tunnel, trees on either side, clouds overhead, and, somewhere to the left and right, the mountains. Suddenly, the clouds dropped right to the river, and we flew straight into the fog.

Without even thinking, I put the airplane into a steep turn. I really flipped her up on her side. I did a 180-degree turn over the river, and when I leveled out, I was on a perfect reciprocal course. In a moment, we came out of the cloud. We were flying straight down the river. All that practice paid off in spades in that one moment.

"The training was very, very good," Dick Witt, who arrived in Lima in 1942, recalled. "It was very early in the era of real instrument flight, and we practiced manipulation of the controls on an airplane while not being able to see out. Dinty's classroom was always full of pilots watching other pilots fly these intricate maneuvers that Dinty had designed, which, if done right, would draw a very pretty picture by means of an inked pen that could crawl around on the table top over a large sheet of paper.

"There was always a coffee break when everyone was expected to go across the street," Witt recalled. "There was a man who sold Dr. Pepper and Coca-Cola and everything out of a push cart, who would play a game called 'Queen Bee.' I don't recall how it was played, but it involved matching a lot of coins, and the loser got stuck with the tab for the five, six, or seven pilots who were with Dinty. This was Dinty's big moment of the day, and it was always a good idea to try to let Dinty win because he got an enormous thrill out of this, and it vastly improved your chances of getting through his training course."

One of the things Moore demanded of Panagra pilots was the ability to float in, barely above stalling speed, and land on a short runway, of which Panagra had many. Loyal Domning got to be so good at this that he was christened "Death-Glide" Domning. Others weren't so skilled.

One day Chuck Beatley, one of my housemates, said he didn't like it down in Lima any more. The problem really related to Dinty Moore. Beatley would cross the fence (i.e., make the final runway approach) at 90 knots, and Dinty would tell him to do it again, at 80 knots. Chuck would say, "But I like the safety factor of the other ten miles per hour."

Dinty would come back with, "I'm not interested in what you like. I'm telling you how I want you to fly the airplane, and you have to be able to fly it the way I want you to." It was a training procedure Chuck took offense to, and eventually he left South America.

Jack Miller, on the other hand, liked to make an extremely steep, side-slipping approach to the airport. "The last thousand feet," Ernie Hummel recalled, "would consist of a side-slip, power off, so steep that the airplane's left wing tip was pointed vertically straight at the end of the field. At the last second, he would recover in a swooping slide out and usually plunk the airplane pretty close to the end of the field on three points and then rap the copilot on the leg and ask him how he liked that."

Charles Schultz recalls teaching Civilian Pilot Training (CPT) at the University of Toledo from 1939 to 1943. Four of his students, Homer Compton, Cecil Richardson, Wayne Martin, and Leonard Griffin, graduated and reported for work with Panagra. In 1943, when the CPT program was ended, Schultz himself came to work for Panagra and found himself junior in seniority to his former students.

Other pilots who came to Panagra via the Civilian Pilot Training program were Paul Willey, Allen Kopp, Dick Witt, Joe Betty, William Dripps, and Cecil Richardson

"We were enrolled in the Northeast Flight Officer Training Program," Willey recalled. "That eventually became part of the Air Transport Command. Some of the people stayed with the ATC, and I don't know if they actually flew overseas in Burma, or where. But a bunch of us came to Panagra."

Starting the latter part of 1941, Panagra had gone on a hiring tour. They didn't have adequate personnel to train for captains, so they hired people who were already flying for Northwest, American Airlines, Braniff, and Delta. I was one of those pilots, having flown for Braniff. It was one of those fortunate instances of perfect timing, with Panagra looking to hire at the very time I had decided to make a move.

It generally worked out well for my group, for those of us who had the capability to check out. In fact, I was with Panagra for just a little over ten months before being checked out as captain on DC-2s. That was the summer of 1943, and I was 22.

Hiring and keeping qualified pilots became a personnel nightmare during the war. "It was tough to expand our routes," Douglas Campbell recalled, "because we not only had to buy airplanes, but we couldn't hire pilots without Uncle Sam's consent. He needed them all."

Furthermore, the civilian pilots often chafed at the need to fly freight and passengers in South America when there was glory to be won in the combat theaters. I wrote a letter to the naval attaché at the U.S. Embassy in Buenos Aires asking to be drafted into the service. I eventually received my letter back from Washington with the request denied because I was involved in Panagra's military support activities. It was followed by a summons from Frank Havelick, Panagra's chief pilot. "Don't ever do this again," Havelick said. "It took me a lot of time and trouble to get this straightened out."

In fact, Army Chief of Staff General G. C. Marshall considered our work as pilots so essential that, though I didn't know it at the time, he had written in a letter of November 6, 1942, to General Hap Arnold, "My principal concern would be that they do not forget that in their personal desire to get into the active fighting they must not let us down in the tremendously important service of the transportation operations in which they are now engaged. Although in a civilian status, [they] have been performing not only a very great service for the Army and Navy and therefore the nation, but to my mind an equally patriotic service with that of Army and Navy pilots."

The war brought increased passengers and freight down to Panama, and thence over to eastern Brazil, where a flight to Africa was possible. With the outbreak of the war, the fast steamers that had moved passengers and freight between South American cities vanished almost overnight. Those passengers, and much of that freight now had to move by air. In addition, the Allies insisted that German airlines must get out of South America entirely. Panagra was suddenly called upon to fill the vacuum left by the departure of German pilots and ground personnel—and their equipment—in Colombia, Ecuador, and Bolivia.

As if all this were not enough, the war had its own peculiar demands. Rubber, cinchona bark (the raw material for quinine), and high-grade mineral concentrates were suddenly essential, so essential that it was sometimes deemed worth the cost to transport them by air.

By the end of 1942 records indicate that passenger traffic had increased by 500% since the start of the war. To handle this increase, Panagra instituted a number of new routes and schedules.

The most important route from the point of view of moving war-related materials and passengers was Panama-to-Lima, then to Arequipa and across Bolivia to Brazil.

On January 3 a second weekly *Transcontinental* service connected to the "Sawtooth" route and thence to Corumbá, Brazil, where Panagra aircraft linked up with Panair do Brasil flights. By July 17, the two weekly *Transcontinental* flights could move passengers from Rio de Janeiro to Lima in two days and from Lima to Rio in less than a day and a half. Pan Am's Brazilian subsidiary, Panair do Brasil, also commenced a direct Corumbá-Asunción service, permitting two-day service direct from Lima to Asunción.

Panagra's other Atlantic connection, through Chile to Buenos Aires, saw dramatic increases, too. On February 15 a fifth weekly service began between Balboa and Buenos Aires. With this route Panagra had increased its weekly air mileage flown from the 23,112 statute miles flown

The Panagra Express route map for 1941, redrawn by R. E. G. Davies of the Aeronautics Department of the Smithsonian Institution National Air and Space Museum.

just before the U.S. entry into the war to 55,239 statute miles, an increase of 239%. The advantage in passenger capacity of the larger DC-3s can be clearly understood when this mileage increase is compared with the 500% increase in the number of passengers.

On April 21 Panagra instituted a sixth weekly international service between Balboa and Buenos Aires, via Santiago. Chile now had four direct weekly flights to Balboa and on to the U.S. The other direct international flights from Buenos Aires flew up the *Diagonal* route to Tucumán and Salta in Argentina, and then on to Uyuni and La Paz in Bolivia, thence across to Arequipa, Peru.

Flying the route one day with an empty plane bound for the maintenance shop in Lima, Bill Chamberlin had to make an emergency landing at Chala, about 180 miles northwest of Arequipa. The story he remembers illustrates the skill and resourcefulness of the Panagra pilots, and their support of one another. "I was coming from Arequipa to Lima with an old DC-3 which had two Wright-powered engines," Chamberlin said. "They only had 1,000-hp; they weren't the bigger 1,200-hp, you know. And they were always falling apart. In fact, I had a special letter from [John] Shannon authorizing me to fly that DC-3 from Santiago to Lima because it was over-consuming oil. It was the right engine that leaked oil, so I kept worrying about the right engine, and about the time I got my lunch tray on my lap, all hell broke loose. The plane started to shake, and everything was coming apart. I was sure it was the right engine, but it wasn't. We'd lost the left engine. It had blown a cylinder.

"I threw the lunch tray back. I had a bad engine on the right and no engine at all on the left, but there was a little airport I'd never been in, at Chala on the coast. It was a little seal town where they made these seal pocketbooks and all that. I found this out after landing, but it didn't look like a town at all from the air. It was barren, but that was where I was going. I just couldn't fly any farther, and as I was making my approach with a copilot who was fairly new and nervous as hell, I asked him to put the gear down. Instead, he put the flaps down."

Already flying at a dangerously slow speed, and now with the flaps extended, Chamberlin suddenly found himself flying a crippled aircraft that was about to stall in mid-air and drop like a stone. "He'd given me full flaps, and I was losing altitude like crazy," Chamberlin explained. "We didn't have normal hydraulic capacity with only one engine. It just takes too long to get the flaps up and then back down again, so I had to push the throttle just about to the stop to make it to the airport. I had to hold the gear up until the last minute. I made it, and at the end, because it was a very narrow strip, I thought that I had best turn it around and taxi so the tail was off the runway because I knew somebody was going to have to come and get us.

"It was a Sunday afternoon. I called [Bob] Disher, and he said that he'd be down, and just before he hung up he said, 'I suppose you're sitting right in the middle of the runway, so I can't land.' I said, 'No, I'm not. I turned it around with most of the plane off the runway.' 'Runway,' that's a laugh!

"That poor copilot apologized and apologized. He was afraid Disher was going to come down and fire him. I felt really sorry for him, and since we'd made it anyway, I didn't bring it up again."

By May 8 there was daily service between Balboa and Lima, and by September 6 there was daily service continuing over to Buenos Aires, a new flight being added from Antofagasta in northern Chile, through the Monturaqui Pass to Salta, Argentina, and on to Buenos Aires on the *Diagonal* route.

It was on a flight from Arica to Antofagasta, along the Pacific seashore and over the Atacama desert, that Chuck Schultz learned of a new Panagra "policy." It wasn't an official one, certainly, but it was original.

"About the middle of the flight," he recalled, "I heeded the call of nature and went back to the head. Naturally, at this point the right engine began to backfire. I hurried to the cockpit as fast as decency would permit, to find that my copilot had already shut down the engine and feathered the propeller. There was nothing more for me to do but review the appropriate checklist.

"Jack Marta, from Panagra's sales department, was on board, and when we got into Antofagasta, he told me that when we shut down the right engine, our fast-thinking purser, in order to relieve the minds of the passengers, announced that this was a normal procedure used by Panagra to save fuel."

Freight movements took on added importance during the war. "We had actually started the air express business back around 1934," Douglas Campbell recalled. "But it really didn't get much volume until the war came around. Very shortly after the U.S. got into World War II, all the ocean steamers disappeared, and Panagra was the only means of transporting people or anything else. There were still freighters, but no big steamers any more." In fact, all of Grace's passenger steamers were pressed into service as well.

There was a shortage of aircraft, too, and the U.S. government stripped aircraft from most domestic airlines. Panagra was different. It was located astride a main supply route, and it was now one of the few transportation links left in South America. Campbell spent part of the summer of 1942 in Washington, where he not only talked the military into letting Panagra keep its aircraft, but put the company on the factory delivery schedule for three new DC-3s.

On July 9, Panagra instituted its first all-cargo service, between Balboa and Lima, using two DC-2s. This was the first regular commercial all-freight operation by any airline certified by the Civil Aeronautics Board.

The DC-2s were by this time no longer a major part of Panagra's fleet, which on May 4, 1942, consisted of nine DC-3As, just two DC-2s, several miscellaneous aircraft, and one Stinson Reliant that had been converted to a hood trainer.

A "hood" trainer is simply an aircraft flown by a man who is trying to learn to fly without visual aids. His vision is obscured by a hood that surrounds his head, and he learns to fly entirely by instruments. A second pilot, the safety pilot, who can see out and who can take over to prevent accidents, is always along for the ride. Bill Chamberlin remembered the Fairchild and the trainer with a mixture of fondness and hatred. His curiosity got him into trouble:

"When I first went to Lima there was still an old Wasp-powered Fairchild, which had been bought back from the Runcie Photographic Company. It was in the hangar, being overhauled to go to Lloyd Aéreo Boliviano as a hood trainer. But when it was finished, Peru would not allow it to leave the country. So to make some use of it, Panagra said that, as part of their upgrading, the copilots had to solo in it. After I soloed it, Floyd "Nellie" Nelson found out that I didn't much like flying it, so he made me fly it before he'd give me my rating to fly as safety pilot in the Stinson.

"I decided that if I had to fly it, I wanted to know something about running the engine, etc. So I dug around in some old records until I found a handbook for it. McClesky found out I had done that and said that now I was the Fairchild instructor and had to check out the other copilots," Chamberlin explained.

The Fairchild and the Stinson weren't the only relics left behind by Panagra's explosive expansion. "There was an old OX-5 biplane, a Travelair, I believe, stored in a hangar at Limatambo," Chamberlin recalled. "I was told it was an old Panagra plane. At the same time, there was an ex-Panagra S-38 parked at the airport at La Paz that belonged to a mining company."

What on earth a Bolivian mining company needed with an amphibian aircraft, Chamberlin never found out. "I never knew it to fly," he recalled. "And it eventually disappeared."

During the week of September 30 to October 6, Panagra aircraft carried 14,000 kilos of cargo out of Balboa, most of it destined for Argentina, Chile, and Peru, on a special freight service. These large shipments brought the total cargo carried to date on the all-freight flights to 43,000 kilos.

On October 3, 881 kilos of medicines, made in Quito by the Laboratorios Industriales Farmacéuticos, were carried north to Central America.

On a related note, Panagra continued its reputation in South America as a good friend in time of need. On May 15, 1942, working with the Ecuadorean Red Cross, Panagra transported doctors, nurses, and medicines from Quito to other towns in Ecuador which had been hit by earthquakes. And on July 16 a Panagra flight rushed from Balboa to Santiago with 270 kilos of sulphadiazine, urgently needed in Chile to combat a meningitis epidemic. On June 1, Captain Warren Smith was made "Knight of the Andes" by the Chilean government, for having crossed the "hump" one thousand times. As we shall see later, Smith was to become one of the most beloved Americans in Chile.

These actions helped Panagra to deal with the growing nationalism of South American governments, most of whom by this time wanted their own national airlines. However, any movement in this

Capt. Warren B. Smith's 1,000th crossing of the Uspallata Pass between Argentina and Chile. Smith was the first to do so, and received congratulations from President Roosevelt and many others. Smith (r), copilot William Hankins (2nd from r), radio operator, and purser pose for a commemorative photo in Santiago. The plane is a DC-3.

direction was stymied during the war because new aircraft were not available to them. Nevertheless, Panagra attempted to maintain its profitability and service while still accommodating the various governments with which it worked.

To this end, Panagra announced the establishment of Aerovias del Ecuador Panagra on March 1. This subsidiary would operate the internal routes within Ecuador, which were to expand by year's end to 4,254 statute miles flown per week, an increase of 230% in two years. Wayne Ballentine was made manager of the subsidiary, with headquarters in Guayaquil. Walter Jones was transferred from the Panagra SAGO office in Lima to take charge of the Quito office.

Throughout 1942, both the radio and the meteorological services were strengthened. Radio stations began operation at Ascazubi, Ecuador (February 6), at San Antonio de los Cobres, Argentina (May 14, just nine days after installation started), at Buenos Aires, Argentina (May 26), at Vallenar, Chile (June 11), and at Villa Mercedes, Argentina on September 15.

Valmore La Pierre was appointed communications superintendent on August 4, just in time to oversee an ambitious three-week, five-city program from August 4 through August 26. Installations were completed along the *Diagonal* route at Córdoba and Salta, Argentina, and at Arequipa, Peru, as well as in Ecuador, at Manta, and Cuenca.

In June five more professional meteorologists were hired, bringing the total on staff to seven. In September Panagra finally came to grips with the crucial and difficult weather situation on the *altiplano*, building a weather forecast center at Cochabamba, Bolivia, to provide forecasts for both the Bolivian sector of Panagra operations and for Lloyd Aéreo Boliviano, now being operated under Panagra's control.

On the administrative side in 1942, in addition to the appointment of La Pierre as communications superintendent and the loss to the Army Air Force of Harold Harris, Panagra appointed B. H. Young as maintenance engineer and Captain Frederick T. "Fritz" Sterling as acting operations manager. In December, reacting to the 500% passenger traffic increase, Panagra established a passenger service department. The first unit consisted of five Argentine women, who, after extensive training, worked at Morón Airport outside Buenos Aires.

Panagra was joining the mainstream airlines in terms of standardization of training.

"From 1939 on," Loyal Domning recalled, "most of the young men recruited for flight duty were recent products of standardized courses and could follow routines and emergency procedures which had been developed in close coordination with aircraft manufacturers and with Pan American.

"Panagra organized its training program into several steps. It had bought a Link Trainer for instrument flight training in 1938, and Dinty Moore was put in charge. When the growing pilot staff overloaded this machine, a second Trainer and instructor were added in 1941 and another instructor added. In 1943 Bill Denham and I were designated as flight instructors, and we began systematic training of all new pilots in the DC-2 airplane. By that time, Dinty Moore was conducting instrument flight training in a Stinson V-77 which Pan Am had obtained from the U.S. Navy."

Wilbur M. Denham had been an Army Air Corps pilot when, in 1934, the U.S. government canceled all domestic air mail contracts, charging collusion and price-fixing among the airlines. For a few months, military pilots had attempted to fly the mail. The tiny fighters were not night-rated and were dangerous in bad weather. Many pilots crashed, some died, and the air mail went back to the civilian airlines. Bill Denham survived this fiasco, although he said that at times he was "scared to death," and came to Panagra in 1937. He was one of the pilots who carried heavy cargo to gold mines in the Ford Tri-Motors. He retired just before Panagra merged with Braniff.

As the training load increased, professional instructors were used to teach emergency and instrument flight training. Sometimes Pan Am instructors came in to help. Domning, now first assistant chief pilot for training, supervised all of the aspects of both local and line training, when he wasn't doing his share of the flying as well.

1943

In January 1943 Panagra began using flight plans for the first time. It happened almost casually. I had some old Braniff flight plans from my days with that company. I took them into the chief pilot's office one day and said, "You know, we really ought to be operating on flight plans, instead of just keeping our plans on the back of a paper pad or something." They modified the Braniff plans to our conditions, and we used them from then on.

Panagra had never done many things by procedure. They had excellent pilots who had learned to survive without a lot of help from anybody else. The CAA couldn't help them. The Pan Am boys out of Miami were basically boat pilots—they were good navigators, but they were not used to flying in and out of those mountains. We Panagra pilots had to adapt to a different world, and we did. As time went by, we were able to incorporate more of the procedures used elsewhere into the unique aspects of our situation.

The biggest efforts in 1943 were to increase passenger- and cargo-handling capacity and to improve meteorological forecasting. Fortunately, equipment was becoming available through U.S. government channels; Panagra was now considered a strategically important part of the war effort.

The all-cargo service, established from Balboa to Lima the previous year, was extended to Santiago and across to Buenos Aires on February 3. For the first time, air freight could fly the full length of Panagra's 5,300-mile north-south route without being unloaded.

On February 18 a weekly service was begun by Panagra's subsidiary, Aerovias del Ecuador, between Quito, Ecuador, and Ipiales, Colombia, in the mountains bordering Ecuador. By March 2, Panagra was operating into Ipiales as well. The next day, March 3, Panagra announced an average 10% reduction in its ticket price.

On August 24, 1943, the first of three DC-3A aircraft that Panagra had purchased from the U.S. Government arrived at Limatambo Airport. These extra aircraft were to help the airline handle the swelling volume of passenger traffic.

The airline and the Allied war effort could ill-afford to lose a single airplane. But there were losses and close calls.

"Panagra needed more captains as fast as possible," Bill Chamberlin recalled. "Some of us new-hires were checked out as captains ahead of our seniority ranking because we had logged enough flying time to qualify for airline transport licenses. During our training, since we needed experience, we were approved for DC-2s and DC-3s and encouraged to practice any time we could get a plane from maintenance and somebody to copilot for us.

"Some time after I had checked out on DC-3s, we got a new DC-3

A DC-3 at Quito, Ecuador. With an altitude of 9,200 feet, Quito was one of the highest airports Panagra operated into, until the Panagra expansion into still-

in. Wayne Martin had been practicing in it one morning and left it at the hangar for refueling while he went to lunch. When he returned, the plane was gone. Some people on the beach reported having seen a plane go over, climbing at a steep angle, and an oil slick and some cushions were spotted in the water off Chorillos. Two mechanics from the hangar, one of whom had a little flight training with the Aero Club, never came back to work after lunch."

Cy Collins recalled the same incident, adding, "Doug Campbell, our general manager resident in New York was in Lima, and we were standing around trying to figure out what had happened. It was obvious; the airplane was gone, and the mechanics were gone. I remember saying to Doug, about two hours after it happened, that maybe we should send a cable to New York and tell them about this. Doug looked at me said, 'By God, you're right,' and he went off and composed a cable.

"It was hard to convince Harold Roig, who was then president, and the people at W. R. Grace in New York that two mechanics could simply take off and fly an airplane into the drink. Grace reacted predictably and said we should put ignition locks on all the planes.

There were other accidents. Tommy Grimm and Floyd "Nellie" Nelson belly-landed number P-47, a DC-3, at Talara, Peru, after one engine caught fire and fell off on take-off. An accident at Chala in January, 1943, took another DC-3, number P-45, out of service.

"I'm sure the one in the accident at Chala was P-45," Bill Chamberlin recalled, "because it doesn't appear in my logbooks after December 1942. It was built for United originally. Number P-44 was built for American with the door on the right side. I thought it always flew sideways like a crab, but even so, it went as fast as the others."

The DC-2s were being relegated to freight roles. They too suffered losses. "P-28, a DC-2, was a freighter when I knew it," Chamberlin recalled. "It was wrecked in Arajuno when McCleskey decided that we should not go down to the oil camp at Shell Mera to haul for Shell without being checked out by a check pilot.

"He went down there to check out Gene Christianson, and they wrecked P-28 in Arajuno. The other DC-2s were eventually given to the Peruvian air force about the end of 1945. I understand that the company found some cracks in the center section of one or both of them."

"Jack Mehrmann was captain on one of the Wright-powered DC-3s that, as I remember, was en route from Mendoza to Córdoba," Bill Chamberlin recalled. "Somewhere in the Córdoba Hills, he had to shut an engine off. Then he shut the other one off when it overheated, and landed dead-stick in a pasture. I heard that he rolled between two trees that were so close together that they had to jockey the airplane around to tow it out."

Ernie Hummel remembered more details about the story:

"Jack and copilot Bob Frough were cruising at 11,000 feet when Jack noticed that Bob was staring intently out the right window.

"'Bob,' he said, 'what in the hell are you looking at?'

"'I see a lot of stud bolts rattling around and collecting in the bottom of the cowling,' Frough said.

"Sure enough, more than a handful of cylinder hold-down bolts were loose. So Mehrmann shut the engine down and feathered the prop. He shoved the power up on the left engine and anticipated no problem holding 11,000 feet until he could go a few more miles and pass the summit of the Córdoba Hills.

"Just as he was crossing the summit, the purser came forward and said that a vast amount of oil was collecting on top of the left wing. At that moment, the left engine oil pressure dropped, and the temperature started to climb. They barely skimmed across the tops of the Córdoba Hills, but now they had lots of good landing sites in the flat country around Córdoba.

"Mehrmann picked out a nice long field, and down they went, one engine feathered and the other barely pulling. At the last second they realized that the field had tall grass in it, and in the tall grass were lots of sheep. So they quickly picked out another field, landed, and barely squeezed the airplane between two trees at the far end.

"The airplane, as I understand it, actually ended up on the patio of a farmhouse there. Of course, with no engines, it didn't make much noise. A small boy saw all this and ran into the house to tell his grandfather.

"'*Abuelo, Abuelo, llegó Panagra,*' the boy said.

"'*Sí hijito, llega Panagra todos los días de la semana,*' Grandpa said.

"'*Pero Abuelo,*' the grandson yelled. '*Está en el patio.*'"

Chamberlin had a very similar close call in the same area shortly thereafter:

"I was flying a Pratt & Whitney-powered DC-3 from Buenos Aires to Santiago when, out of Córdoba for Mendoza, I looked out of the cockpit and noticed that all but one or two of the cowling fasteners in the row on the left engine were loose. They probably had been loose since Buenos Aires, but I didn't notice them until we were crossing the Córdoba Hills.

"I sent a message to our emergency field at Villa Dolores just to the west to have them bring a ladder to the field. We landed, but nobody showed up. I unloaded enough baggage to stand on so I could reach the row of fasteners, secured them, and continued on to Mendoza."

Most of the passenger volume increase was on existing routes at this time, but on December 8 a third weekly service went into effect on the *Transcontinental* route through Bolivia to link up with Panair do Brasil, and on to the east coast. Meanwhile, a fifth weekly service commenced between Lima and Santiago, the latter rounding out five trips weekly between Santiago and the United States.

On the weather front, Panagra began taking upper air soundings at Arica, Chile and at Cochabamba and Trinidad, Bolivia. These stations were equipped with high-altitude "pilot" balloons for this service. In December, two similar stations were established at Guayaquil, Ecuador, and at Santa Cruz, Bolivia.

In May an Airways Forecast Center was established at Lima, increasing coverage to those parts of the Panagra schedule south of Lima. In October Panagra submitted requisitions to the United States government for the equipment and instruments to establish fifty-five first-class weather stations, including fifteen high-altitude stations capable of taking measurements in the upper atmosphere.

To staff this increased effort, four more meteorologists came on board in November. At the same time, the Bolivian Forecast Center was moved from Cochabamba to Santa Cruz, combining with the high-altitude equipment at that location. This provided improved forecasts for the pilots who normally overnighted at Santa Cruz.

In July a new terminal was opened at Albrook Field on Panama's Pacific Coast. Panagra shared the Canal Zone Air Terminal with Pan Am, UMCA, and TACA airlines. It offered all the amenities of the day: air conditioning, fluorescent lighting, a public address system, even pneumatic tubes, through which messages were sent from one part of the building to another.

Also in July, the Panagra Operations Center moved into new quarters at Limatambo Airport in Lima. It included a new medical department for flight personnel and employees.

This was just part of a massive Panagra upgrade in administration. In August, H.E. Benham, Panagra's navigation instructor, was made director of ground training. He began at once to organize a systematic ground training program for pilots to supplement the already extensive flight program. Benham at first worked only with the apprentice copilots, but the program soon expanded to include dispatchers, flight radio operators (FROs), airport traffic control operators, and maintenance personnel. By November there was a full-time instructor of meteorology for both flight and station personnel.

Perhaps the highlight of 1943 was when Vice President Henry A. Wallace and his aides made an official diplomatic tour of South America. Captain Floyd Nelson picked up the group in Lima and took them to Panama. Nelson chose that flight to be my check as captain.

1944

On January 1, 1944, Panagra technicians completed the conversion of a DC-3A (number P-49) into a cargo plane, installing a cargo hatch in the top rear. A separate, smaller cargo compartment was provided in the same aircraft for valuables.

Cargo was becoming more diversified. Pilots now sometimes flew to the sounds of croaking frogs or chirping insects as air freight opened up possibilities never before dreamed of in international trade. On January 21, for example, Panagra carried a shipment of trout and whitefish eggs, a gift from the U.S. government, to Peru. The fish eggs were bound for the International Fish Hatcheries at Chucuito, Lake Titicaca. The 500,000 whitefish and 40,000 lake trout eggs arrived in perfect condition. South America repaid the favor on March 15, sending seventy giant bug-eating frogs (*Bufo Paracnemis* and *Bufo Arenarum*) from the low-lying Chaco region, to Balboa, and then on to Miami, where sixty-nine of the frogs were released in hopes of exterminating plant parasites in Florida. One of the pie-plate-sized frogs died en route; the rest reproduced happily and are now a considerable problem in south Florida. And on March 22, in an ironic twist of fate, a shipment of insect eggs, intended, upon hatching, to control the boll weevil, left Tucumán, Argentina, for the Cotton Belt of the United States. Panagra, formed originally from a boll-weevil dusting operation which left the United States to seek its fortune in South America, was in a way returning to its roots.

Meantime Chuck Schultz, in his own twist of fate, was flying around South America as copilot to some of the same students he had trained back in Ohio. He seemed quite cheerful about it. After all, there was no better way to find out if your students had learned anything.

Chuck Schultz also teamed up with Herbie Schultz (no relation–and not a former student) on a flight up to Panama that got into bad weather:

"It was very unusual for the weather at Panama to close," Schultz said. "But it does occur. We deviated to Turbo, Colombia. Seventeen training planes had already landed at Turbo, with their crews, and there were also two Pan American planes with crews and passengers. The field was very crowded, and when we arrived, everyone ahead of us had eaten.

"We had to wait, along with our passengers, until the station manager sent a dugout canoe over to the mainland for some staple goods and a live pig. Then we had to wait until the pig was slaughtered and cooked before we could have any supper.

"Most of the passengers slept in the airplane. The rest of us slept in the station on the floor, or anywhere else we could find. The next morning when we got ready to leave, the station manager showed me that the only thing left to eat in the station was a half bottle of catsup."

In September 1944 Panagra successfully flew a 1,040-kilo shipment of Fleischmann's yeast from Lima up to Guayaquil. Cargoes of less commercial importance included a Peruvian cinchona tree, sent to Miami by the Rotary Club in Lima, and an air express shipment, on October 12, of a dozen black siskins, a rare and delicate variety of canary from the Amazon jungles, sent to Baltimore as part of a breeding program.

Other cargoes were humanitarian in nature. In April and May of 1944 Panagra carried 8,275 pounds of quinine, valued at $150,000, from La Paz to Lima, where the shipment was picked up by U.S. military aircraft to be rushed to the United States. Quinine, of course, was an essential drug for an army engaged in fighting in malarial climates.

On June 29 a Panagra plane carried a shipment of penicillin into Chachani Airport at Arequipa, and in September an emergency flight from Santiago, Chile, to Río Tercero, Argentina, brought a shipment of gambusias, mosquito-eating fish, to help fight a malaria outbreak.

Pilots at this time often flew very long routes, and fifteen-hour days were not unusual. In fact, I just might hold the record for long flights. I used to fly two Buenos Aires-Santiago round trips each week. The round trip was about 15 hours. One day, after I had flown Buenos Aires-Santiago, operations sent word for me to bring a flight back up to Lima. I got to Lima on the second day, and operations said, 'Well, we'd been planning to send someone else on to Panama, but that flight's a day late, so we're going to send you up there tomorrow.' I said, 'That's all right with me.' So the next day, I flew to Panama, and the following day I flew from Panama straight back to Lima. Operations said, "Well, you may as well go back to Buenos Aires with this flight."

In six days I'd flown the entire route for the airline, round trip, which was about as fast as you could fly. Today a pilot would never be permitted to fly 72 hours in six days. That's a lot of flying, and there is too much fatigue involved.

One passenger even stopped me when I went back into the cabin for coffee. He said, "I've been on this airline for two or three days, and I've never seen anybody fly but you. Are you the only pilot they've got?"

During their long hours in the cockpits, Panagra air crews either

DC-3, number P-43, unloading at Limatambo. The passengers used to wait until the flight crew had dissembarked before leaving themselves. The captain here (middle of the flight crew group) is William Krusen.

became good friends, or got on one another's nerves, or both. One pilot complained of his copilot that, "he stops whatever he's doing to take a picture every time he sees a beautiful sight. And I never saw anybody eat as much. That, of course, makes him sleepy, so when he's through eating, he takes a nice nap. When he wakes up from his nap he wants to practice his Spanish, so he gets the steward to talk to him. There's really not much point in having him aboard the airplane."

Three more meteorologists were added to the staff in 1944, and the forecast service finally extended over all Panagra routes, from Balboa, Panama, to Buenos Aires, Argentina. Other administrative changes included a 24-hour service by the new medical department at Limatambo.

For the convenience of the passengers, an airport limousine service was established in Buenos Aires, almost identical to the famous La Guardia Field limousines. Each car had a capacity of ten passengers and driver. This was one of the few instances of an airport limousine service outside of the United States.

In personnel matters, Harold Roig was re-elected president of Panagra at a meeting on April 15, and a new subsidiary, Compañía de Avación Pan American Argentina, S.A., was formed in May, with George P. Smith named general manager. J. B. Ottiker took over as commercial advisor for Lloyd Aéreo Boliviano, with an office at LAB headquarters in Cochabamba, Bolivia. Harry "Pop" Colliver, longtime Panagra pilot, retired in a ceremony at the Lima Country Club. And Colonel Harold R. Harris, Panagra senior vice president, now on active duty with the U.S. Army, was appointed chief of staff of the U.S. Air Transport Command.

One personnel problem to contend with was that pilots were unhappy if their long trips took them away from their families for very long. I was one of the bachelors, and, as a result, I was shuffled from one end of the Panagra route to the other, on the theory that no one would miss me. I really enjoyed it. I got a lot more flying out of it, because a lot of times they ended up giving me additional flights. If anyone got sick, they'd say, "Let's send Krusen, and he can live down there for three months." There were several months when I was flying 150-160 hours a month, about double what we normally flew.

I didn't complain. I was a company man, and I loved the flying. However, after a while, I didn't like the fact that I was a nomad. I was in Argentina, my clothes were in Lima, and my laundry was in Santiago. I had no real base. I lived out of a suitcase.

I probably should have taken notes from a Pan Am pilot, flying on the east coast of South America, who was known as "one-shirt Willy." This gentleman wore his uniform shirt only to walk to and from the airplane. Once in the cockpit, he stripped to his undershirt to fly the plane. At the end of a week of flying, he had an assortment of dirty undershirts and one rather tired uniform shirt.

Although we were all required to learn Spanish, most of the Panagra pilots tended to socialize only with one another and sometimes with the passengers. We had little contact with the natives in each country. During free time in Buenos Aires I occasionally went over to Uruguay to be with some friends. I had an old single-shot shotgun, and we would go out to one of the ranches there to shoot perdices, which were like pheasant. Occasionally, we would go horseback riding. I swam at the Buenos Aires YMCA, played a little golf, and played tennis once in a while at the Hurlingham Club. That was about it. If I had a break in Lima, I'd sleep late, then go to the beach. I didn't have much social life. My life, like that of most other Panagra pilots, was flying that airplane, and I lived pretty much in that world. I was interested in anything related to that. So I enjoyed watching the changes as they happened within each area of Panagra.

A new section known as flight control was created within the operations department and placed under the control of Chief Dispatcher H.G. Kitchens. All members of this section were CAA-licensed aircraft dispatchers or apprentices. To handle flight control problems over the entire system, Panagra routes were broken down into "flight control areas" with a "flight control office" being established in each area. The system started with offices in Cali, Colombia; Guayaquil, Ecuador; Lima, Peru; Santiago, Chile; Buenos Aires and Salta, Argentina; and Santa Cruz, Bolivia. Each office was staffed with a dispatcher-in-charge, a flight dispatcher, apprentice dispatchers and control clerks.

A good manager works with the human material at hand, encouraging each person to give the best of which he or she is capable. Cy Collins remembered one young executive who eventually left Panagra for new worlds to conquer:

"Peter Morrison was a very bright and very interesting young man, whom we didn't know what to do with. He got into everybody's hair, and it became my job to find a place for Peter. I put him in as manager of the Chiclayo station, perhaps the least important job in the whole company.

"But Peter turned that station around. He sent us reports almost three times a day, telling us of the tremendous activity that was going on down there. Well, he did communicate, entirely too much, but it's why I remember Peter with affection. We couldn't bury the guy, he insisted on letting us know every single thing that went on in that little place.

"I don't mean to poke fun at Peter. He was a kid who was hard to handle, a character who made my life in South America more interesting, and, as I've said, went on to do very well on his own."

In terms of route expansions, a second weekly service between Quito, Ecuador, and Ipiales, Colombia began on February 18, 1944, by Aerovias del Ecuador. In addition to connecting with an Avianca flight at Ipiales, this service linked Quito and Bogota, the capitals of the two nations, with just five hours of flying time.

On April 6 another subsidiary, Lloyd Aéreo Boliviano (LAB), began direct weekly service to Tarija, capital of an important agricultural and mining province in southeast Bolivia. This was a significant step for the Allied war effort, tapping the rich mineral and petroleum reserves of this region bordering upon the vast Chaco desert. In May LAB also extended its Cochabamba-Yacuiba service to Santa Cruz and return.

During an uprising in Bolivia, a band of revolutionaries seized the Panagra bus that carried passengers out to the La Paz airport from the town. "Carl Rooth, the stationmaster, was an old-timer, a Scandinavian," Cy Collins recalled. "The Panagra bus was admitted to the airport on the assumption that it was full of passengers, but it was really full of armed revolutionaries who promptly started a battle to take over the airport.

"Bullets started coming through the station, and there was Carl reporting all this with his Scandinavian coolness on the radio. After the revolutionaries won, he sat down and wrote a letter to Bob Disher. 'Things are calm now,' he wrote. 'The new government is in power and everything is O.K. A few repairs are needed to the station where the bullets went through. And will you please tell Mr. Collins that I think it's time for my sea-level rest.' I agreed, and we gave him that."

As previously discussed, Panagra had signed a number of mining contracts, among them one with Shell Oil company to transport by

Planes at Shell Mera were driven to locations where the landing gear rolled into trenches to bring the cabin nearer to ground level for loading.

Loading mining equipment into a DC-3, number P-50, at Shell Mera. The plane, a converted military C-47, is shown parked in the loading trenches, with its door at a convenient height.

A crew at Shell Mera loading oil drilling pipe for delivery to Arajuno, Ecuador. This plane, a converted C-47, has a larger cargo door (the smaller passenger door is set into it) and vents in some windows for the comfort of paratroopers.

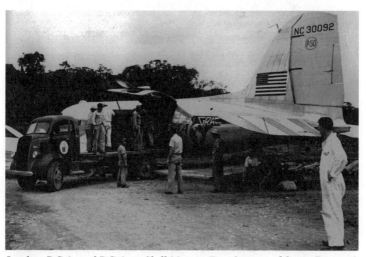

Loading DC-2s and DC-3s at Shell Mera in Ecuador, east of Quito. Panagra's ability to deliver so many types of equipment as air freight was especially important in areas where the mountains had proven to be a major transportation obstacle in the past.

air over 1,000 tons of oil-well drilling machinery from Shell's base camp at Shell Mera into the jungle-bound Arajuno region of Ecuador.

I guess I was one of the first pilots to fly into Shell Mera. You flew up the Mera River and turned off the river into a slot cut into the jungle. The trees must have been 150 feet high all around. The Shell people had floated a disassembled bulldozer down the river on dugouts, put it together, and used it to knock down the trees. Then they brought in fill dirt from somewhere, and that was the runway. It was about 2,000 feet long, but if you didn't stop in time, you went straight into the trees at the end opposite the river.

"The Shell people had found a German oil rig, still in its crates, abandoned on the docks at Salinas," Dick Witt recalled. "It was left there at the start of World War II. Panagra, hired to move this equipment to Arajuno, sent five people to live at the base camp of Shell Mera. There was a pilot, a copilot, a radio operator, a mechanic, and an accountant to keep the books on this operation. At first, we used a DC-2.

"Many of the girders were heavy and much too long to load into the airplane. These were cut into pieces and reassembled at the other end. Even with the smaller pieces, it would sometimes take a day and a half to load one piece into the airplane.

"Eventually, Bob Disher brought over a DC-3 and took the DC-2 back to Lima. But even with the larger airplane, it took a very long time to load. Sometimes we had to take the front windshield out and load the girders in through the cockpit.

"We also carried a lot of vegetables and supplies to the men who were at the camp at Arajuno. It was very primitive country over there. We used to fly down over the Auca village—by this time they had moved about six miles away from the camp and were no longer a threat to anyone—and they would come out and, thinking this big bird was coming after them, throw their spears up at us. Of course, we were too high, but they didn't know that at first."

Insurance regulations forbade Panagra pilots from taking passengers on freight runs. "We turned our heads a few times, I admit," Witt recalled. "It just wasn't right for those poor guys to have to spend three days hacking their way through the jungle with machetes, exposed to all the bugs, snakes, and whatever else they had there."

On September 13 Panagra celebrated its 16th birthday. Records through the end of the previous year, 1943, showed traffic increases of 660% from 1939 to 1943, with 68,700 people transported in 1943. Cargo in that same period was up 1,850% to a 1943 total of 1,980,000 pounds. Mail was up 474%. Route miles had increased to 8,800 and total miles flown in 1943 (not passenger miles but actual route miles) were 4,686,303.

Since 1939, service from the Panama Canal south to Lima, Santiago, and Buenos Aires had increased from twice weekly to daily.

Plans were afoot to institute more "express" routes to speed up the time-table, and applications were in with the CAB for two such routes out of Panama.

Panagra could also look back on a pioneering effort in the fields of radio communications and weather forecasting in South America. Now there was point-to-point contact between airports as well as radio bea-con navigational aids. Crystal-controlled transmitters could broadcast radio telegraphy, both modulated and unmodulated, and radio tele-phone. The original 1,020-watt antenna power of the network had in-creased to 14,900 watts. Limatambo alone employed 25 radio opera-tors and 16 technicians for shop maintenance of ground and aircraft radio equipment. In all, Panagra owned or controlled some 75 radio stations in the countries that it served.

Coinciding with the 16th anniversary celebrations, Panagra Presi-dent Roig announced contracts for the purchase of three four-engine Douglas DC-4s of 52-passenger capacity. These were to be used on a Panagra "great circle" route and would offer night flying service in both directions.

Panagra's 16th year was also the 15th year for air mail service in Panagra's service area. On May 18-26 Panagra observed the anniver-sary of the first flight between the United States and the western part of South America. Congratulatory messages were exchanged between the presidents of the United States and Ecuador. On July 21 the scene was repeated with messages between the presidents of the United States and Chile and between Harold Roig and the Chilean foreign minister. Chilean postal authorities authorized the use of a special stamp for the occasion.

This exchanging of letters and celebration was, of course, a fine way for the management of Panagra to remind the leaders of the various countries within its operational area of the contributions of the U. S. airline to their nations' economic (and social) integration into the world economy.

As another way of reminding political and business leaders of its importance to their countries, Panagra could be counted upon to whisk dignitaries about the continent as needed. On June 22 President Prado of Peru and members of his staff took a tour of southern Peru via Panagra, making stops at Arequipa, Cuzco, and Puerto Maldonado. When Major General Fulgencio Batista, former president of Cuba, wanted to make a goodwill tour of South America, Panagra was there to accommodate him; not a bad policy as Batista was to return to power in his country, remaining until the Communist revolution of 1959.

Panagra did not receive the coveted Inter-American Safety Award for 1943. Instead, it was awarded on September 28, 1944, to Lloyd Aéreo Boliviano, which had operated under Panagra supervision since

August of 1941. Along the way, on January 8, 1944, Panagra Vice President John Shannon and Panagra Captain Harold A. Speer, technical advisor to LAB, were awarded the Order of the Condor of the Andes, the highest civilian honor conferred by the Bolivian government.

Frank Havelick noted that during the Second World War, Bolivia opened its doors to Jewish refugees fleeing persecution in Europe. The nation benefitted from this influx of technically-advanced immigrants.

"At first," he noted, "the only available accommodations were offered by the Stranger's Club in La Paz. The influx of Jewish refugees completely changed the face of the urban centers. It seemed to be a catalyst for development and modernization. The Sucre Palace Hotel was built and opened in record time. Clean meat markets sprang up. The first no-grit white bread was on the dinner table, and hot water was available for bathing. Soon there was even a medicinal-oxygen plant, allowing Panagra to replenish passenger and crew oxygen bottles there."

1945

By 1945 the momentum in the war had swung to the Allies. This lessened the need for supplies and equipment transhipped via South America for Africa. Nevertheless, Panagra continued to be a mainline supply route, partly because of the geographic situation and the limited over-water range of the aircraft of the day, and partly because of the well-established infrastructure along Panagra's routes.

The first of three more Douglas transports, allocated to Panagra by the U.S. War Property Administration, arrived in Limatambo on January 24, 1945, piloted by Capt. Ernie Hummel. At the ceremony marking the arrival, Panagra officials announced the scorecard for 1944: 84,206 passengers carried (up 22% over 1943), 5,143,422 miles flown (up 9.5%), 158 tons of mail (up 4%), and more than a thousand tons of air cargo carried on regularly scheduled flights—and exclusive of any special contracts.

On March 1 Vice President Thomas Kirkland took a leave of absence from Panagra to undertake a special assignment for the U.S. Navy, with the rank of commander. Harold Harris was promoted to brigadier general in the U.S. Army Air Force on June 9.

Cargo operations continued. On April 10 aircraft number P-50 carried its largest commercial air express shipment to date, some 1,316 kilos of generator parts, which it brought from Balboa, Panama, to Guayaquil, Ecuador. These parts were urgently needed for the resumption of mining operations by the South American Development Company in the Portobello sector of Ecuador.

On May 13, just a few days after V-E Day, Panagra celebrated its tenth anniversary of service into Bolivia with a party at El Alto, the La Paz airport. The playbill was the usual: John Shannon, Panagra vice president, took the Bolivian president and some of his cabinet for a ride. The president congratulated the airline in the form of a letter to U.S. President Harry S Truman. The Bolivian minister of foreign affairs sent a congratulatory message to Panagra President Harold Roig in New York. The Bolivians, not to be outdone by the Chileans of the year before, issued their own Panagra postage stamp. Since they printed eight million of them, it must have taken a while to use them all.

Even with first-rate meterological reports, flying across the *altiplano* at this time still meant having to solve the problem of late-morning turbulence, caused by the sun's heating up the bare rocks. From Salta, Argentina, we'd climb up through a canyon and onto the *altiplano*. It was 12,000 or 13,000 feet high, and we would cruise at 16,000 or 17,000 feet. At that altitude, a DC-3 could only do about 130 knots. We'd land at Uyuni, take on or drop off passengers, no fueling there, and head on north to Oruro, where we would do the same thing. The next town was La Paz, and then through the western *cordillera* and down to Arequipa, then on north to Lima. The whole trip took eight or nine hours. If you left Salta at 9 a.m., you got turbulent air on the *altiplano* because of the temperature. So I said, "Heck, I'll just leave at 6 a.m. and be through the *altiplano* before the heat builds up." That's what I did, and it was ideal.

Unfortunately, the management got up in arms and said that I couldn't do that. What if someone went to the airport to catch the flight and it had left three hours earlier? I said, "Well, they'd have to find out about it. Why don't you change the schedule?" But they wouldn't do that.

I still left early. I'd send word ahead that, "Due to weather, I request an early departure."

Route mileage had by this time reached its maximum extent for the time being, subject to minor adjustments. On September 1, 1945, just days before the Japanese surrender, Panagra added two new flights from Balboa to Lima, for a total of nine trips per week. At the same time, one additional flight from Lima to Santiago was added, raising the number of weekly flights over this sector to six.

The Ecuador routes received the greatest increase in equipment. Four new weekly flights were added between Guayaquil and Quito, beefing up this vital link. Quito had been dropped from the longer routes, as the airline switched over to "longer-legged aircraft," in favor of the more populous Guayaquil.

With this change, there were twelve weekly flights between Quito and Guayaquil. At the same time, a second flight was added between Quito and Esmeraldas and another between Quito and Ipiales.

The Ecuadoreans had already expressed their gratitude to Panagra earlier in the year when they honored Captain William Sindo in a ceremony at Eloy Alfaro Airport at Manta in March. Ecuadorian officials took special note of the efforts by Panagra and Aerovias del Ecuador in furthering commercial aviation links between Ecuador and the rest of the world. Considering the size of this airborne pipeline that had been funneling goods and manpower through South America en route to Africa, most of the credit goes to Panagra.

Bill Sindo had been on duty with the Army Air Corps in Panama when he decided to leave the service and join Panagra in 1936. (Fritz Sterling had done the same thing two years earlier, and Sindo may have known of this.) Sindo served at the Lima and Buenos Aires bases until the Through Flight Agreement between Panagra, Pan American, W. R. Grace Co., and National Airlines in the late 1940s opened up the United States to Panagra flights. Sindo then moved to Panagra and Pan Am's Miami base where he worked until his retirement.

On September 13 Panagra celebrated 17 years of existence and the end of the war. In more than five years of wartime operations, the company had flown 13,650,661 miles, carried 206,384 passengers, 1,011,561 pounds of mail, and 5,268,257 pounds of express air cargo. This latter figure did not count special charters, mining assists, and assorted disaster relief missions. Some indication of the effect of the war upon Panagra can be seen from one statistic: in 1945 the airline carried 10,000 more passengers than it had carried in the previous year, and that increase alone was more than the total passenger load in 1939.

On November 7 General H. L. George, commanding general of the U.S. Air Transport Command, sent a letter to Panagra President Roig, on behalf of the ATC, thanking Panagra for "a wartime job magnificently done." At the same time, an ATC unit assigned to the Panagra base at Miami was dissolved.

The next day, November 8, 1945, Chuck Schultz took his ATR (Air Transport Rating) test on the DC-2. It was the last such test issued, at least for the Panagra fleet. "A few days later, Chief Pilot McCleskey called me into his office for a lecture on the Panagra captain's code of ethics," Schultz recalled. "He stressed very strongly that all Panagra captains were considered equal. For example, he said, if you are flying as second section, and the lead plane finds the weather conditions too rough and decides to turn back, the second pilot should abide by this decision and do likewise.

"The following day, November 25, I took my first solo trip, on a C-47 freighter from Lima to Balboa. At Cali, Colombia, I was sandwiched in between McCleskey, flying a DC-3A passenger flight, and John Biller, following me with another passenger flight.

"McCleskey flew ahead, at 10,000 feet, looking for an opening through the ridge. As he went by each pass, he radioed back that it was closed. To stay out of his way, Biller and I went up to 12,000 feet. In a short time we found an opening and went through. Shortly after, I heard McCleskey on the radio, reporting that all the passes were closed and that he was turning back. Then I heard Biller saying that he, too, was turning back. We were already on the other side, and I didn't see any sense in turning around to find the hole again, to over-night at Cali. I just kept going to Panama.

"But I was anxious about what McCleskey would have to say. I asked for an early departure out of Panama to avoid the confrontation as long as possible, and I left a note for McCleskey with the station manager. I spent the next few days in Lima waiting for the call from McCleskey's office. It never came. Instead, I ran into Bob Disher, who had my note. 'Did you really write this?' he asked. I owned up to it. 'Oh hell, that's the breaks of the game,' was all he said. And that was the last I heard of it."

The war was over when Panagra took delivery of its last DC-3A at Limatambo on December 5. It was time to reorganize, to look at still larger aircraft, and to build on those extensive routes and ground bases that Panagra had established during the war.

A Panagra DC-4. The four-engine planes, soon also joined by new DC-6s, helped relieve congestion on the routes after the war.

Mt. Cotopaxi, Ecuador (6,843 meters), from the cockpit of a four-engine DC-6.

CHAPTER 9

POSTWAR OPERATIONS, 1946-1959

1946

On February 3, 1946, Panagra Vice President Douglas Campbell announced changes in the executive organization that would get the airline moving forward on a post-war footing. Thomas Kirkland had returned as a vice-president after his brief tour of duty with the U.S. Navy. He would be assigned to the New York office. Vice President John Shannon was to devote his time entirely to the four-engined aircraft that Panagra would be receiving. Shannon would make all necessary arrangements for operation and maintenance. Captain Charles Disher, operations manager, was promoted to supervise the operations, maintenance, and communications departments. He would be assisted by F. L. Achilles, Jr., and a new operations "superintendent," J. T. Scholtz.

A. J. Phelan, formerly the assistant comptroller, was put in charge of the newly-organized financial department in South America. One of two assistant treasurers, W. F. Lewis, was assigned the management of financial affairs for the New York office. The other assistant treasurer, E. E. Spencer, was given the job of recruiting personnel and handling any business matters associated with that activity. Lastly, J. H. Nelowet was to work with Vice President Campbell on any special projects Campbell might assign.

The round-trip from Santiago to Buenos Aires had originally been a two-day affair. By the end of the war, faster aircraft made possible a single-day round trip. It was still a challenge for the pilots, though.

Whenever I flew that route, I started early from Buenos Aires, and I didn't fool around. I would have the radio operator call ahead to get the passengers standing out on the ramp. Then we would stow luggage according to destination. When I landed, I would only shut off the left engine long enough to get the passengers and baggage off and take the new ones aboard. I wouldn't let the other passengers disembark and stand around. We could cut a normal 50-minute stop to five minutes this way.

I always carried extra fuel, so I didn't have to re-fuel every place. We had plenty of tanks and tank capacity, but nobody ever put the extra fuel in. Maybe they thought it cost extra money to haul it around, but fuel was cheaper in Buenos Aires than it was anyplace else. So I put in all I could in B.A., and when I got to Córdoba and Mendoza, I didn't need any. I put more in at Santiago, and started back. Even so, it was a long day, about 15 hours of flying time. You had to push all the way.

On April 1 there had been an attempted coup in Ecuador. The government arrested the ten ringleaders, but was afraid to execute them because they were so popular with the people. Instead, on April 2, Chuck Schultz found himself dragooned into flying the men into exile: six to Ipiales, Colombia, four to Talara, Peru.

"When the first bedraggled group was brought out of a van and saw the ring of soldiers with fixed bayonets surrounding them, I'm certain they were very scared," Schultz recalled. "They probably assumed that this was a firing squad. They were loaded into the airplane along with two of the soldiers. The soldiers had trouble with their rifles and bayonets in the small cabin of the DC-2.

"When we got into Ipiales, only the station manager was on duty, and no flights were scheduled at that hour to transfer the men. We explained the problem to the station manager and said that he had to hold these men for a later flight. He had no guards, he said, and the Ecuadorean border was just off the south end of the runway. He asked if he could borrow the two Ecuadorean soldiers, and we said sure." In Talara things were more organized, with a proper reception for the four plotters.

What the Colombian government might have thought about two Ecuadorean soldiers acting as guards on Colombian territory, Schultz never learned.

He also never learned how the two soldiers found their way home again, because when he returned to Quito after completing his second "pest-removal" mission of the day, a grateful Ecuadorean government kicked him out of the country.

"I was told to get myself and family ready for departure from Quito to the United States on the first available flight, which happened to be the next day," Schultz recalled. "Jack Willey came to Quito to replace me, and he took over the rental of our house. After a furious night of packing and sorting our belongings, we made the flight the next morning, April 3, 1946, which was the start of a very pleasant three-month vacation in the United States."

It wasn't Schultz's last revolution in Ecuador. A few years later he helped to organize an evacuation flight out of Quito just as a rebel force reached the northern end of the airport runway in their push towards the city.

"Bob Farmer taxied south and made a hurried take-off toward the north, using only half the field and banking sharply to the right, away from the fighting," Schultz recalled. Schultz went home, and he, his wife, and several women from the American Embassy spent the night listening to the radio and to the fighting outside their doors as the rebellion was put down.

Panagra continued its relentless pursuit of records, particularly safety records. On April 5 Captain Warren Smith chalked up 1,500 runs across the Andes from Santiago to Buenos Aires, and upon his return to Los Cerrillos airport in Santiago, received a warm welcome from Chilean air officials and a large Chilean crowd.

On April 9 Panagra received the Aviation Safety Award from the Inter-American Safety Council for the fifth time, in a ceremony held at the Biltmore Hotel in New York. However, this event, and previous awards of a similar nature, revealed a subtle problem. While the South American people–and government officials, too–personally loved the North Americans who worked for Panagra, actions such as giving out safety awards for South American aviation in far away New York City could only irritate sensitive Latin American governments.

Another sore point was Panagra's control over radio transmitters within the countries it served. Today this would seem an irrelevancy, but the Second World War, just ended, had demonstrated the capabilities of air power and had turned radio and radar technologies into powerful intelligence tools. Many nations, not just South American ones, were wary of foreign radio transmitters on their soil.

Panagra had already taken steps to integrate itself as much as possible into South American governmental and business worlds. Of the 2,300 Panagra employees and *obreros* in South America, fully 95% were local nationals, rather than *norteamericanos*. The rising nationalism of the Latin American countries was a problem with which Panagra management was fully cognizant. Short of abandoning all profitability, Panagra would take any steps necessary to preserve its position.

One thing the airline never did was to hire native pilots. This was not because of a shortage of talent; most of them would have worked far more cheaply. "Pilots had to be licensed under American rules in order to fly the U.S. Mail," Frank Havelick recalled. "They generally frowned upon any foreign airline carrying the U.S. Mail. If it hadn't been for the mail, and the mail pay, we would never have made any profit. We got paid per pound and per mile. That's what kept Panagra going."

The mechanics, however, were almost all locals, supervised by a few Americans.

"As the years went by," Havelick recalled, "they trained some splendid mechanics–just tremendous! They would work their hearts out for the company. Union rules didn't mean anything. They took pride in their work, and they kept the airline going."

But when asked if he socialized with the local mechanics, Havelick could recall only big, special occasions. "We didn't go out with them or have them over to dinner," he said. "They had their own lives to lead. But in our day-to-day relations on the job, we were just like brothers."

For example, on April 19 Panagra did something unique, chartering two DC-4 aircraft from Dodero Aviation, an Argentine company. Ironically, Panagra had actually been one of the earliest airlines to order the DC-4, and the Panagra name had already been painted on one of the first to come off the production line, when the U.S. Army Air Force stepped in and requisitioned it at the start of the war.

"Dodero was a huge shipping company," Frank Havelick recalled. "They had been anxious to get into air operations, so they bought some military DC-4s and converted them to passenger use. Of course, everything was C-54s (the military version of the DC-4) in those days. They tried to operate an airline in Argentina using these planes and didn't make a go of it."

These planes were to be used on the Balboa-Lima section to relieve congestion there until the new DC-4s and DC-6s that Panagra had ordered were delivered. Panagra could have chartered DC-4s elsewhere, but by chartering them from an Argentine company, Panagra received more than the aircraft—it won points for diplomacy.

For the same reason, Panagra always made a celebration out of an air mail route anniversary. It was an opportunity to arrange for a letter, albeit almost a form letter, to be sent from the U.S. president to the president of the country being served. Panagra did this again on May 18, 1946, celebrating seventeen years of air mail service to Peru and the renewal of Panagra's airmail contract.

On May 22, after two years of hearings, the Civil Aeronautics Board (CAB) in Washington, D.C., approved a proposal by Panagra to extend its service to the U.S. mainland.

"The DC-6s had been ordered for delivery late in 1946," Loyal Domning recalled. "But these were delayed several months for modification to a fire-prone fuel system. When they were finally available, Panagra was able to conclude a package agreement with Pan Am which permitted the extension of our route from Panama to Miami. That, in turn, set the stage for a subsequent interchange agreement with National Airlines, adding Washington and New York to the system."

At first, Panagra had not wanted the DC-6. "Immediately after the war, Panagra ordered the Lockheed Constellation as part of the joint Panagra-Pan American procurement program," Domning recalled. "A contingent of flight engineers came to Lima to train Panagra's flight crews in the operation of the Connie and its Wright-3350 engines. This program was nearly completed, and the Pan American-Grace name had been painted on the airplanes when a decision was made to stick with Douglas and to buy the DC-6s."

For most of its life Panagra's route was to end at Panama, where it joined the Pan Am Miami-Panama route. Panagra, as an "extra-national" airline, was supposed to wave the American flag overseas and carry out, as it had during the war, certain American policies. But it wasn't supposed to offer competition to airlines operating within the United States. It was not a new argument, and it was one that would continue long past Panagra's existence. Nor did endorsement by the CAB guarantee immediate U.S. routes; Panagra still had to deal with Pan Am, which was doing just fine, thank you, with its Miami-Balboa route.

Panagra flirted briefly with another expansion route immediately after the war. "There was a plan to fly from Santiago, Chile, across the Pacific to Australia by way of some South Pacific islands," Ernie Hummel recalled. "Panagra bought a C-54 (a military DC-4) configured with extra fuselage fuel tanks. All pilots and copilots had to take a navigation course that included celestial navigation.

"When it was time to get type-rated on the DC-4, it was very cold in Lima, so we moved the school up to France Field in Panama. The pilot in charge, sitting in the right seat one day, was shouting so many orders to the pilot undergoing training that things got confused. They were slowing the engines to idle, one at a time; sometimes they had props feathered, too, and the training got pretty wild," according to Hummel. The pilots took turns in the left seat, and if they were not flying, they watched over the shoulders of whoever was, or sat back in the cabin. "On one maneuver, with two engines shut down, gear down, approach flaps down, the operation got well behind the power curve, and they lost air speed and altitude. It was obvious that they weren't going to make the airport. The instructor shouted still more orders to the pilot, who couldn't carry them all out fast enough.

"In the last few seconds one of the other captains got down and crawled through the legs of all the ones who were standing in the cockpit watching. He grabbed the flap lever and bled the flaps up at a rate that permitted them to hang on to the last few knots of air speed. They just missed the trees getting down onto the runway."

The CAB had, in 1945, requested the Department of Justice to investigate Pan Am for anti-trust violations. The Justice Department never took any action, but in 1963 the case eventually found its way to the U.S. Supreme Court, which returned airline-related anti-trust jurisdiction to the CAB.

Doubtless influenced by the CAB's actions, and by the desire of W. R. Grace to have Panagra fly into the U.S., Pan Am agreed to let Panagra fly into Miami using Pan Am's own route certificate. Ultimately, Panagra was even given routes to New York and Washington,

D.C., although those flights were flown by National Airlines pilots. The CAB also approved plans for a "Great Circle" route, essentially a high-speed Balboa-Santiago-Buenos Aires run with relatively few stops, and a resumption of service to Montevideo, Uruguay.

On July 19 in a ceremony held at the Lima Country Club, the first class of Panagra flight hostesses was graduated. Fifteen Peruvian girls had been selected and carefully trained. They were the first female flight attendants to be used by an airline in South America.

Panagra was rapidly deploying the new four-engined DC-4s, putting them into long-range service as fast as the airline could take them. On August 5 the airline announced direct daily through-flight service from the continental U.S. to Buenos Aires without any change of plane. However, when the new service went into effect on August 18, Panagra did not have the Balboa-Miami route. Passengers changed planes in Panama, but thereafter flew straight through South America on one of the new DC-4s.

The DC-4s were especially important between Santiago, Chile, and Buenos Aires, Argentina, where "The main route is, and always has been, via the Uspallata (La Cumbre) Pass, which is the shortest one," Loyal Domning recalled. "That's the route which passes over Mendoza, Argentina.

"There are two other routes: one via the South Pass, over somewhat lower terrain and about 240 miles longer, and the Las Ramadas, or North Pass, which is 175 miles farther than the Uspallata route. These passes were not used to a significant extent by unpressurized airplanes because when the weather was bad enough to close La Cumbre, the others were also usually not open at altitudes low enough to be used by those planes.

"The arrival of the DC-4 ended the era of long delays on either side of the *cordillera*," Domning continued. "It had the range required to go as far as necessary either to the north or south of La Cumbre to circumnavigate foul weather with no payload penalty."

Ernie Hummel remembered when Panagra hosted a number of FAA/CAA people, down from the States to do 'proving runs' of the DC-4: "'Weeping Willy' Denham was flying them from Panama to Lima when the weather at Lima went below minimum. They landed at Trujillo, and the crew and the officials went to the National Hotel on the square at Trujillo to overnight.

"By late in the evening their luggage still hadn't arrived, so the whole group walked around town looking for a *farmacia* (drug store), to buy some toothbrushes, toothpaste, and a few odds and ends. Finally, they found one and pounded on the door, standing there in the dark. A hole in the door opened, and a very old Chinese man looked out. None of them spoke Spanish, and they stood in the street trying to make this old druggist understand what they wanted. Finally, he nodded, and they passed all their money in through the hole in the door.

"In a few minutes he was back, with a sack, which he squeezed out through the hole. The men walked back to the hotel and opened the sack in the lobby where they could see to pass out their toothbrushes. It turned out that all the bag contained was condoms."

The traffic between Lima and Santiago continued to increase, and on September 17, two additional flights were added, these with DC-3s. Several more DC-4s went into Panagra service on October 11, and were put onto the Balboa-Buenos Aires "Great Circle" run. On November 1, Panagra extended its *Transcontinental* route from Corumbá, on the Brazilian side of the Brazil/Bolivia border, into Campo Grande, Brazil.

"I flew a plane load of soccer players on a DC-3 flight from Campo Grande to Santa Cruz, Bolivia," Chuck Schultz recalled. "It was a clear day, beautiful weather conditions and perfectly smooth air. We were 45 minutes out when the purser came to the cockpit and told me there was a sight in the cabin I might enjoy. I went and looked. The entire soccer team was trying to talk to one another while they had 'sick sacks' covering their mouths. Someone had told them that the proper procedure when flying was to get airsick."

DC-4 service between Lima and Santiago was beefed up on November 17, with flights that stopped only at Antofagasta, Chile. The southbound flight was Panagra's first regularly-scheduled night flight. It left Lima at one a.m. and arrived at Los Cerillos Airport in Santiago at 10:15 a.m. With these flights taking up the slack, the supplementary DC-3 schedule of daily service between these two cities was cut back to twice weekly.

On December 26, for the first time, Buenos Aires was connected to Balboa and onward to United States destinations via four-engined aircraft. DC-4s now flew daily between Santiago and Buenos Aires.

There were changes on the *Diagonal* and *Transcontinental* routes as well, with Arica added as a stop on the *Diagonal*, and Oruro eliminated as a stop on the *Transcontinental.*

In November and December the maintenance program was revised. The old maintenance engineering department was split, with O. Z. Johnson taking over the new maintenance department, Ed Trippe the engineering department, and C. A. Jorgenson the stores department. As of December 15, 1946, the DC-3s would receive engine overhauls at the Pan Am shops in Brownsville, Texas.

Toward the end of 1946 Panagra took steps to attempt to head off the increasing nationalism of the governments of the nations it served. Panagra Vice President John Shannon was involved in the procedures that resulted in establishing an organization known as PICAO (Provisional International Civil Aviation Organization) on October 12.

Los Cerillos Airport in Santiago, Chile.

PICAO was to facilitate relations with the various governments of western South America. It also laid the groundwork for standardizing operating and performance standards for airlines. It became ICAO (i.e., the word "provisional" was dropped) in 1941, after the necessary twenty-six signatories had been obtained from member nations.

1947

On January 1, 1947, Argentina banned *cabotage* service by international airlines. Panagra and its non-Argentine competitors were prohibited from picking up and discharging passengers traveling only within Argentina. Panagra was most affected on its *Diagonal* route, in the cities of Córdoba, Mendoza, Salta, and Tucumán.

At the same time, the airline continued to expand its four-engine flights. By April 20 all Panagra DC-4s were converted into 44-seat configurations, replacing the more crowded 55-seat original passenger capacity. The airline advertised this change as, "maintaining the Panagra tradition of providing the ultimate in service for its clients." The resulting actual passenger load factor was not changed significantly, but those who flew could be more comfortable.

Then on May 20 the first of the DC-6s arrived. Ordered years earlier, immediately after the end of the war, Panagra's aircraft were the first DC-6s in South America. On the first, or "survey," flight, the aircraft flew some 7,434 miles, from the factory at Santa Monica, California, to Buenos Aires, in 23 hours and 25 minutes flying time, for an average speed of more than 300 knots.

The average speed did not count the time spent repairing engines. "The chief pilot was flying the airplane and had landed at Guayaquil, Ecuador," Ernie Hummel recalled. "When he restarted the engines, there was a nacelle explosion in the left inboard engine, a loud bang, and then flames shooting out.

"This really startled the passengers, including lots of company personnel and FAA people who were on board. George McTigue, a pilot himself and one of Panagra's aeronautical engineers, flung open the emergency door, grabbed the emergency escape rope, and leapt into space.

"But the idea was that you lowered the rope first, then slid down it. George had grabbed the loose end and just jumped. When the slack came out of the rope it jerked out of George's hands, and he just kept going, hitting the ramp so hard that he sprained an ankle." Fortunately, it wasn't a serious injury.

In May the CAB, following up on its earlier permissions, formally authorized Panagra to fly into Miami on its own "ticket," and the company began the new service on May 31 using DC-4s. On July 17 the new DC-6s took over. Flying on a thrice-weekly basis, the "6's" left Miami at 7:45 p.m. and arrived in Buenos Aires at 6:10 the following evening. With two hours lost because of time changes, this meant a passenger could fly between the two cities in a little more than twenty hours. This not only marked the first time that Balboa and Buenos Aires had been joined by less than a day's flying, but it meant that New York and Buenos Aires were now only about one day's flight apart.

Panagra President Harold Roig, his wife, and their daughter Leila, were aboard the inaugural DC-6 flight. Mrs. Roig had taken an active part in the design of the interior of these aircraft.

The greater altitude and range of the DC-6s were improvements on the Santiago-Buenos Aires route. By July 1947 the larger aircraft were flying regularly over the Andes.

"The pressurized DC-6 was able to cross the Andes at levels up to 25,000 feet and could use whichever pass was open at that height," Loyal Domning recalled. "Most of the time the Uspallata Pass was available under those conditions.

"The minimum Uspallata crossing altitude for instrument or night flight was 26,000 feet, comfortably above the nearby peak of Aconcagua at 23,000, but too high for piston-powered airplanes."

To bolster use of this new pass, Panagra built a new radio station near Ovalle, Chile, to monitor weather in the pass. The Ovalle station sent reports on to Panagra stations in Mendoza and Santiago.

By October 11 Panagra had the bugs worked out of this new long route, and inaugurated, with unprecedented fanfare, the *El Inter Americano* service, featuring DC-6 aircraft and fast flights between Miami and Buenos Aires. The event was publicized widely and celebrated at all DC-6 stops along the route–Balboa, Lima, Santiago, and Buenos Aires–including the new Panagra terminal in Miami. There was band music; there were military escorts; there were messages from presidents, from postal officials, even from school children. Actress Dolores del Rio was on hand to lead the festivities in Buenos Aires. Panagra was learning to appeal to Latin sensibilities.

Ernie Hummel recalled the party in Miami on October 17: "The DC-6 was vastly different from the then-familiar DC-4. Considerable schooling, ground and flight training, and enroute operation experience, plus a new CAA (later FAA) license, or type rating, were necessary. This project was still underway when October 11, the date of the start of the *El Inter Americano* service, rolled around.

"There was a party with a polished '6' in a hangar, tables of food and drink, and aviation dignitaries. A small hurricane, with a very confused trajectory, had brushed by Miami, headed west, earlier in the day. Delta and Eastern, plus most private aircraft, acted conservatively and ferried their aircraft out. Pan Am, however, decided to leave theirs on the deck. At the height of the festivities, the storm reversed course southwest of Miami and headed back, dead-centered on the Pan Am 36th Street airport. The rain which hit was torrential; in no time the water inside the hangar was knee-deep. Pan Am had DC-4s on the ramp, and began calling in crews to ferry them out. Panagra had one DC-6 outside, and it was decided to get it out, too. Since Warren Smith and I were on the spot, we were picked to fly."

When the eye of the storm passed across Miami, Hummel and Smith rushed out to the DC-6 and got the engines going as quickly as they could. They knew they would have only about twenty minutes before the eye passed over and the wind came up from the opposite direction.

Hummel recalled how the airport was so eerily quiet in the eye of the storm that he could hear frogs croaking in the grass. He and Smith taxied through water that was over the aircraft's wheels. They found a runway that was still above the flood waters, at least in the very center of the runway, and started a takeoff roll.

"Just as we lifted off and crossed the fence, a big Florida Power & Light electrical transformer exploded right underneath us," Hummel recalled. "It was like having a giant flash bulb go off. It lit up the whole city.

"Just about that time, we hit the on-coming wall of the hurricane, and the airplane seemed to stop dead." The vibration and noise were severe; Hummel and Smith fought to control the bucking aircraft which, between its take-off speed and the speed of the oncoming wind, was enduring forces well beyond its design parameters.

Making very little forward movement, they rode the hurricane wall vertically until they topped out above the storm at about 30,000 feet.

"Suddenly, we came out of the clouds into a beautiful night sky," Hummel recalled. "We could see the storm below us, and the stars in a clear sky above. We settled things down and headed for Havana.

The DC-6 had been subjected to stresses far beyond what it was designed to endure. Engineers from the Douglas plant came to take a look. The airplane was undamaged, and the engineers were delighted at the evidence of quality construction.

Panagra continued to do everything in its power to convince the South American governments that, even if they wanted to have national airlines for prestige purposes, it was still wise to let Panagra operate there, bringing both passengers and mail across all national borders impartially. The effort seemed to be an uphill one. "I thought our relations with the countries we served were very good," Douglas Campbell recalled. "Up through the end of World War II, they were delighted to have us. We were providing them with the service that they couldn't provide for themselves, and it was costing them nothing.

"In fact, we even made deals with them, before airports became so expensive. We built some airports, like the one in Guayaquil, and were paid by remissions . . . that is to say, they didn't charge us the gasoline taxes or other airport charges. So they recognized that we were providing a very important service.

"But after World War II, they began to have their own airlines. Every country had to have its own airline. Then it wasn't quite so easy."

One country, Campbell recalled, had never been easy: "The Chileans were always pretty tough because they had their own airline." This was LAN, which had co-existed alongside Panagra almost from the start. "Chile was the only country which never permitted us to carry what we called '*cabotage*'traffic, that is between points within the country. The other countries, even Argentina, did, at one time or another."

A half-step backward for Panagra occurred when it agreed to help found CORPAC, a quasi-governmental Peruvian corporation which would control radio facilities within Peru. On November 24, CORPAC took over all commercial aviation communications and operational facilities in Peru. Because a very large part of these had been built and maintained over a twenty-year span by Panagra, this represented a severe blow to the airline's inventory and its real estate cash value. Ironically, the move by CORPAC came little more than two weeks after Panagra had mounted yet another earthquake relief effort into San Ramón, Peru, 125 miles northeast of Lima, flying scientists into the stricken area and carrying out full loads of refugees over 16,000-foot mountains.

A few days after CORPAC seized Panagra assets in Peru, Avianca, the Pan American Airways subsidiary operating in Colombia, took over all Panagra communications facilities in that country. Again, Panagra lost its considerable investment in building up this infrastructure.

Panagra fought back. On December 1 a new sales promotion organization for South America, to be run by Granville Bourne, started operating in Buenos Aires. J. W. Walker had already taken over, on October 17, as regional manager for South America.

On the last day of 1947 Panagra announced air express rate reductions of from 7 to 36 percent below former tariffs. It was the first time that Panagra had offered an "over and under" rate, i.e., a rate structure benefitting shippers of light as well as of heavy freight.

The airline was to adjust these tariffs almost constantly from then on, raising them a trifle here, dropping them to respond to competition there. In fact, some tariffs were raised just 32 days later, on February 1, 1948. Panagra had started out dependent upon air mail, whose rates were set in Washington and other capitals and not by day-to-day competition. Then it had expanded explosively down the west coast and across to Argentina and even into the Mato Grosso of Brazil, routes where there was light competition. With the war, Panagra had taken over much of the competition and had benefitted as well from the huge United States-Africa trade. Now it was different; there was competition everywhere, in passenger and freight traffic alike. Some of that competition was beginning to come from the very countries Panagra served, and from airlines which enjoyed government subsidies, preferential routes, and often outright government collusion.

To put the trend into perspective, remember that but for some early rule-bending on the part of various United States postmasters-general, the U.S. government had never formally supported any airline. It was the only government of an aircraft-producing nation not to establish and directly support a state airline. It still is.

1948

Panagra started 1948 shuffling its route patterns and equipment to try to adapt to the changing conditions and ended the year by losing still more equipment to local governments.

On February 7, Salinas, Ecuador, was dropped as a stop for Aerovias del Ecuador, the Panagra subsidiary airline. On April 15, the *El Inter Americano*, the showpiece Panagra flight from Miami to Buenos Aires, resumed after a short break. The new schedule called for three flights weekly, with daily service to go into effect as soon as possible. The forward berths had been removed and the interior redesigned for the greater comfort of the passengers. Panagra even had Peruvian silversmiths design trademark silverware—of real silver.

Greater comfort, however, was not always possible. Bill Chamberlin recalls flying a Lima-Panama flight that ran into bad weather: "I was out of Quito for Cali and was unable to get through because of bad weather south of Cali. We received a report from our alternate field at Dos Ríos that said the field was wet, but fit, so we planned to stop in Dos Ríos to wait for the weather to clear between there and Cali. "Just at the instant of touchdown, I saw that the field was a solid sheet of water under the grass. We got stuck and were unable to get out before dark, so we had to stay overnight.

"The experience was memorable because we had Douglas Bader on board. He was the famous English fighter pilot who had fought World War II with prostheses instead of legs. He was such a good sport and such good company that none of the other passengers dared complain about the primitive conditions. The next morning Bader said he had had an advantage over the rest of us because he could remove his legs and just fit to sleep in a double seat in the airplane."

Chuck Schultz remembered a less famous passenger he encountered while flying from Quito to Guayaquil. "The purser came into the cockpit and told me to go back and look at this woman. She was a very well-dressed, middle-aged English lady, rather buxom, in a low-cut dress. Poking up from the v-neckline of her dress was the head of her pet snake, observing all around him."

I once had my own weather problems involving a famous passenger who needed to go to Quito. During the rainy season it was important to arrive at Quito by 1:30 or 2 p.m. before the passes into the airfield were closed by clouds and rain. On that day, we were in Guayaquil, and we were told to wait two hours for the international flight out of Lima. This flight had been delayed somewhere down the line.

It was very unusual to hold the local flight to Quito unless some VIP needed to make the connection. It seems that Orson Welles was to be the guest of honor at a reception that evening.

So, we waited. We kept getting reports from George Mansfield, the station agent in Quito, about the worsening weather. When we finally left for Quito with our famous passenger aboard, I figured that we had less than a 50% chance of getting into the valley, not only because of the weather, but also because of the late hour.

All the passes were indeed closed. So we went on oxygen and climbed up over most of the weather, hoping to find a hole through which we could descend into the Quito valley. After a lot of milling around, we did manage to get into Quito shortly before sunset.

It was not a pleasant flight, but I thought the extra effort was justified for the sake of our VIP on board. The next day George Mansfield told me that Welles had never shown up for his reception. He had locked himself in his hotel room with a bottle and left on the early flight north the next morning. Personally, I hadn't thought the flight was all *that* bad.

Fellow pilot Chuck Schultz had problems with important people *leaving* Quito. "Some of the minor officials liked to show their importance by arriving in a cloud of dust, just as the plane was about to leave the ramp," Schultz said. "The plane would have to be delayed long enough to complete their documentation and load them. As a result, the schedule for the whole day was jeopardized.

"It finally got to the point where something had to be done. Col. Flores Guerra, who was in charge of operations in Ecuador, together with the station manager, Russ Hoyt, got together and decided that, ten minutes before scheduled departure, the books would be closed. Anyone arriving after that time would not be loaded.

"The next morning we left the ramp on schedule and taxied out to the runway. The tower called. There were two passengers who had just arrived, and could we hold until they could drive the passengers out to us? I told them I was sorry and took off.

"When I got back, Russ Hoyt asked me if I knew who it was I had left behind. It turned out to have been the president's son and daughter-in-law. A few days later, on a morning flight from Quito to Guayaquil, I went back through the cabin to see how the passengers were doing, and there was President Arosemena. He spoke excellent English, and I knew him quite well from many other flights. I tried to slide by without being seen, but he pulled at my sleeve, and I bent down to hear what he had to say.

"'My son and daughter-in-law were left behind a few days ago,' he said. 'Did you happen to be the pilot of that plane?'

"'Yes sir,' I said. 'I was that pilot.'

"'Thanks,' he replied. 'They needed that.'"

On May 6 Panagra tried something novel. One of the problems that the airline had always faced, and about which it could do nothing, was the poor state of telephone service in South American countries. This was a kinder and gentler era, when passengers received telephone calls at their hotel rooms to notify them of flights. Crews, too, got wake-up calls at the appropriate times.

In Lima, Panagra set up a private 5-watt radio station whose sole purpose was to announce Panagra arrivals and departures, news, and crew calls. The announcements came in English and Spanish and were transmitted by the crew-scheduling office at Limatambo.

In 1948 the La Paz, Bolivia, station manager was Peter Radulovich, a protegé of Cy Collins. Radulovich, a young Yale graduate from a mining town in Pennsylvania who had gone to college on a football scholarship, had interviewed with W. R. Grace. Grace didn't have a job for Radulovich, but sent him over to Collins's office, and Cy had hired him on impulse.

"I talked to him for about five minutes and decided this guy was just what we were looking for," Collins recalled. "So I hired him. He had various adventures and eventually ended up as station manager at La Paz."

Radulovich replaced the cool-under-gunfire Carl Rooth. Later, he was almost replaced himself. He discovered a jewelry smuggling ring that loaded jewelry aboard Panagra planes in Lima, consigned to Arequipa. The Panagra planes flew by way of La Paz, and there the smugglers took the jewels off the flight, having smuggled them into Bolivia without paying duty.

Peter became wise to this, and instituted an arrangement whereby Bolivian Customs would have one key to the customs storehouse in La Paz, and he would have the other. But when the smuggled jewels came into La Paz, they were confiscated and locked up in the customs house.

Of course, Peter knew perfectly well that the smugglers were somehow going to manage to get into the customs house, either through bribery or by force, and take the jewels. They could then file a claim on the lost cargo. Having failed to deliver the jewels to the consigned destination (Arequipa), Panagra would be forced to pay the loss. The smugglers could steal their own cargo, and then make Panagra pay for it.

"When the next plane came along that was destined for Arequipa," Collins recalled, "Peter made the mistake of breaking open the customs' lock, unlocking the house with his key, and putting the cargo back on the airplane to Arequipa. Well, Bolivian customs screamed to high heaven. They considered it a terrible violation of trust . . . . I was sitting in New York, having hired this kid, and Doug Campbell was sort of twitching his moustache and saying, 'What kind of nincompoop do you have down there?' Doug made it quite clear to me that the best thing I could do was to fire Peter.

"I didn't, and a few months later Doug and I were in Bolivia on other business. At a dinner, the American ambassador's wife said to Doug, 'I just want you to know that you have here in La Paz one of the most charming young men that I've ever met, and our daughter is interested in him. They're seeing a lot of each other, and I just hope it works out because there's nobody I'd rather have as a son-in-law than Peter Radulovich.'

"Well, Doug squirmed visibly, and I enjoyed it. When we arrived at the airport, Doug was obviously pleased to find that somebody besides myself liked Peter. I said, 'Peter, you'd better watch out what you do with the ambassador's daughter.' Naturally, Peter promptly avoided her from there on, but Doug forgave him, and Peter got back into Doug's good graces."

On May 16 the *El Inter Americano* went to daily service. All five of Panagra's DC-6s were devoted to this run alone. With the additional aircraft, a new schedule was possible, including stops at Guayaquil and Antofagasta on alternate days. These aircraft had always been set up as "lounge/sleepers," with sleeping berths that could be folded out of the way to create a lounge for daytime use. On July 7 the five aircraft were further modified, with the back portion of the cabin holding four single and four double permanent berths. The forward portion of the cabin was now the lounge, with 36 lounge-type chairs.

On July 1 Captain Frank Havelick replaced retiring Captain J.R. McCleskey as chief pilot. McCleskey had requested transfer to Panagra's new Miami base. With the new aircraft and changes in technology, Havelick was going to have his hands full. Just for starters, Panagra air crews were about to switch from continuous-wave (CW) radio that used Morse code to radio-telephone communications.

Also on July 1 the Panagra meteorological section in Chile was combined with the meteorological section of Linea Aérea Nacional (LAN). If this wasn't an outright takeover by the Chilean government, it was the next worst thing.

However, to put the trends into perspective again, governments the world over were beginning to assume responsibility for weather forecasting for air travel. It was just too expensive an operation to be duplicated, within each country, by each airline operating there. If each nation were to enjoy the benefits of air travel, a centralized weather operation was in everyone's best interests. Panagra didn't mind the idea of the centralized weather reporting—as long as it was up to Panagra standards, but somehow the airline was rarely reimbursed for its set-up expenses when Panagra stations became the property of the respective governments.

The combined Panagra/LAN meteorological section must have been up to snuff, for on July 20 a Panagra DC-3 piloted by Loyal Domning crossed the Monturaqui pass between Chile and Argentina at night, relying on weather information and communications from the station near Ovalle, Chile. This navigational test flight was the first ever night crossing of the Andes by any airline, and Domning was accompanied by a CAA inspector.

On August 2 the first of eight new radio-telephone communicators arrived at Lima. These people were to train South American apprentice communicators as part of Panagra's plan for changing over to radio-telephone. By August 24 a class of Peruvian nationals was training, and on September 2 some Ecuadoreans also began to work with the new technology. On November 1 flights within Ecuador began using the new radio-telephone equipment with pilots speaking directly to ground stations. Panagra's ground-based CW radio operators were removed from that country.

As Panagra phased out its CW stations, the host nations, already nervous to the point of paranoia about foreigners operating radio stations within their borders, took them over. Sometimes the host country didn't wait for Panagra to finish the transition from CW to radio-telephone. In Argentina, where Panagra had supervised government-built stations, the radio contract terminated on November 4, and all equipment and personnel reverted to government control. Training of Argentine apprentice communicators didn't begin until December 1.

Peru also continued to tighten the noose. On September 13 Panagra had celebrated its twentieth anniversary in Peru, hosting a party for employees and visitors, giving out 20-year service pins to a number of employees and pilots, and giving away a free trip to Buenos Aires to Sr. Benjamin Romero, who had been one of Panagra's first passengers.

Just ten days later, on September 23, the Peruvian government inaugurated a new CORPAC terminal building at Limatambo (in which, incidentally, Panagra operated a traffic office). Aircraft number P-1, Panagra's original 4-passenger Fairchild airplane, was parked outside the new terminal building as a pointed reminder of just who it was who had brought passenger aviation to Peru.

On November 22 the Peruvian government announced that, as of January 1, 1949, Panagra's operations within Peru were to be restricted to international flights only, with all internal traffic being handled by Peru's national airline. Despite this prospect, 1948 did see some notable Panagra accomplishments. Introduction of the 300-mph DC-6s meant that flying times had been reduced by more than 90 percent over those early days of the 1920s. On August 16 Captain Donald McArthur crossed the Andes at 30,500 feet, while flying from Buenos Aires to Santiago, establishing a new altitude record for a DC-6. McArthur made the crossing at this altitude to avoid heavy storm clouds that reached to more than 30,000 feet in height.

In the cargo department, on August 2 Panagra inaugurated an all-cargo service intended to increase such operations between the United States and the west coast of South American by 50%. A Douglas DC-4 freighter with a 15,000-pound payload was used, flying from Buenos Aires to Balboa early in the week and making the return trip by the weekend. The flight stopped at Santiago. Talara and Antofagasta were designated as flag stops only. The *Diagonal* flight that operated between Lima and Buenos Aires on Thursdays was eliminated, reducing the *Diagonal* route to one flight a week.

On September 21 Panagra announced that in 20 years of operation it had carried more than 24 million pounds of cargo and more than four million tons of mail. Among cargoes carried were insect eggs, toads, chinchillas, bullfighting horses, lobsters, fish eggs, trees, furs, rare serums, and false teeth.

On October 8 some of the DC-6s began operating a "cutoff" route, stopping at Antofagasta instead of Santiago, then flying through the Andes at Monturaqui pass and on to Buenos Aires.

On a scientific note, Captain Frank W. McGann discovered a new comet while piloting the *El Inter Americano* from Lima to Miami on November 4. McGann notified the Panagra Meteorology Department in Miami of the sighting. The notice appeared in the press, and the comet was first designated 1948-L. Some U.S. observatories denied McGann's claim until a Professor Paraskevopoulos, with a Harvard-sponsored observatory in South Africa, confirmed the sighting three days later. At this point, the scientific community hailed Paraskevopoulos as the discoverer, despite newspaper accounts predating by days the professor's announcement. Some magazines and newspapers took to calling the comet the McGann-Paraskevopoulos Comet, which was a mouthful. McGann himself always preferred to call it the Panagra Comet.

The day after McGann's discovery, the *El Inter Americano* figured in the news again. On November 5, 1948, the first shipment of radioactive materials ever to go to South America was loaded aboard the flight. This shipment of research materials was supplied by the Oak Ridge, Tennessee, laboratories to Dr. Oscar Ortega, head of the pathological department of the *Hospital Dos de Mayo* in Lima.

1949

The year 1949 opened with Panagra's training of Chilean apprentice communicators at Limatambo in January. On January 10 the Ecuadorean government issued Ecuadorean tourist cards, an attempt by that government to increase tourism by making it possible for a tourist to visit Ecuador without a 90-day standard visa. Under an arrangement with the government, Panagra bought the first 160 of these cards, for $1 apiece, for re-sale to passengers at Panagra offices on two continents. James Gilbert of Greenville, North Carolina, the first tourist to use the service, bought a card at the Balboa office on January 25.

Throughout the year Panagra increased its use of the DC-4s and the DC-6s in the fleet, and made considerable adjustments in fares.

The first fare reductions were announced on February 8. The *El Inter Americano* sleeper service, Miami-Buenos Aires, was reduced from $125 per berth to only $45. On March 1 Panagra followed up with fare reductions on key parts of its route. Depending upon the circumstances, passengers could save between $25 and $45 on any round trip ticket between New York and Buenos Aires. By May 19 a DC-4 (NC-88817) was ferried up to Miami for conversion to a new "tourist" class of service to be shared by Panagra and Pan American. The aircraft would have a seating capacity of 44 (with plans to increase that to 46 in August) and a forward bulkhead to permit storage of freight at the front of the cabin. The seats were removable, as well, so that the entire plane could quickly be converted for freight operations if needed.

Then on March 30 Panagra entered into a four-way agreement with Pan Am, W. R. Grace and Co., and National Airlines. National would issue additional stock, and Pan American had the option to acquire up to 30% of that; W. R. Grace could own up to 18%. A one-plane, American-flag service would be established between New York and South America via Miami and Panama. The agreement was subject to the approval of the Civil Aeronautics Board. The matter was still under CAB scrutiny when, three weeks later, President Truman's DC-6, *The Independence,* damaged its landing gear at Key West. In a great public relations move, Panagra rushed spare parts to the scene.

A second DC-4 (NC-88904) was ferried up to Miami on June 12

for similar conversion, and on June 19 the new service started. Tourist-class flights left Miami on Tuesdays and Saturdays, and Buenos Aires on Wednesdays and Saturdays, connecting with the Pan American east coast flights at New York and Buenos Aires. Food service was limited to light breakfasts, box lunches, and dinners, and the seating and other cabin comforts were different from the normal-tariff flights.

With the cost of a ticket as much as 27% below first class, it was now possible to make a trip over the entire Panagra-Pan Am route in South America for as little as $855. This was $133 less than the first class fare for comparable travel. Here is how some of those savings broke down:

Route	First Class	Tourist Class	Savings
Miami-Balboa	$137	$110	$ 27
Miami-Lima	319	240	79
Miami-Santiago	484	364	120
Buenos-Aires-Miami	514	374	140
New York-Rio de Janeiro	460	360	100
New York-Montevideo	543	443	100

Operations in Bolivia–and particularly in the eastern part of that nation, where the Panagra *Intercontinental* route connected to Pan Am's routes–were interrupted by a revolution for two weeks, September 1-15, 1949.

As of September 19 the CAA granted Panagra permission to test a new dispatching set-up. The office at Guayaquil would control all DC-3 flights in the Guayaquil-Balboa sector, while the Limatambo office would control all DC-4 and DC-6 flights in the Lima-Balboa sector. After a three-month test, the final approval to make the arrangement permanent came on December 5. On that date, approval was also granted to control all Miami-Balboa flights from Panagra's office in Miami.

On October 2, with no increase in fares, the tourist-class flights received full-course hot meals. At the same time, hostess service was added. Previously, there had been only the box lunches and dinners, with one steward assigned to each flight. On December 17, however, the full-course hot meals were discontinued, apparently to emphasize the difference between tourist and first-class service. Nevertheless, the reduced service was equal to, or superior to, the food served on today's aircraft; passengers enjoyed hot soup, then cold chicken, roast beef, or ham and cheese. There was a "real" salad and dessert, rolls and butter, and coffee. On December 17 a new liquor service was introduced on the *El Inter Americano.*

Cargo operations in 1949 included the northbound shipment inside Panagra's DC-4 freighter, of P-1, the partially disassembled four-passenger Fairchild with which H. R. Harris had started the airline. On March 5 the aircraft flew to Miami and thence to Park Ridge, Illinois, to be turned over to the Smithsonian Institution. It was one of the first aircraft to comprise the nucleus of the new National Air Museum. Today, still flying its green-and-white Panagra colors, P-1 hangs from the ceiling in the huge National Air and Space Museum on the Mall in Washington, D.C.

On August 1 Panagra reduced air cargo tariffs between 15% and 50% for goods traveling between the U.S. and South America. Further, the paperwork was simplified; from then on goods would travel the entire way on a single airway bill.

Panagra responded to a wide variety of emergencies in 1949, including one of its own which turned out to be minor. On March 7 a hangar owned by Línea Aérea del Pacífico Sur (LAPA) caught fire at Santiago. Panagra personnel worked with the local Chilean Air Force fire brigade to extinguish the blaze, but not before aircraft and equipment belonging to LIPA, as well as FAMA and ZONDA (two Argentine airlines), were burned. Losses to equipment, exclusive of the building itself, were pegged at sixty million Chilean pesos.

Panagra's response to two medical emergencies had more positive results. On March 18 a Panagra DC-4 landed at Quito carrying an iron lung for a North American stricken with polio. This was also the first time a DC-4 had visited that city. And on April 2 Panagra rushed a shipment of whooping cough serum from the U.S. to Guayaquil to save the life of the son of the president of Ecuador. A radio message requesting the serum had been sent from Guayaquil to the Panagra office in Miami on Friday, April 1. The serum was located at the Serum Exchange of the Children's Hospital in Philadelphia and was immediately flown to Miami and then on to South America aboard the *El Inter Americano.* The serum arrived at Guayaquil at 4:40 a.m. on Saturday, April 2, less than 24 hours after the request. Today, such a delivery would seem routine; in South America in 1949, it was astounding.

Laboring away in frustrated boredom in New York, Cy Collins longed to be back in Lima, but at the same time he realized that his post as assistant to Douglas Campbell was a step up the corporate ladder. On one occasion, he nearly fell off the ladder:

"Jimmy Walker, assigned to the general manager's office in South America, was one of the characters I will never forget," Collins said. "He played hard; he worked hard; and he was a lot of fun. He was a good practical joker.

"Our communications were sent by cable, coded, through the Grace cable department. One Friday afternoon in New York I wrote up a cable to Jimmy Walker, to which I signed the name of our president, Harold Roig. It was a fake cable, but I did it just as if it were a real one. I knew that one of our secretaries was going down to Lima and I asked her to take the cable form with her and put it on Jimmy Walker's desk first thing Monday morning.

"The fake cable, supposedly signed by Harold Roig, said that we'd experimented with air transportation for some years now and that the experiment had not proved a success. So it was decided by the Board of Directors that we would revert to crop dusting. The cable said to Walker, 'Will you please make immediate arrangements to sell all our aircraft to anybody that wants them and give me a full report on your plans for returning to crop dusting.'

"I knew that Walker would figure that some clown was behind this and would probably figure out that it was me. But I wasn't prepared when I came into the office the next Monday morning in New York to see a cable in front of me that said–addressed to Roig, of course–'Have your cable. Taking immediate steps to sell aircraft. Have three sold already and will proceed immediately into crop dusting.'

"This gave me about five minutes of anguish. I had played a joke that had boomeranged to a hideous proportion. It was about a half hour before another secretary, who had been in Lima and who had come back to New York over the weekend, confessed that Walker, having figured out who the culprit was, had instructed her to put this answer on my desk. I was greatly relieved!"

On July 26 the daily flight into Santiago made an emergency landing at Los Cerrillos airport with one engine in flames. Engine fires were rare, though not unheard of, and Panagra had been relatively trouble-free. Just four months before the July 26 incident, Panagra had received a special award from the Inter-American Safety Council for having had a perfect safety record over the previous five years. The July incident would not affect Panagra's record because it did not result in any injury or death. On August 2 Panagra had its award for safe flying in 1948, its fourth in a row.

Three days later, on August 5, Panagra put its aircraft and other facilities at the disposal of the Ecuadorean government in the aftermath of the terrible Ambato earthquake. Panagra employees also took up a collection of money which they donated on September 12 to the president of Ecuador, Sr. Galo Plaza.

In 1948 the implementation of the new radio system had started with the training of some radio operators for the ground stations. On March 10, 1949, Panagra put into service the new Curico, Chile, weather station, about 150 miles south of Santiago. The upgrading continued throughout the year including additional training for cockpit crews. On March 18 copilots trained as flight engineers were made flight crew members aboard all DC-6 flights south of Lima.

In addition to building stations and upgrading equipment–the little that Panagra still operated, most radio equipment having been taken over by the various host governments–Panagra had to thread its way through a paperwork maze to implement the new voice-radio system. Looking back, it seems odd that anyone would think for a moment that voice-radio was not superior to the old CW system, which required the use of Morse code. But, in fact, there were genuine and very real concerns. CW, whatever else you could say about it, was reliable. The Morse code could be transmitted by a relatively low-power set and be picked up with good comprehension a very long way off, with little interference from the weather. Voice-radio required more transmitting power and a more sophisticated receiving set to screen out the background noise. In addition, it introduced all the vagaries of human speech to the process. Panagra had fought hard for decades to improve safety through the use of on-board radio. With the modern aircraft and long-range routes more dependent than ever before upon up-to-the-minute meteorological data transmitted to the pilots as they flew, Panagra was very careful in its use of this new technology.

On March 12 the CAA granted Panagra approval for a new communicator system on international flights over Guayaquil and Quito, Ecuador; over Cali, Colombia; and over Balboa, Panama. On April 30 permission was granted to use voice-radio for en-route communications on all international DC-3 flights between Lima and Guayaquil, as well as on all international DC-4 and DC-6 flights between Lima and Balboa. On May 6 this CAA approval was extended to include all flights between Lima and Santiago, although at first only a "test" was allowed. On July 18 the "test" was discontinued; permission was granted to use voice-radio for en-route communications between Lima and Santiago and across to Buenos Aires. The same permissions were granted July 25 in the Bolivian sector, from Lima and Arequipa to La Paz, and from Lima to Arica and on to Antofagasta. A few days later, on August 1, voice became the standard on the *Diagonal* route also (La Paz-Oruro-Uyuni in Bolivia and on to Salta-Tucumán-Córdoba-Buenos Aires.)

There were celebrations and awards in 1949, too. On September 13 Panagra celebrated the 21st anniversary of that first flight from the Lima racetrack to Talara, Peru. The year marked the twentieth year of airmail service between South America and the United States. On May 18 Peru commemorated the two decades by issuing special stamps and holding a formal celebration. On July 21 it was Chile's turn, with a birthday party in Santiago coinciding with the presentation of the first 20-year service pin to a Panagra employee in Chile, C. H. Brunson. On October 12 a celebration in Buenos Aires followed a birthday cake and gala party on board the *El Inter Americano* flight as it crossed the Andes.

For twenty years Harold Roig had played a major role in the pioneering and development of Panagra. He retired as Panagra's first president on July 11, remaining as a vice-chairman of W. R. Grace, half-owners of Panagra. He was succeeded by Andrew Shea, a director and senior vice president at W. R. Grace.

In a ceremony at the Peruvian Embassy in Washington, D.C., on September 12 the Peruvian government honored Roig and Douglas Campbell. Both men were made Commanders of the Order of the Sun, the highest decoration the Peruvian government granted to a civilian.

Andrew Shea started his administration with a 25-day inspection trip, beginning on October 5. In the course of his inspection he covered 15,000 miles of routes, visiting twelve cities in seven Latin American countries.

At a special celebration on December 5 Captain Jack Miller, a Panagra veteran, was honored for completing 25,000 flying hours. He had been flying for thirty years and in August had completed eighteen years with the company. Miller was one of Panagra's most colorful pilots. Born a full-blooded Indian in Nebraska, he had learned to fly in 1921. "Among other things," Dick Witt remembered, "Jack was always inventing things, like vacuum cleaners that could vacuum your uniform in flight by using the suction out the window when the cockpit window was opened on a DC-3."

Miller may have picked up the trick from Warren B. Smith, who used to read his mail while crossing the Andes, slowly feeding the envelopes out the window, which he would open a quarter-inch. The slipstream would shred the paper as finely as anyone could wish.

"Everyone liked Jack," Witt continued. "When Frank Havelick was sitting at Dos Ríos, Colombia, waiting out some bad weather in the passes he needed to traverse to reach Cali, Jack swooped down and landed on the old dirt field, threw out the day's English-language newspaper from Panama, shouted over to Havelick, 'Here's the paper for you to read,' and took off again. He and his wife had a parrot in their home which had been taught to say a great many things, most of which are unprintable."

1950

In 1950 Panagra finally obtained the last permissions to use voice-radio—or RTO (Radio Telephone Operator)—on its aircraft. On January 6 the CAA granted approval for the new communications equipment to be used in Bolivia on the La Paz-Campo Grande and the Sawtooth routes (Santa Cruz-Concepción-San Ignacio-San José-Robore-Puerto Suarez.) Shortly after this, the CAB approved DC-4 service to La Paz, which to date had been served by the DC-3s.

CAB decisions, finance decisions, squabbling over routes, mail contracts, and the like all happened far from where we flew and required a very different mentality on the part of Panagra employees in New York.

"It was kind of frustrating," Cy Collins recalled of his first days in

New York after working in Lima for three years. "We didn't get very much day-to-day information about what was going on, and it bothered me. I remember saying to Douglas Campbell one time, 'Hell, we don't even know whether all the planes got home last night. We don't know anything.' Campbell sort of twisted his moustache and said, 'Well, we've got people down there we're paying to take care of that.' That put me down, and I knew exactly what he was saying. We had to do our thing, which was more in the financial and political arena, dealing with the parent companies, buying and selling aircraft . . . all the stuff that's so boring after you've been in the field."

The DC-4s and DC-6s were of such a size that only well-built runways could handle them. Many cities had runways that were either too short, too narrow, or both. Nevertheless, Panagra made better use of its DC-4s in 1950 by putting them to work between Panama and Houston and between Panama and New Orleans. Panagra was permitted into these latter cities only by virtue of a Through Flight Agreement with Pan Am. A new schedule, intended to supplement the *El Inter Americano* and using only DC-4s, could take a passenger from Houston to Buenos Aires in a little over 33 hours of flying time. From New Orleans the time was about two hours less.

By June 20 Panagra was flying DC-4s into Bolivia's interior, supplementing the regular DC-3 service to Cochabamba and Santa Cruz. La Paz now had six flights a week from the United States.

Quito, Ecuador, was an example of the problems associated with the newer, heavier aircraft. The Quito runway was too short for a fully loaded DC-4. A special flight the previous year had successfully carried in a single iron lung for a polio patient, and had carried out nothing, but that lightly loaded trial had not solved the runway problem. On July 28 Panagra successfully tested a DC-4 equipped with Jet-Assisted Take-Off (JATO) at Quito. The JATO equipment wasn't really a jet, but a system of rockets which were attached to the aircraft and set off by pilot command. The rockets burned for only a few moments, but they greatly boosted the takeoff speed of the aircraft. The test was a success from the standpoint of runway length, but it was decided that the pavement needed strengthening to absorb the greater impact of a DC-4 landing before any regular service could be considered.

Panagra lost one DC-4 on December 13, 1950, when it was lent to the airlift supporting United Nations forces in Korea. The aircraft was actually delivered to Pan Am in San Francisco on December 30, after modifications had been made at the Pan Am base in Brownsville, Texas. Panagra captains and pilots would fly it on a rotating volunteer basis throughout the Korean conflict.

New kinds of freight, principally medicines, and supplies associated with disaster relief flights dominated the year in cargo operations, showing in some cases the advantages of the faster DC-6s and the DC-

Top: Jet-Assisted Take-Off (JATO) high-altitude testing at Quito, Ecuador, in May 1957. The aircraft is a DC-7. Personnel are (l-r) unidentified Panagra PR man; Ernie Werner, FAA; Col. M. Fernande, of the Ecuadorean Air Force; and Panagra Captain Loyal Domning. Bottom: JATO testing at Quito, April 1957. Standing (l-r) are John Laws, Chief Engineer; Ernie Werner, FAA; Capt. Loyal Domning, Panagra; "Chico" Vargas, Panagra mechanic; and Manuel Correa, Panagra's station manager at Quito.

4s. On April 14 two hundred rare chinchillas–almost extinct then in South America–were shipped to New York for breeding. On May 22 Panagra responded to an earthquake in the Cuzco region of Peru. Company aircraft transported medicines, food, supplies, and personnel from all over South America and the United States for the relief of the victims. The day after the Cuzco disaster Panagra shipped more than seven tons of medicines, said to be the largest airborne medicine delivery in the history of commercial aviation from the United States to Brazil. The shipment, consigned to Squibb & Sons in São Paulo, included penicillin and liver extract.

On June 6 a shipment of seventeen kilos of blood plasma arrived in Cochabamba, Bolivia, just two and one-half days after a Panagra plane picked it up in Houston, Texas. This shipment was for medical research at the Foster-Wheeler Company in Cochabamba. Within a year Panagra aircraft would be flying in plasma, in iced containers, for relief of wounded victims of a revolution.

Other cargo shipments were remarkably diverse. On July 4 an air cargo shipment of spare parts, weighing 800 pounds, arrived in Lima from Switzerland. Required for the repair of the city's electric power plant, the parts from the Brown-Boveri factory in Zurich were delivered by Panagra in little more than two days. On July 18 a Spectacle Bear, one of the world's rarest, was shipped to New York from Lima. This specimen, believed to be the only female in captivity, was to be used for breeding. The Liberty Bell of Huara was flown to Buenos Aires on August 11 to take part in a homage to liberator General José de San Martín. The bell, which weighed 1,400 kilos, was loaded aboard a DC-4. A military delegation, headed by General Felipe de la Barra, accompanied the bell.

For the *El Inter Americano* flights, Panagra's showpiece operation, the year included many highlights. On April 22 the *El Inter Americano* schedule was published in Chinese. This not only emphasized the influence of the large Chinese population in western South America, but pointed out the connections that Panagra had with Pan Am and the overseas routes available through the latter to the Far East. On July 5, the price of berths on the *El Inter Americano* was reduced to $10 for an upper and $5 for a lower. This was in addition to a ticket on the aircraft; not everyone bought berths. On August 14 some of the DC-6s on the route were re-configured, with an expanded lounge area forward. While they were at it, designers painted the tops of the aircraft white, reducing the internal temperature by as much as fifteen degrees. These aircraft, newly designated as the "Fiesta-Lounge" Service, took the Antofagasta-Buenos Aires "Cut-off" route, bypassing Santiago and arriving in the Argentine capital just 19 hours after leaving Miami.

A baby boy was born aboard the *El Inter Americano* between Balboa and Guayaquil on November 6. The child's parents, Mr. and Mrs. Rafael Undurraga, were returning to their home in Santiago. Hostess Violetta Laureys of Lima and Mrs. Dexter Farnsworth, wife of a Panagra pilot, assisted in the delivery. The Undurragas named the boy Carlos Antonio Panagra Undurraga. Panagra officials made sure that the entire world knew about it.

There was other good news to share as well. On May 31 Panagra celebrated its 15th year of carrying passengers and mail into Bolivia, giving officials of the government a special trip to Buenos Aires. The Peruvian government awarded the airline a gold medal on July 28, honoring its services as the first commercial airline in Peru. And Lloyd Aéreo Boliviano (LAB) awarded another gold medal to Panagra on September 27 in recognition of services performed during the period from 1941 to 1946 when Panagra had operated LAB.

In the one major personnel change of the year, Kenneth A. Lawder was elected vice president and comptroller of the airline, succeeding Gustavo Vidal. Vidal left to take up other duties with the W. R. Grace Company.

In December National Airlines terminated the interlocking four-way agreement between itself, Panagra, Pan Am, and the Grace Company. When National canceled the stock options held by Grace and Pan American to buy unissued National Airlines stock, Grace held 17.4% of National's stock, part of which was, in turn, under option to Pan Am.

1951

Commencing on January 13, 1951, Panagra began refitting all its DC-6s with more powerful engines, converting them from Pratt & Whitney R-2800 CA-15s to CB-16s. These were the same engines used on the newer DC-6Bs. At the same time, Panagra fitted all engines with Hamilton Hi-Activity propellers, improving the performance of its fleet.

The improvements came in handy on May 18 when Panagra aircraft began an emergency assist in Ecuador, where fires had devastated the Esmeraldas region. Panagra ground crews had hardly cleaned up the aircraft used in that emergency when the Ecuadorean government celebrated Panagra's 20,000th crossing of the equator with a special in-flight radio broadcast and a bronze plaque, which was attached to the Equatorial monument commemorating the event. The by-now-usual commemorative stamps were also issued—no reason why the Ecuadorean government shouldn't profit from this—and several thousand first-day covers were sold.

Equator crossings were observed in unique ways by some of the pilots. "Jack Miller had operated a flying circus before going with Panagra," Ernie Hummel recalled. "He flew according to his own whims and his own entertainment, and the rest of the crew and the passengers went along for the ride. One of his favorite tricks, on trips crossing the equator, was to haul the thing up into a steep power-off stall. After recovery, he'd call the purser up and have him take a note back to the passengers saying that they had just passed the equator—and congratulations!"

The airport at Esmeraldas, Ecuador, was across the river from the small town, and in the early days passengers had to come over by boat or canoe. I once flew into Esmeraldas in an old DC-2 to pick up a char-

On April 17 the Chileans threw a party for Captain Warren B. Smith, who had just completed 20,000 flying hours. In the early 1950s the company name was painted in an artistic, cursive script.

ter party consisting of a wealthy Ecuadorean shoe-manufacturer and his friends, who had gone down for a week-end celebration of some kind. When we landed at the airport, there was no sign of the passengers. When they finally showed up, the cause of the delay was obvious. The party was still going strong, and our would-be passengers were drunk. With some difficulty we got them all on board. Then when we tried to start the right engine, no amount of coaxing would get it to fire. The purser was having his own problems back in the cabin, so I told him to unload the passengers until the local mechanic could do some troubleshooting on the engine. As it turned out, there was a broken primer line. The mechanic fixed it, and we soon had the engine running again. All we had to do was re-embark our passengers and head for home, or so I thought. By this time the party was going full-swing again, and we couldn't get them near the airplane. Finally, the host of the expedition explained to me that any engine that was that hard to start wasn't going to keep running long. They thought, in fact, that they might as well go back into town.

All the persuading that we could do fell on deaf ears. At last, I advised Lima of the situation and asked for advice. Bob Disher wired back, saying, "If persuasion does not work, head for the barn." As we took off, the party-goers were all in their canoes, paddling back to town.

Panagra's safety record was widely known. There might have been some real worry about the engine, but it is far more likely that it served as a convenient excuse to re-schedule their departure.

By September 13, Panagra's 23rd birthday, the airline could boast of flying more than one billion passenger miles. The Houston and New

Orleans routes had begun to catch on with the flying public, and the larger DC-4s and DC-6s rolled up the passenger-miles far faster than the smaller DC-3s. In 1951, as a result, there was a 23% increase in revenue passenger miles over the previous year.

CAB statistics for 1951 show that Panagra then served 23 cities, covering a route 6,149 miles long. Its aircraft flew some 15,983 miles per day, filling an average of 58.4% of total passenger capacity. Of the 12,695 annual aircraft departures, almost 99% completed their flights— a statistic that says nothing about how "on-time" the airline was, but speaks volumes for the quality of maintenance. Today's airlines have a far worse record of breakdowns and flight cancellations for maintenance reasons.

1952

As the new year began, Edward Bern was elected a vice president of Panagra on January 14, and he continued as sales manager as well. Panagra would face a new year of changes in politics, business, and technology.

A few months later, on April 10, Panagra flights rushed medicine and blood plasma into Bolivia, where yet another revolution was underway. However, the company now had years of experience coping with radical political changes along its routes. While helping with the medical supplies, it carried on with its own commercial plans. On the same day, Panagra announced the lowest tourist-class fares in South American history. A round-trip Miami-Lima ticket was now $300. For $870 a tourist could fly throughout the entire Panagra route. The fare was valid from May 1 to October 31.

When that special rate started on May 1, Panagra unveiled a new DC-6B tourist service, called *El Pacífico*. Fast, pressurized planes made this the most luxurious low-fare service on the continent; the high density seating of 72 passengers made it a reasonably profitable run for the airline. Panagra offered three flights weekly from Miami to Lima, with two of those continuing on to Buenos Aires.

The first major approach lighting system in South America was inaugurated at Limatambo on May 21. The system had been financed and installed by Panagra, in cooperation with CORPAC. A special flight, carrying the Peruvian minister of aeronautics and other government and airline officials, including Peruvian Vice President Hector Boza, marked the occasion.

Carrying everything from top political figures to pragmatic cargo, Panagra continued to offer a full range of services throughout the continent. A special shipment of 6,500 flies was sent from the United States to Santiago on July 2 to combat a crop plague. Such an action today might horrify agricultural inspection officials, who have a better understanding of the danger of introducing a new species into an environment where it has no natural enemies. But speedy air travel, making possible live shipments of this sort, long preceded better scientific studies. Today, biological pesticide treatment is making a resurgence, albeit with better precautions.

Summer proved to be a time for administrative changes. James Walker, Jr., resigned from his position as Panagra's regional manager for South America on July 11 to take a position with Pan Am, and James T. Scholtz was appointed in his place. A few days later, F. S. Kidd replaced J. B. Ottiker as maintenance superintendent. Ottiker, who had been one of Panagra's first employees, was promoted to superintendent of passenger service.

Beginning August 1 the Panagra hostesses started to wear new uniforms of pastel green, instead of the gray uniforms they had previously worn. The new styles were selected to better match the fuselage colors. A week later, on August 8, Panagra proudly accepted its eighth consecutive safety award. The airline had averaged more than 100 million passenger miles each year during the past eight years without a fatality.

On September 11 the conversion of DC-6s to the new engines and propellers was completed. The ambitious program had taken just over a year and had cost $600,000. The type R-2800 CB-16 Pratt & Whitney engines, combined with the Hamilton Hi-Activity propellers, gave Panagra the fastest civil air transport in regular daily scheduled service anywhere in the world. With upgraded engines, the Miami to Buenos Aires schedule speeded up. The "Fiesta Lounge" flights of the *El Inter Americano* route now took just short of eighteen hours of flying time. The speedier aircraft also permitted, for the first time, weekly daylight flights on the *El Pacífico* tourist service between Miami and Lima.

The first day of *El Inter Americano*'s daylight flights from Miami to Lima, Captain Fritz Sterling set a new speed record going the other direction, flying between Lima and Panama with Mrs. Eleanor Roosevelt aboard. By December 11 the service had established such a standard that the very first Frye Trophy, one of aviation's most prestigious awards, went to Panagra for its "Fiesta Lounge" service on *El Inter Americano*. The service was lauded as the fastest passenger service on a regularly scheduled run operated by a United States airline. Jack Frye himself, a well-known figure in aviation for many years, and then-president of Trans-World Airlines (TWA), presented the trophy to Douglas Campbell in a ceremony at New York's "21" Club.

1953

Safety and progress were matters of company pride. On March 1, 1953 Panagra installed its first instrument landing system (ILS). The system, set up at Limatambo, was officially inaugurated by CORPAC. In conjunction with the high-intensity approach lights installed on May

21 of the previous year, the ILS reduced minimum ceiling and visibility requirements, making Limatambo one of the most modern airfields in South America.

Attuned as usual to the value of good public relations, Panagra officials took the president of Peru, General Manuel A. Odría, and a large party of Peruvian dignitaries to Brazil on August 24. Panagra's president, Andrew Shea, came down for the occasion and hosted the flight. A DC-6 was used for the delegation, which flew from Lima to São Paulo to meet with Chilean President Getulio Vargas.

Continuing with the public-relations campaign, Panagra, on September 13, announced the "Junior Ambassador" program. Thirty-five boys, aged 14-16, were selected, five by each of the presidents of the seven nations Panagra served in South America. The boys were taken on a three-week tour of eleven North American cities. September 13 was Panagra's 25th anniversary, and Andrew Shea made sure that announcements of the goodwill trip included that information. On September 24, Panagra unveiled its order for five DC-7 aircraft, to be delivered by mid-1955. Panagra may have had trouble competing with national airlines in the countries it served, due to government bias, but it would always have more modern equipment.

Despite competitive tensions, in a further show of solidarity with South America (and in a brilliant publicity coup), Panagra and the Macy's Department Store got together on December 19 to send Santa

Displaying another safety award are (l-r) O. Z. Johnson, superintendent of maintenance; Capt. Ernie Hummel, regional chief pilot and fleet superintendent; L. R. "Dinty" Moore, instrument flying instructor, and one of the pilots on the U. S. Navy's first transatlantic flight; and Andy Anderson, flight radio operator. The trophy was just one of many Premio de Seguridad *awards given Panagra by the Inter-American Safety Council.*

Claus throughout the Panagra service area. "Papa Noel," as he was known, was met at all stops by hundreds of underprivileged children, to whom toys were distributed. Presidential families, local charities, and newspapers all cooperated to make this a very successful event. The event was so popular that Panagra made it a tradition, and Ed Sullivan, of Panagra's personnel office, was the Santa for several years.

1954

Panagra President Andrew Shea was the guest of honor when Panagra was lauded for 25 years of of uninterrupted service between the Americas at the annual Newcomen Society dinner on February 25, 1954. A few days later, on March 3, the airline celebrated its 20,000th crossing of the Andes.

After extensive trials at El Alto airport, Panagra began its first regularly-scheduled DC-6 service to La Paz, Bolivia on March 20. To do this, Panagra began routing the *El Pacifico* flights through Bolivia and down the *Diagonal* route to Buenos Aires, replacing the once-weekly service. This new schedule marked the first one-plane DC-6 flights from the U.S. to Panama, Ecuador, Peru, Bolivia, and Argentina, and raised the number of through tourist flights to Argentina to three.

On May 19 the president of Ecuador recognized Panagra's 25th year in that nation with a ceremony and a personal award to Col. Flores Guerra, Panagra's Quito office manager. Panagra had done well in the public relations department since the Second World War, but local governments still wanted their own airlines and control over all aircraft and equipment–especially radio equipment, meteorological stations, and expensive airport facilities–within their borders. On June 1 Panagra began to move pilots and their families back to the United States. By September, thirty-five pilots and families had been relocated to Miami. This trend would continue for several years until, by 1960, no Panagra pilots were still stationed in South America.

Even while the pilot moves were taking place, Panagra flight schedules moved ahead. The *El Pacifico* service was beefed up with a second weekly flight that stopped at Cali and at Quito, where the troublesome runway had been improved. On June 14 Panagra placed an order for five Douglas DC-7B aircraft to replace five DC-7s ordered the year before. Placed in service in 1955, they cost $2 million each, were equipped with on-board radar and air conditioning, and were capable of speeds of 360 m.p.h. On June 25 Panagra received its tenth consecutive Inter-American Safety Council award. But this time the airline also qualified for the National Safety Council's annual Aviation Safety award for flying within the United States.

Economic growth and business opportunities were continuing interests. On October 8, 1954, Panagra organized and sponsored a "Trade Tour" of South America, giving U.S. businessmen an escorted visit to eleven cities in nine countries. On this trip, which today would be called a trade mission, the group explored trade and investment possibilities through inspection tours, Chamber of Commerce contacts, and talks with government officials.

On November 5 Panagra flew a special flight to La Paz with the entire household effects (all 8,000 pounds) of the newly-appointed United States ambassador to Bolivia. This was the first time that the United States State Department had ever authorized such a shipment by commercial air freight. The year was also a significant one for Panagra's mail-carrying business: it was the year the airline became totally independent of mail subsidies.

On December 19 Panagra repeated its resounding Christmas success of the previous year. Macy's wasn't along for the ride this time, but Santa Claus distributed toys and good cheer to underprivileged children in stops in Peru, Chile, and Argentina. Again, presidential families, charities, and local newspapers rallied to make the program a success.

"The Post Office contract never paid us for more than two trips a week, and as our frequency increased, we had to make them cost-effective without any increase in subsidy," Douglas Campbell recalled. "The CAB established a rate which was supposed to give us an after-tax profit of 'X' percent on what they recognized as our investment." Campbell also noted that Pan Am's own subsidy continued for some years after 1954. "Eastern, I think, was the first airline to get off subsidy," he said.

1955

Tommy Kirkland, Panagra's vice president of operations, began the new year by announcing faster service and improved performances on local flights within Peru, Bolivia, and Ecuador. This announcement, made on March 8, followed a month of regular operations with modernized high-performance DC-3s. The new Panagra "Hi-Per" DC-3s had a maximum cruising speed of 214 m.p.h. and a maximum gross weight of 26,900 pounds. This was a substantial increase over the 180 m.p.h. and 25,200 pound weight limit of the original model. Pilots appreciated the fact that, equipped with R-2000 Pratt & Whitney engines, these aircraft had 20% more power on takeoff.

"This was especially important," Loyal Domning recalled, "because these airplanes provided service in Ecuador and Bolivia, which have some of the highest airports in the world."

On April 1 Panagra began to serve liquor on its tourist service, the *El Pacífico* flights. This had been prohibited earlier by the IATA, the International Air Traffic Association. A glass of wine cost ten cents, while a highball cost seventy-five cents.

The next month, on May 8 Panagra began to use television in the

United States to advertise its services in South America. On a "Meet the Press" segment, Panagra representatives extolled the wonders of the various South American countries along the airline's route and showed films highlighting Argentina, Bolivia, Chile, Ecuador, and Peru. Two more DC-6B tourist flights were added between Miami and Lima on June 1, bringing to seven the total number of such flights per week–a daily service.

While the company worked to increase tourist interest, it continued research and development to enhance the overall operations, completing a six-year meteorological study on May 15. This was a statistical analysis of surface temperature at twelve major Panagra terminals. A new study of surface winds was initiated at the same time. Panagra wanted to know about seasonal average winds up to forty thousand feet over its routes. An upper wind study for all of South America was started to arrive at a statistical representation of winds up to twenty thousand feet. These data would be much needed in the years to come, when Panagra converted to jet aircraft.

On July 12 in cooperation with Panagra, the Argentine government installed the first of two VOR radio ranges–very-high-frequency, omnidirectional radio range stations. The first installation was at Ezeiza, near Buenos Aires. A second system at Malarsue, in the foothills of the Andes near Mendoza, was completed on August 22. "These were the first steps in creating the first international VOR airway in the world," Loyal Domning recalled. "The airway between Buenos Aires and Santiago was completed in the same year."

Using the just-delivered DC-7B aircraft, Panagra instituted twice-weekly service between Miami and Buenos Aires on August 1.With flying speeds in excess of 300 knots, Panama was just four flying hours from Miami. It was another five hours to Lima, and a further five and a half hours to Santiago. In all, a passenger could fly from Miami to Buenos Aires in sixteen hours and fifteen minutes of flying time, with just three intermediate stops. The new DC-7Bs had seats for 58 passengers. There was also a five-seat lounge and bar, and 15 bed-sized berths. The cabin was air-conditioned, and the cockpit came equipped with a Bendix RDR-1 airborne radar.

The DC-7B also had Wright-3350 "compound" engines. The exhaust gases were recycled in a rudimentary power-recovery system. The exhaust was on the left side of each engine, and it was pretty spectacular. The pilot, looking out his window at the left wing, could just see the tips of the blue flames coming from the engines. However, to the copilot looking out on the right, it sometimes seemed as though the wing was on fire. The high-pressure blowers that cut in to recycle the exhaust and boost the engine's power also put a considerable strain on the mechanism. The engines could blow up, and when one did, it lit up the night sky pretty well."

"Some airlines had trouble with those engines," Loyal Domning recalled, "but we operated and maintained them very carefully. The one scary event was caused by a prop reversing in flight—no fault of the engine."

On August 8 Panagra flew the president of Bolivia and a party of more than 40 people through Peru, Ecuador, and Colombia. The good-will trip, made aboard a DC-6, actually lasted almost two weeks, and the distance covered was over 3,000 miles. The Bolivian government was very impressed by Panagra's service.

Panagra started daily service for the first time on September 14—both first class and tourist—from New York, via Washington, D.C., and on to Miami. This route was a beneficiary of Pan Am's part-owner-ship of National Airlines, and Panagra flew the route on National's route certificate, as authority for such use had been agreed upon the previous year. National Airlines flight crews took the airplanes north from Miami to New York and return.

This was the new route of *El Inter Americano*; the DC-7Bs used could take a passenger from Idlewild Airport in New York (now John F. Kennedy International Airport) to Morón airport outside Buenos Aires in just 21 hours of flying time. The new service also linked, for the first time, cities such as Cali, Quito, Talara, Antofagasta, and Santiago with direct one-plane flights to New York. By December, Panagra began a new freight service, rushing Chilean cherries to markets in Ecuador. In all, nearly one hundred tons of cherries were brought into Guayaquil during the picking season in Chile.

Just before Christmas, on December 22, Panagra President Andrew Shea announced that the airline had ordered four Douglas DC-8 jet-liners, with an option for two more. The new jet aircraft would not be delivered before 1960, but already Panagra, and the South American governments which now ran most of the airports and electronics equip-ment, were preparing for the vastly heavier models and their larger passenger loads.

1956

Panagra President Andrew Shea pointed out in a speech made on January 1 that more Americans had visited South America in 1955 than ever before. Some of this was for pleasure, he noted, but most of it had to do with the nearly seven billion dollars in trade between the United States and the South American nations.

Shea was justifiably proud of the company's role in building eco-nomic ties, and tourism continued to be of paramount importance. On March 22 Panagra lowered its rates across the board with a year-round excursion fare scheduled to go into effect on April 23. Under the new fare, two persons traveling together could tour the continent with stop-overs at Panama, Colombia, Ecuador, Peru, Chile, Argentina, Uruguay, and Brazil. The cost was to be $576.80 for tourist class, compared to the former price of $779. First class passengers on the same plan would pay $714 instead of $918.

Taking an excursion of their own, the New Orleans Symphony Orchestra chartered Panagra aircraft, beginning on April 6, to move 90 people, 200 pieces of luggage, and some 4,000 pounds of instruments.

"We had a DC-4 and two DC-6s, all freshly painted, with *City of New Orleans* on the noses," Ernie Hummel recalled. "We had them lined up at the New Orleans airport, and a huge crowd showed up to see the orchestra off.

"Now, New Orleans is a very religious city, so they had Catholic, Protestant, and Jewish prayers for us. The Catholic priest and the Protestant minister said the usual general things; the rabbi got to the meat of the matter. He said he hoped that the crews who were going to fly these airplanes knew what they were doing, had studied flying conditions, the airports and so forth. He hoped the mechanics who maintained the airplanes knew exactly what they were doing and were willing to devote long hours to seeing to it that, while on the ground, the airplanes would be prepared for the next day's flying. He hoped that the flight attendants knew their emergency procedures." Following this somewhat sobering send-off, the orchestra toured 22 cities, including Havana, Mexico City, Bogotá, Caracas, and Lima, flying some 10,000 miles in the process.

Panagra missed an opportunity to buy out its principal competition in this year. It was to prove a fatal mistake.

"Vice President Wright Rex Brack of Braniff Airways went to New York to talk to Andy Shea," Ernie Hummel recalls. "He had instructions to offer all of Braniff's holdings in South America, the routes, facilities, DC-6 aircraft and equipment, and any other property that went with those, for the low sum of $5 million. Braniff had consistently lost huge amounts of money in their South American operation, and they had finally decided to get rid of it once and for all.

"It wasn't the first time Panagra had been handed an opportunity on a silver platter. Well back in the 1940s, Eastern Air Lines was on the ropes financially and made an offer to the Grace Company. With CAB authority, Grace could have bought Eastern and merged it with Panagra, a natural merger thanks to the north-south orientation of both airlines. Grace turned the offer down as a bad investment, although the selling price was something that they could have met out of their petty cash.

"Now the Braniff offer was the opportunity of a lifetime," Hummel reflected. "And the selling price was peanuts. However, Braniff never got to make the offer formally. Rex Brack waited outside Andy Shea's office and was never allowed inside. Had Panagra taken the offer, it would have given us the Lima-Rio route that was so badly needed for so many years, while at the same time getting a thorn out of our side. To let this opportunity slip through their hands seemed unconscionable to all of us, contributed to tremendously bad personnel relations and really shattered the dreams and hopes of just about every Panagra crew member."

Loyal Domning didn't think the CAB would have approved the sale even if Shea had agreed to buy Braniff: "The opportunity to buy Braniff's South American routes was really too good to be true. The fact was, such a deal would have needed government approval, and anything related to Pan Am was in political disfavor."

A combination of circumstance resulted in no further negotiations, and Panagra carried on with its shifting range of air transport challenges. On July 23-27, Panagra freighters flew 55.5 tons of pre-fabricated building materials to help the Point Four Program's Bolivian office build a public health hospital in San Ignacio. The airlift required 22 flights, covering 5,785 miles.

Later in the year, on September 21 and again on December 20, Panagra aircraft made urgent freight shipments. In the September flight, two cases of machinery, weighing 460 pounds, were rushed from New York City to Lima to help the Backus & Johnson Brewery del Perú. The brewery's bottling plant had been shut down because of broken equipment. In December more than 17,000 pounds of ocean vessel salvage equipment was brought from the United States to aid a C-3 cargo vessel, the S.S.P.T. *Seafarer*. The ship, based in San Diego, had been beached on the coast near Los Villos, Chile, and was in danger of breaking up in rough surf.

Panagra had never served much of Central America, even though its aircraft occasionally flew up and down the isthmus en route to and from the Pan Am service shops in Brownsville, Texas. There was a good reason for this lack of corporate interest at the Panama/Costa Rica border; Pan Am had other subsidiaries operating in the Central American countries and saw no reason to compete with itself to drive its own prices down. There was competition enough as it was.

In Panama, of course, Panagra flew into one airport where passengers could change to or from Pan Am aircraft. At various times in its history, Panagra operated from airfields at either end of the Panama Canal, where passengers could fly from one side to the other for a few dollars, making Panagra a de facto in-country carrier for that nation.

It was never a deliberate policy of Panagra's to compete with Pan Am. In fact, the two companies could cooperate to their mutual advantage. One example was the series of advertisements sent around Argentina promoting a route from Buenos Aires to Mexico City "via" Panagra. In reality, Panagra would carry passengers to Panama, where, the ad promised, "immediate" transfer to a Pan Am plane would be available to fly north to Guatemala and on to Mexico City. Passengers could leave Buenos Aires three times weekly aboard the *El Inter Americano*'s DC-7B and be in the Mexican capital the following day.

1957

On January 2, 1957, Cy Collins was appointed vice president for sales and traffic. A few days later, on January 11, Panagra launched its most extensive advertising and promotional campaign to date. The advertising was increased to include more newspapers and national magazines within the United States and throughout South America. Advertisements in trade and travel publications and on the radio were used, too. The campaign tried to focus the public's attention on Panagra's low-cost group excursion fares. Hollywood fame and glamour brought additional attention to the airline when, on February 28, a Panagra charter flight from New York to Montevideo carried U.S. movie stars to a film festival. The passenger list included Lana Turner, Yul Brynner, Craig Stevens, Alexis Smith, Anatole Litvak, Mitchell Leisen, Anita Ekberg, Van Heflin, Joanne Dru, Joanne Gilbert, Del Armstrong, Hedda Hopper, Beverly Tyler, and Ann Miller.

Panagra doubled its cargo service to La Paz on April 1, with the inauguration of a new DC-4 flight from Lima to La Paz via Arica. At the same time, it reduced the cargo rate on that run to thirteen cents per kilo.

These improvements naturally led to increased demand, but the DC-4s were still having trouble carrying the heavier freight loads into high-altitude airports such as Quito and La Paz. On April 29 Panagra engineers, assisted by specialists from Douglas Aircraft, the Pratt & Whitney Aircraft Company, Aerojet General Corporation and the CAA, began a series of high altitude performance tests of the DC-7B. Jet-Assisted Take-Off (JATO) equipment was carried as a safety factor.

In May Panagra crews carried out additional performance tests on the new DC-7B. Loyal Domning recalled how Panagra was always required to perform these tests which no other airline was required to do:

> From the beginning Panagra had flown to and from the highest airports in the world. Such operations were and still are considered to be more difficult and hazardous than those at lower elevations, and Panagra's pilots liked to brag about them to flatlanders. Making these flights both safe and profitable was one of the company's proudest achievements.
>
> The Andes Mountains contain the highest terrain in the western hemisphere. They also cover much of the territory of all of the countries which lie along the routes flown by Panagra. The airports of Bogotá, Colombia; Quito, Ecuador; Arequipa, Peru; and La Paz, Bolivia; all lie at more than 7,000 feet above sea level, with Quito at 9,200 feet and La Paz at 13,400.

In the early days the capabilities of airplanes used at these airports were evaluated by the pilots themselves, using whatever empirical performance standards suited them. In the late thirties, the U.S. Civil Aviation Administration established standardized levels of performance which were required to be met by airline aircraft. Airplanes built after the adoption of these rules were denominated as "Transport Category" aircraft. The DC-3, having received its "type certificate" before the establishment of the new regulation, was exempt from compliance. It continued to fly in accord with the operating policies which had been established by collaboration between the company and the manufacturer.

These policies had been developed with the assistance of Eddie Allen, at that time a test pilot for Donald Douglas's factory at Santa Monica, California, when the DC-2 was brought into Panagra service. Allen achieved considerable fame as a test pilot but was killed in a wartime test flight of the Boeing B-29.

Not only was it necessary to prove that airplanes such as the DC-4 and DC-6 could operate safely at Quito and La Paz, but it was necessary to conduct a full-fledged flight test program to do it. The performance data provided by Douglas covered airports from sea level to 8,300 feet—the altitude of the highest U.S. airport.

The Panagra team which conducted the testing for the DC-4, DC-6, and DC-7 consisted of John Laws, chief engineer; Bill Murray, maintenance engineer; Sy Michener, power plant engineer; Al Secada, performance engineer, and Loyal Domning, technical chief pilot, who did all the flying. CAA and FAA personnel participated in the planning and approved the results. Any of the company's line pilots who were sufficiently interested to endure the cold and rarified atmosphere of La Paz were encouraged to participate.

The DC-4 tests were done in January/February, 1950. DC-6 work was done in January of 1954, and the DC-7 was tested in May of 1957. In all cases the certified performance was better than that which had been projected.

In each case, it was Panagra's position that the tests were unnecessary because Douglas had provided sufficient data to establish the high altitude performance by mathematical means. The government authorities were adamant, however, and the expensive testing was carried out.

As an example of the functioning of the bureaucratic mind, at the outset of the DC-4 program we were told by the FAA that our target take-off weight for La Paz was 54,000 pounds. At the completion of testing we had demonstrated that we could comply with a maximum weight of more than 55,000 pounds and requested approval accordingly. The response was, "You asked for 54,000, and that is all you're going to get."

No other airline in the world had ever been required to test its airplanes as thoroughly as had Panagra. The performance data it developed were purchased and used by other operators in many countries. A side benefit to the company was that its operating and maintenance personnel became much better acquainted with its airplanes and their capabilities than would otherwise have been the case.

In all of the thousands of Panagra's passenger flights at these high airports, carried out over a span of 32 years, no one was injured.

Panagra's media blitz had an unexpected side effect on July 8, when the American Public Relations Association presented the airline with its highest award, the Silver Anvil, for "meritorious public relations service which stimulated trade and tourism between the two Americas." The recognition was nice, but Panagra officials would have traded any number of silver anvils for a long-term contract with the Argentine government permitting the company to book tickets for passengers flying between cities within Argentina.

Of course, it was this trend to national airlines, with their government-backed monopolies over intra-national passenger traffic, that had spurred Panagra to launch the media campaign. Henceforth, Panagra was going to have to rely largely upon two sources of passenger revenue: South Americans flying from country to country within the continent or northward to the United States, and North Americans (and others) that Panagra could draw to its ticket counters in New York, Washington, D.C., and Miami, who wished to fly to destinations within South America.

At the same time, freight operations, once the backbone of the airline, were again assuming an increasingly important position. Air cargo to South America increased 19% during the third quarter of 1957, with a total of 1,164,266 revenue ton miles flown in that period, compared to 940,847 in 1956.

As the trend toward nationalization continued, on November 19, the Argentine government and Panagra signed an agreement for the purchase, installation, and maintenance of seven VOR radios. The airline also agreed to train the Argentine communication personnel in the United States. This modern short wave navigational equipment was to be installed at the Argentine airports of Ezeiza, Mendoza, Córdoba, Tucumán, Villa Reynolds, and Junín to cover the air routes between Buenos Aires and Santiago and between Buenos Aires, Córdoba, and Tucumán within Argentina.

1958

The year started with a reduced tariff on both Panagra and Pan American aircraft for groups of eight or more traveling together to South America. Intended to encourage group travel, the tariff was 30% below regular fares.

The low tariffs were part of an industry-wide fare war. These had become more frequent as the skies became more crowded with competing aircraft. Panagra by this time had 13 IATA (International Air Transport Association) competitors and 10 non-IATA competitors who did not have to abide by the conference rates that IATA set for its members. By October, due to "cut-rate, uneconomical fare levels" among its non-IATA competitors as well as rising costs, Panagra was forced to ask the Civil Aeronautics Board for a subsidy. Panagra said it needed $6.8 million per year and wanted payments to start immediately.

American airline companies were traditionally at a disadvantage because there was no regularized national support. Many of them began with mail routes, which amounted to subsidies for expanding the passenger side of their business, grew to profitability in an open market, then filled that market and saw their profits slip away. Panagra, operating almost entirely overseas, was among the first to find itself competing head-to-head with airlines subsidized by the very nations Panagra served. Add a xenophobic indifference to the fate of an outside airline to the *mañana* mentality of Latin American governments when it came to processing paperwork, and you had real frustration.

In fact, Panagra was operating at critically low levels. Its "load factor," the percentage of seats booked on each flight, had dropped from an average of 60% to a break-even level of 53%. Passenger revenues had declined from $10,086,000 for the first eight months of 1957 to $8,993,000 for the same period in 1958. This was despite the fact that lower rates seemed to bring more business in the form of group travel. The airline was flying women's clubs, professional associations, trade groups, and others all over South America, but it was giving away the store to do so. The airline's rate of return on invested money was 9%, a figure Panagra's accountants termed "wholly inadequate." None of this was good news for a company on the verge of spending $27 million to upgrade to jets, $18 million of which it would have to borrow from banks.

On the bright side, revenues from air cargo were up, thanks to a surge of oil and mineral exploration in areas served by Panagra. Ever-innovative, the company's freight specialists had developed a special plywood crate, the "Casapak," which was now used to transport household goods (thus the name) or other small items that needed to travel together. The Casapak was the forerunner of today's container shipment.

All of this helped. In the first half of the year, freight-ton-miles increased 26% and Panagra was maintaining a 15-times-per-week freight schedule by year's end. However, air cargo was too dependent on factors beyond Panagra's control to be a reliable resource in long-range planning.

The *Dirección Aeronáutica* of Chile conferred upon Panagra its "Diploma of Honor" on January 2, 1958, for having been the first foreign company to operate an airline in Chile. The diploma was presented to Carlos Brunson, Panagra's manager in Chile, by General Eduardo Iensen, Chile's director of aeronautics, during ceremonies commemorating Aviation Day.

There was another earthquake that year in Peru, and on April 17 the Peruvian Red Cross honored Panagra for its help to the people of Arequipa.

Panagra continued the publicity blitz. In February figures were released pointing to higher revenue ton miles flown. The continued expansion of the South American industrial base, combined with increased oil and mineral exploration, accounted for most of the 12.5% increase.

On September 12 Panagra celebrated the 30th year of the start of airline service from the U.S. to South America. It was a bang-up display; Panagra arranged a special "Salute to the Americas" at Rockefeller Plaza in New York honoring the Latin American republics. Victor Andrés Belaunde, Peruvian ambassador to the United Nations, was there, as was the Most Rev. Philip Furlong, representing Cardinal Spellman. The consuls-general of the other Latin American republics were there as well, along with the postmaster-general and an assortment of people distinguished in either aviation or South American business circles. Andrew Shea, Panagra's president, presided, but they were all upstaged by the star of the show, flown in for the occasion. Panagra had arranged the loan, from the Smithsonian, of P-1. A radio broadcast of the ceremonies was sent to every nation in South America, as were written press descriptions.

In October Panagra petitioned the CAB to grant subsidy payments for mail, citing the "cut-rate uneconomical fare levels" of its non-IATA competitors and rising operating costs. Panagra estimated it needed a subsidy of $6,818,000 for the year beginning October 3, 1958.

The company had done without any subsidy since the end of 1954. Now it competed with 13 IATA carriers and 10 non-IATA carriers. Four more non-IATA carriers were expected to start up soon. The pie was being split into wedges too small to satisfy anyone's appetite.

Nonetheless, on December 15 Panagra once again staged a "Santa Claus" trip to the principal cities on the route, bringing gifts to underprivileged children and more name recognition to itself.

1959

Panagra Senior Pilot Floyd Nelson died in Miami after a brief illness on January 29, 1959. Nelson had worked for Panagra for 22 years, flying everything from the first Fairchild four-passenger monoplane to the latest four-engine equipment. He had pioneered many of the Panagra routes in South America and had flown 21,000 hours on those routes alone. In addition to his work for Panagra, Nelson had flown for the U.S. military and for China National Aviation Corporation, the Pan Am affiliate in China before the communist revolution there.

On March 1 Panagra extended its first class service to additional key cities in South America. Cali, Quito, and La Paz had been served up to this date with tourist flights only; thereafter, those cities would have combined first class and tourist class flights. Mixed-class flights had been in use in the United States for some time already, but this was the first use of a split-class aircraft by Panagra.

The entire DC-6B fleet was converted to dual-class service at this time, with a 12-passenger first-class compartment in the rear, and a 55-passenger tourist class compartment in the front. The rear compartment also featured carpeting, fully reclining seats, and four sleeping berths. A third cabin attendant was added to the crew.

Aircraft of this type had passenger loading doors in both front and rear, and the two classes did not mingle while boarding or departing the plane. Passengers used a rolling stairway to disembark, then walked into the terminal building through whatever the weather condition was at the time. Not until the advent of the covered passenger walkways used today did everyone get on or off the airplane through the same door. When this happened, the first-class compartment was moved to the front of the aircraft so that first-class passengers could leave first. That this advantage only allows them to wait longer for their luggage is a problem that airlines have yet to work out.

Of course, one could make the argument that the *El Inter Americano* flights out of Miami and on through to Buenos Aires had been *de facto* mixed-class flights all along; each passenger bought a seat, while only some passengers also bought sleeping berth accommodations.

In any case, the modification of the fleet had a wider effect. Guayaquil, Talara, Lima, Antofagasta, Santiago, and Buenos Aires all saw an increase in the number of first-class seats on flights to those cities.

On May 20 the National Symphony Orchestra left Washington, D.C., on a 17,000-mile, 12-week flying tour of 19 Latin American countries. Pan American and Panagra flew the orchestra throughout their entire tour. Three aircraft were used to move the 108 musicians and staff and the 18,000 pounds of luggage, instruments, and equipment. This was the longest tour to date planned by President Eisenhower's Special International Program for Cultural Presentation in cooperation with the American National Theater Academy.

The ongoing Pan Am/W. R. Grace dispute boiled over again in

May 1959. This time it was precipitated by the U.S. Department of Justice, which brought an antitrust suit against both companies. Suing to force Pan American to divest itself of its Panagra stock, the Justice Department asked the court at the same time to enjoin both companies from combining to conspire in restraint of trade. The Justice Department accused Pan American and Grace of violating the Sherman Anti-Trust Act, saying that they had formed Panagra, "for the purpose of obtaining and maintaining domination and control" of U.S.-South America air transportation and intending to exclude the establishment of a competitive, independent airline. Under that agreement, the Justice Department said, Panagra had refrained from asking for rights on the east coast of South America, and Pan Am had refrained from asking for west coast rights.

Pan Am, Panagra, and Grace denied any wrongdoing. Pan Am said it had formed Panagra to obtain the capital necessary to bid on air mail contracts to Latin America. Furthermore, the ownership of Panagra had been studied by the Justice Department in 1928. Panagra, it said, had been selected to pioneer air travel service along the west coast of South America. Pan Am argued that the U.S. Government was prevented from contending there was a violation of the antitrust laws because (in the form of the CAB) it had studied and approved the relationship itself. Grace said the divestiture would be unnecessary and contrary to the public interest. It stated that Grace did not have a monopoly in air transportation, that there was no clear violation of the antitrust laws, and that the CAB had already approved its interest in Panagra.

The defendants fell to pointing fingers at one another, somewhat to the Department of Justice's amusement. Grace said that it had fostered Panagra's growth despite Pan Am's refusal to extend the airline's routes to the U.S. west coast or to South America's east coast. Pan Am, for its part, said that Grace was supposed to leave the running of the airline to Pan Am, and was instead trying to "convert Panagra to its own instrumentality as a part of the Grace empire." Grace did, in fact, have offices and shipping interests all along the U.S. west coast, and there is no doubt that it would have been at least convenient to have its own private airline serving those cities. Pan Am resisted Grace's demands, it said, because its own routes were complementary with Panagra's, and any such extension would prevent it from competing effectively.

These issues became part of an ongoing argument that would last as long as the unstable marriage of the two corporate giants survived. Where their mutual interests ran together, which was most of the time and over most of the South American routes, Pan Am and Grace were happy. However, when Grace wanted route extensions to serve the U.S. portions of its "empire," or extensions to tap the lucrative Brazilian coast business, Pan Am resisted for the very logical reason that it was already providing service over those routes. Sometimes, as when Grace helped Panagra to add the New York and Washington stops, Grace had its way. Sometimes, as in the case of the U.S. west coast, Pan Am won the argument.

About the only thing Pan Am and Grace could agree upon in court was that the Justice Department had no business bringing the matter up. The CAB had approved the unique half-and-half ownership arrangement back in 1928; the CAB had never complained about the way Pan Am and Panagra shared the South American pie. As for Grace, whatever else you called it, the company was not monopolizing air traffic. Why should it be punished?

The court this time ruled in favor of Pan Am's and W. R. Grace's arguments and let things stand. The CAB in turn sought a higher-level ruling to the effect that it, and not the Justice Department, had sole authority over such matters, a fight that was to sputter on in courthouse back rooms for several more years.

On March 12 Panagra garnered the by-now-usual Inter-American Safety Council Safety Award for safe flying in 1958, and on June 30, the National Safety Council announced a special award, honoring Panagra for outstanding safety, with an accident rate (*all* accidents and incidents, not just those that caused a fatality) far below the average for the preceding three years.

For the Christmas season, Panagra executives hired Sonny Fox, a popular television personality, to join Santa Claus in giving away toys to children in the seven South American countries that Panagra served. Since the start of this "toylift" in 1954, Panagra had distributed more than 10,000 toys.

On December 21 Panagra received a Christmas present of its own. In France the Nice International Club of the Air recognized Panagra for the "distinguished quality of its service," the first time an airline operating in South America had been so honored. French World War I flying ace Roger Millo made the presentation at a ceremony in Lima. The award, coming from a club of aviation enthusiasts and experts, was very special. The fact that it was presented by a man who was a contemporary of H. R. Harris and the other, older men of Panagra added to the occasion. But there was also an air of poignancy to it all. Panagra, like the rest of the world, was moving on at an accelerating pace. The time when the actions of one individual, be he a pilot or a corporate president, could make a large difference, was passing. The jet age was nearly upon Panagra, bringing faster and more convenient travel for the passenger, but bringing a certain anonymity as well.

The delivery of Panagra's first jet. This DC-8-31, #8274H, flew from Long Beach, California, to Miami, Florida, in just four hours, forty minutes. Captains Frank Havelick, Ernie Hummel, and Charles Schultz made the trip on Easter Sunday, April 17, 1960.

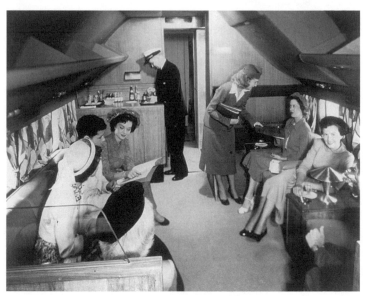

The comfortable lounge on a DC-7 in the 1960s.

CHAPTER 10

THE COMING OF THE JETS;
THE COMING OF THE END, 1960-1967

1960

By January 1, 1960, all Panagra pilots had been transferred to the Miami station. The process had started in 1947, with Tommy Jardine moving north. From then on, the crews would be passing visitors, not residents, in the countries through which they flew.

The airline was changing–had already changed. Pilots were older, procedures more rigid. Efficiency had replaced exuberance.

From the point of view of the passengers, this was probably all to the good. Cy Collins, now vice president for sales and traffic, had other thoughts: "One thing I remember from frequently riding in the cockpit, which I almost always did, was the talk. We were all so young, and the talk mostly drifted to two subjects. Of course, sex and women; that was first. And second was flying. Today I fly a lot in the cockpit on American Airlines, and it's so different. The guys are all older, and what they want to talk about now is the skill of the management, and who's going to get what assignment, very establishment-minded, very dull. No sex unless a pretty stewardess comes up and they haven't seen her before, and someone might say, 'Who's that?' But these are all old guys, and the girls are young enough to be their daughters. It's quite different now, and I think we all remember the good old days when we were all in our twenties and thirties with a special affection."

Collins noted that there is one topic that today's pilots have in common with their predecessors: the union. "Panagra pilots, like pilots today, talked about union matters in the cockpit," he recalls, "though they didn't do so when any management people were present." Collins neglects to point out that *he* was management from the first, not an aircrew member, yet the pilots talked freely in front of him. "At Panagra we had a couple of unused frequencies that we could chit-chat on– about the latest union negotiations, for example–with nobody hearing us, which was good, I guess. Today there are no unused frequencies. Somebody is listening to everything. There is a very constrained atmosphere in the cockpit and a polite reluctance to be too candid. That's partly because we're all grown-up and inclined to be establishment-minded, and partly because of the recorder that's there. If something happens, you don't want your last words to be a criticism of the management or anything else. It all shows a contemporary professionalism, which reflects a vast improvement in one sense, but it isn't as much fun in another sense."

Modernization brought other changes. On February 1, 1960, all DC-4 flights were terminated, and Panagra removed the DC-4s from service. DC-3 flights had already been eliminated everywhere except in parts of Ecuador, where the smaller aircraft still made some economic sense. To accommodate this change, DC-6Bs would henceforth serve Lima, Arica, Cochabamba, and La Paz.

Then on April 18 Cy Collins announced that Panagra's first DC-8 would go into service on May 3. He was close; it actually occurred on May 5, 1960, when a Panagra DC-8 left New York for Buenos Aires, with the usual stops en route. The 5,800-mile flight, which was more than ten times the safe range of the old Sikorsky S-38 amphibians, took eleven hours and forty minutes of flying time to complete. That time, incidentally, was slightly more than half the time that even a DC-6B needed to do the same trip.

Yet, even while Panagra modernized, it faced fundamental difficulties with its routes. By May 1 local service within Bolivia was eliminated. Panagra could no longer effectively compete with government-supported Lloyd Aéreo Boliviano.

A natural disaster in Chile struck just weeks later on May 24, and a Panagra DC-6 immediately left Miami with medical supplies, food, and clothing for victims of an earthquake. The damage proved to be far more extensive than first news reports had indicated; the earthquake had been so severe that it had triggered volcanic eruptions as well. Within three days, Panagra aircraft had moved more than 50,000 pounds of supplies into Chile. Other airlines cooperated by getting supplies to pick-up points for trans-shipment to Chile via Panagra. Throughout the rescue mission, Panagra worked closely with the National Catholic Welfare Committee, the Church World Services, and the Belgian-American Red Cross.

Emergency operations continued into June, when Panagra became a part of "Operation Samaritan," a round-the-clock relief effort that had been taken over by the U.S. Air Force. This was the largest airlift ever attempted in South America. Panagra Flight Superintendent Joseph McCormick reported that Panagra's flight control office at Limatambo had handled more than 200 flights to date of the Air Force's huge Globemasters and C-118s. U.S. Air Force pilots stopping at Lima en route to Santiago were given printed forecasts and personal weather maps; then they received briefings by licensed meteorologists and flight dispatchers. Panagra's radio navigation and communication facilities stayed on the air at all times so that Operation Samaritan aircraft, which flew day and night, could safely navigate south to Santiago.

Some airports south of Santiago were too small or too badly damaged for the larger aircraft, so Panagra lent a DC-3 to the Chilean government. One of the smallest of a huge fleet of participating aircraft, it carried out 310 injured persons to hospitals in Santiago, and carried in 17 tons of relief supplies. While these extraordinary efforts could not undo the untold damage, Panagra's personnel and resources played a major role in the recovery.

Meanwhile, it was business as usual as the airline continued to phase in the new jet aircraft. On July 1 the jet flights between New York and Buenos Aires increased from two to four per week. Piston-engine flights were cut accordingly. The schedules along the west coast were slightly modified to permit more direct connections with other Panagra flights into Bolivia and south to Chile, which was steadily rebuilding from the quake. On the same day, Panagra introduced the first DC-7F air freighter service between the U.S. and South America. It replaced an older DC-6A freighter which had been flying the route between Miami and Bolivia since the first of the year. The DC-7F could fly from Miami to Santiago in less than fifteen hours and had a payload of 29,748 pounds, four times that of a DC-4, and 3,000 pounds more than that of a DC-6A. The aircraft also served Panama, Guayaquil, Lima, La Paz, and Cochabamba on a once-weekly schedule out of Miami.

The DC-8s went into daily service between New York and Lima on October 30, with four of the flights continuing on to Buenos Aires. On those days when the jets did not fly south of Lima, DC-7Bs carried passengers onward. The DC-8s turned east toward Buenos Aires well short of Santiago, passing over the Las Ramadas pass. For a while, Santiago would have to wait to see a jet passenger aircraft.

On December 8 as part of the annual Christmas toylift, Panagra prevailed upon "Uncle" Fred Scott, a popular host of children's television programs, to come south for the event. A film of the trip was subsequently shown on Scott's television show.

1961

Between July 1, 1960, and January 17, 1961, a Panagra memo reported, the DC-7F all-cargo flight between the U.S. and South America transported more than 80 horses and 300 sheep. The same report went on to note that Panagra had, in times past, hauled a rare Bolivian armadillo, pink flamingoes, chinchillas, angora rabbits, Bolivian mountain cats, lion cubs, seals, penguins, hunting dogs, baby chicks, and uncounted numbers of domestic pets.

In fact, the airline had hauled many more animals than the author of the report noted; regardless of their weight, air freight, especially fast air freight, was the best way to transport valuable animals. They suffered much less stress, and the food and water requirements were minimal compared to travel by ship. Often, once cost of stress-related losses was factored in, it was actually cheaper to use air freight.

Panagra showed its leadership with other types of air cargo as well. On May 9 more than 16,000 pounds of cargo, thought to be the largest amount ever carried on a single DC-8 passenger flight, was brought to South America. The shipment ran the gamut from pre-packaged soup, clothing, cola syrup, and television sets, to peanuts and machinery.

On June 15 Panagra finally flew its first DC-8 flight into Santiago. Previous flights had used the Las Ramadas pass, crossing the Andes well north of Santiago, en route to Buenos Aires.

A proud Cyrus Collins, vice president for sales and traffic, announced on August 18 that June, had been the company's best month ever, with revenue passenger miles totalling 20,755,000 for that month alone, more than 14% over previous highs. Collins attributed the increase to the use of the new jets, combined with some timely lowering of tourist fares. Efficiency was better, too; these aircraft were reporting significantly higher load factors, with the planes carrying nearly maximum loads on most flights.

On August 30 the DC-8 frequencies increased to six times weekly to Buenos Aires, with a seventh flight being handled by a DC-7. At the same time, Panagra replaced all five DC-7 flights into Santiago with the new jets.

The star of the annual December toylift was Claude Kirchner, ringmaster of WOR-TV's popular Terrytown Circus show.

1962

Tommy Jardine arrived in Lima on April 13, 1962, to be honored by his many friends, including aviation officials, and by Peruvian industry leaders. Jardine, who had just retired, had started working for Panagra in 1930, had accumulated more than 26,000 hours in the air, and had flown South American air routes longer than any other U.S. pilot. He had pioneered the use of aircraft for heavy freight operations as the first man to land a Ford Tri-Motor loaded with mining machinery at a mining site 12,000 feet up in the Andes. He had also been the first man to fly from Cristóbal to Lima in a single day, and was the one of the first Panagra pilots to take training in the new DC-8s.

On May 16, in a repetition of the rescue missions of earlier years, a Panagra aircraft rushed a 100-pound shipment of Vitron-C to Cochabamba, to help arrest an epidemic of hookworm infection among the Yucarare Indians. The Vitron-C was a specific treatment for the anemia that accompanies such infections.

The third of a series of passenger terminals at Lima, Peru.

During June and July Panagra also hauled more normal cargo; some 75 tons of Argentine beef were air-freighted over the mountains and into Santiago. It was a record for that type of operation. The shipments were carried, approximately 4.5 tons at a time, aboard regularly-scheduled passenger flights.

In August Captain Ernie Hummel found himself rescuing a U.S. Navy flight crew. It was an action he kept a secret for more than thirty years.

Hummel was southbound from Lima to Santiago aboard a DC-8 and was not looking forward to the landing. A massive storm was pounding southern Chile, and Santiago was socked in with a 300-foot ceiling and an official one-mile horizontal visibility. The airport was 1,700 feet above sea level and was surrounded by mountains between 12,000 and 23,800 feet high. Instrument landings started at 25,000 feet, skimmed the slopes of the mountains on the way down, and permitted the pilot only one "pass" at the runway. If he missed his approach, the pilot had to make a steep climb back out of the valley, again skimming the mountains on the way up, then circle around and try again.

As Hummel approached one of his navigation beacon checkpoints near the Chilean coast, he heard the pilot of a Navy A-3, an attack bomber, calling for help. The pilot said he had been launched from the U.S. aircraft carrier *Constellation*, then near Cape Horn, and was en route to Santiago. He was now flying just above the clouds at 37,000 feet and was low on fuel, with barely enough to make the Santiago field. Since he had no foul-weather flying capability and no instrument landing equipment, he was at a loss as to what to do.

Hummel was at a loss, too. The obvious solution was for the pilot and crew to bail out. But the prevailing strong winds would blow their parachutes straight into the mountains, with almost certain fatal results.

Hummel briefly considered having the A-3 fly just off his wingtip during the approach, but that would frighten the passengers. It would also arouse the ire of airline safety officials. Pilots had about the same opinion of safety inspectors as they did of tax collectors.

Finally, Hummel ordered the A-3 pilot to take position just behind and slightly below the DC-8. Hummel would read off each turn and altitude change to the Santiago tower on the way in, and the A-3 pilot would indicate that he had heard by keying his microphone twice, creating audible clicks. In this way Hummel hoped that his help to the Navy pilot would go unnoticed by the authorities.

Hummel, a former military pilot himself, wasn't concerned about the two aircraft colliding. 'Having flown as a military pilot at one time, I knew that pilots who have flown in military squadrons are excellent formation flyers," he said.

Hummel began his descent into Santiago, encountering strong westerly winds, moderate turbulence, and some icing. Each time he reported to the airport tower, he heard a quick click-click in his earphones, so he knew the Navy plane was still with him. Some ground observers later told Hummel, off the record, that the Navy jet was tucked so tightly under the tail of Hummel's DC-8 that the arrangement looked like a single, very long aircraft.

The weather at ground level was even worse than forecast, with light rain, a strong tail wind, and water pooling on the runway. Hummel used every bit of the runway while applying thrust reversers, flaps, slots, and heavy braking and managed to stop just a few feet from the far end of the runway. When he turned the DC-8 to taxi to the ramp, he was delighted to see the A-3 rolling safely down the runway just 100 yards back.

Hummel learned later that the only reason the A-3 was even that far behind him was that the Navy pilot had vigorously skidded, slipped and "essed" at the final approach to back away from the DC-8. "He must have found the interaction of the full flaps, jet tail pipe blast, ejector burble, in ground effect, to be a real handful in maintaining control for the landing," Hummel remarked.

The Navy pilot hopped out of his aircraft, sprinted across the tarmac and up the stairs and into the DC-8 cockpit before the first passenger could debark. He shook hands all around and then, to Hummel's horror, promised to notify his superiors of Hummel's assistance.

"I told him that, although we all appreciated the gesture, it was essential that the matter die right there on the Santiago ramp," Hummel said. "The Air Carrier offices of the Bureau of Commerce, from Buenos Aires to Santiago to the U.S. and back, might have frowned upon the entire incident, despite its humanitarian aspects."

The Navy pilot evidently reined in his enthusiasm, for Hummel never heard more about the incident. However, he recalled his dismay at learning just why a Navy aircraft with no foul-weather capability had been launched, with its entire crew, into a winter storm over southern Chile: a high-ranking officer aboard the aircraft carrier had wanted some letters mailed.

"We were astounded at the apparently indifferent manner in which the flight had been planned," Hummel recalled. "This was an area of the hemisphere where few airports existed, where very few navigational radio beacons were available, where there was an almost complete lack of weather forecasting, and where the second highest range of mountains in the world was located. August is a winter month in South America and is well-known among mariners and aviators as a time to expect violent weather."

Another outstanding flier, Frank Havelick, Panagra's chief pilot, celebrated twenty-five years with the company on November 25. Havelick had been with China National Airways Corporation from 1934 to 1937, then had switched over to Panagra, becoming a check pilot in 1944 and chief pilot in 1947. On that date, Havelick had more than 18,000 hours of flying time in aircraft of all types.

For the annual Christmas toylift, Panagra went all out, managing to collect more than a ton of toys for children in cities along the route. Since 1954, more than 17,000 toys had been distributed to needy children.

1963

Panagra's DC-8 flights routinely overflew Ecuador, the Quito and Guayaquil runways being too short for the newer aircraft. However, on February 1, 1963, Panagra increased the number of departures to Colombia and Ecuador, adding one more to the three weekly flights that had served those nations. This service operated with DC-7Bs via Miami and Panama. On October 28 Panagra DC-8s began service to the Guayaquil airport following the completion of airport facilities for the jets.

Panagra received a bumper crop of awards in 1963, and gave some of its own. On May 6 radio station WQXR in New York cited the airline for "fostering better understanding of the countries, peoples, and culture of South America." The program was transmitted over radio stations world-wide, including Radio Free Europe. The next day, May 7, the Chilean Air Force's "Will of Flight" trophy went to Panagra, the first time it had ever been awarded to a civilian airline, in recognition of the company's contribution to Chilean aviation and to the development of air travel between South America and the United States. Panagra President Andrew Shea received the award from General Eduardo Iensen, commander-in-chief of the Chilean Air Force, at ceremonies in New York.

Shea was back on stage five weeks later, on June 13, when he and

J. Peter Grace, president of
W. R. Grace & Company, received the Order of the Sun at
the rank of Grand Officer. Peruvian Ambassador Fernando
Berkemeyer presented this
award, the highest decoration
given by the Peruvian government, for the important contributions of both Panagra and
W. R. Grace to the economic
and cultural developments of
Peru, and for strengthening
the relationship between Peru
and the United States.

Douglas Campbell, vice
president and general manager of Panagra since 1948,
retired on June 27, 1963.

Panagra President Andrew B. Shea.

Campbell had joined W. R. Grace in 1919 and had been assigned to
assist Panagra in 1932. In addition to taking an active hand in the peri-
odic modernization of the airline as it grew through fast-paced times,
Campbell had personally surveyed many of the routes flown and had
negotiated contracts and agreements with all of the governments involved. Two governments, the Peruvian and Ecuadorean, had awarded
him their highest honors.

The careful planning of men like Campbell paid off in efficiency.
Panagra had the highest passenger load factor of any U.S. airline, international or domestic, in 1963. This was at the same time, and sometimes
on the same flights, that the airline established itself as having the highest percentage of cargo-related ton-miles in a single year. In making the
latter announcement, Panagra officials noted that since the founding of
the airline in 1928, Panagra aircraft had carried 71,000 tons of cargo and
mail–the equivalent of 1,467 fully-loaded all-cargo DC-8 jets.

In September, as Panagra was celebrating its 35th anniversary,
there was more than the usual press notice. Florida Senator George
Smathers read a tribute to the airline into the *Congressional Record.* In
Peru, a monument was erected by Peruvian aviation officials on the
spot where the first commercial flight occurred. So intense was the
publicity, both in the United States and in South America, that *Public
Relations News,* a trade publication, used the airline's knowledge and
experience in public relations as a case study in the application of "skill-
ful and imaginative public relations techniques, which yielded important and lasting values."

The trade magazine was wrong on one count; the value of heavy advertising may have been important in the short term, but no amount of public relations would sway the minds of South American politicians and businessmen bent on kicking the *yanquis* off their continent.

Sometimes it seemed as though the U.S. government, too, wanted Panagra out of South America. The CAB had been pressuring Pan Am to divest itself of all Panagra stock for decades. In 1945 the CAB had tried to persuade the Department of Justice to do something about Pan Am's blocking of efforts to extend the Panagra system north of the Panama Canal and to the mainland U.S. The Justice Department did not act and the CAB had eventually taken the case to the U.S. Supreme Court, which ruled in 1963 that the CAB had sole authority to settle airline antitrust problems.

When Pan Am tried to buy out W. R. Grace and take full control of Panagra, the CAB denied permission. An attempt to force a merger between Panagra and Braniff in 1958, to eliminate Pan American from the west coast position, had foundered upon the question of what to do with W. R. Grace, which was not an airline but which held exactly 50% of the Panagra stock. Braniff at that time did not want half an airline, and unless Grace sold at least one share to Braniff, that's all Braniff would have. Grace did not sell; Braniff and Panagra did not merge.

Back in 1959, when the Justice Department had originally sued to force Pan American to divest itself of its Panagra stock, it had asked the court at the same time to enjoin both companies from combining to conspire in restraint of trade. Pan Am, Panagra, and Grace had denied any wrongdoing. Pan Am said it had originally formed Panagra to obtain the capital necessary to bid on air mail contracts to Latin America, and the ownership of Panagra had been studied and accepted by the Justice Department in 1928. Grace said the divestiture would be unnecessary and contrary to public interest. The unresolved situation had dragged on for nearly four years, but finally the court reached its decision. It argued that Grace did not have a monopoly in air transportation, that there was no clear violation of the antitrust laws, and that the CAB had already approved its interest in Panagra. It was good to have the matter settled at last, though the issue of competition would surface again in just three years during Braniff's negotiations to buy Panagra.

Panagra gave some awards of its own in 1963. On August 8 the airline doubled the number of travel fellowships it granted to South American students. Thirty-three graduate students were selected by the Institute of International Education to represent Bolivia, Chile, Ecuador, and Peru. The total number of such fellowships granted by Panagra since the program had begun stood at 409.

As the year drew to a close, Panagra found some additional ways to assist and support the people of the countries on its routes. On November , the company established the substantial prize of a two-week-long trip to the United States, to be awarded to an outstanding graduating cadet of the Air Force Academy in each of the seven South American countries that the airline served. And Panagra again distributed toys to needy children throughout the service route on December 11. Since starting the program, more than 20,000 toys had been distributed.

1964

Panagra continued to expand its jet service, and on June 2 announced a revision of the schedule to provide the only daily jet service between the United States and Argentina. The DC-8s left New York at 10 p.m. and arrived in Buenos Aires the following afternoon. At this time, Panagra also operated ten weekly flights to Lima, five to Santiago, three to Guayaquil, and one to Antofagasta. When the new runway was finished at Quito on July 1, that city was added to the list of airports serviced by DC-8 jets.

Thirty Latin American and U.S. aviation officials gathered in Santiago early in July to review the state of South American aviation. It was a mixed bag: 19 foreign and 66 scheduled domestic airways serving the continent had put in five billion passenger-miles and carried 94 million ton-miles of air cargo the previous year. South America was obviously one of the most aviation-intensive regions of the world; while average aviation growth world-wide was 117%, in South America it was 175% overall, and far higher than that in some areas.

Yet even in 1964, most of these airlines were making do with hand-me-down DC-3s and DC-6s. Lloyd Aéreo Boliviano pilots still threaded their way through cloud-shrouded mountain passes with the copilot using his wristwatch to count off the seconds to the next turn. Eighty percent of the continent's airports still lacked permanent night landing lights; seventy-five percent had no control towers, radios, or even paved runways. Only five airports in South America had a complete instrument-landing system.

That didn't mean that Panagra had no competition; far from it. "British Overseas Airways Corporation (BOAC) was serving some cities on Panagra's route," Douglas Campbell recalled. "And VARIG, of Brazil, now flew across Bolivia to Lima and onward to Los Angeles. The Chilean national airline, LAN, was flying to Panagra's own home base of Miami. There were lots of them: KLM, Canadian Pacific, Air France–they all started serving large parts of our routes."

And what about Braniff, the airline which would eventually replace Panagra?

"We competed with Braniff," Campbell said, "but there wasn't room for both of us, and the results eventually proved that."

Asked if he thought relations between Panagra and Braniff were cordial at first, Campbell shook his head. "I wouldn't say they were cordial. Uncle Sam said he thought we needed competition, so we said, 'All right, we'll give them competition.' Our idea was that competition consisted not just in trying to sell tickets, but to beat them across the beaches and through the hedgerows and into the streets, to quote Mr. Churchill.

"They thought they were going to come to South America and have the use of all of our radio facilities and our weather forecasting service in the areas where we still operated, in Ecuador and Bolivia, but we said, 'Hell, no; you want to compete with us—we shouldn't help you to run your line.'"

Braniff did set up its own navigation and weather stations where necessary, but, Campbell recalled, that was not the end of the friction.

"One of their planes, flying from Lima to Brazil, had to land at Oruro in Bolivia. I don't know if it was weather, mechanical trouble, or what, but they had flown around, and their fuel was getting low. Oruro was then an emergency field of ours, and we kept a stock of fuel there. We were required to do this by the FAA, which didn't require Braniff to do the same. I told our man there to go ahead and give them the gas they needed to get to their next stop. We couldn't refuse them that. However, I had a bill prepared, whatever it cost us to get that fuel there. It amounted to about $500, and Braniff refused to pay it.

"I got a letter of protest from some vice-president at Braniff, and I knew I would have to give in. Before I did, I wrote back, quoting the story of the turn-of-the-century businessman in Boston who had to have an appendix operation. The doctor sent him a bill for $1,000, and a few days later the bill came back with a note attached that said, 'Please itemize.' So the doctor did. He sent a second bill that read, 'For performing operation: $1. For knowing how: $999.'"

On August 8 Panagra's chief pilot, Frank Havelick, assisted by Loyal Domning and C.A. Schultz, flew a DC-8 into La Paz. The three men were testing the runway and facilities at the highest airport in the world before scheduled jet operations began later in the year. Aboard were James Scholtz, Panagra vice president of operations; James Butler, Panagra's regional manager for South America; officials of both the Bolivian and American governments; FAA representatives; and other Panagra staff. The flight was the first 4-engine jet to land at La Paz. Bolivian President Paz Estenssoro cut the ceremonial ribbon inaugurating the new runway, which had been built with United States Agency for International Development (AID) funds.

A three-engine Boeing 727 on a demonstration flight for the factory had flown into La Paz in June. Airport officials rounded up bowler-hatted Bolivian women in brightly-colored shawls, together with two llamas and a portable sign announcing that La Paz, at 13,358 feet (4,071 meters), was the highest airport in the world. Ladies and llamas were

High altitude testing of the DC-8 at La Paz, Bolivia, August 1964. (l-r) Captain Frank McGann, First Officer Ray Sullivan, Captain Loyal Domning; Panagra Vice President Thomas Kirkland, Captain Ernie Hummel, Chief Pilot Frank Havelick, and Purser Phil Jacobs.

photographed standing between the sign and the nose of the jet. No one noticed that the largest lettering on the sign was an advertisement for Panagra–which never used Boeing jets.

On October 25, the Bolivian jet service began with three weekly southbound and two northbound flights. Panagra had now been serving Bolivia since 1935 and had hitherto been the only airline offering jet service.

Panagra continued to do what it could to influence favorably the South American peoples and governments, awarding another 33 postgraduate fellowships on September 23 to permit Latin American students to travel in the United States. The Christmas toylift continued, with flights in mid-December bringing toys to Panama City, Quito, Guayaquil, Lima, La Paz, and Santiago.

In the closing days of 1964 Panagra earned the coveted "E" award from President Lyndon Johnson. This award, presented to American businesses for work benefitting the United States as a whole, was given to Panagra for its accomplishments in increasing tourism to the U.S. through a vigorous and imaginative *Visit USA* campaign in Central and South America.

1965

Captain Frederick Sterling retired on January 15, 1966. Sterling had flown more than 23,000 hours during his career, thirty-one years of which were spent with Panagra. He had worked for three years with

Isthmian Airways in Panama before joining Panagra in 1934, and he had participated in the earliest experiments with flying heavy mining machinery into remote parts of Peru and Ecuador.

Sterling had brought the first DC-3 down from the plant in Santa Monica, California, puddle-jumping his way to the Pan Am shop in Brownsville, Texas, and then down the Central American isthmus and on to Lima. In more recent times, he had been the first Panagra pilot to be checked out in DC-8 jets and had flown the proving runs in those aircraft from Miami to Panama, Peru, Chile, and Argentina. He had also been very active in the Air Line Pilots Association (ALPA), serving variously as the representative for the South American region, as chairman of several councils, and as delegate to the International Federation of the Air Line Pilots Association. In 1939, the Chilean government had decorated him for his assistance in evacuating 700 earthquake victims.

The earthquakes kept on coming, and Panagra kept on doing what it could. On April 9, 1965, a Panagra jet made a special non-stop flight, Miami to Santiago, carrying 13,000 pounds of urgently needed medical supplies to victims of the most recent earthquake. This was the first commercial non-stop flight between the two cities. The aircraft covered the 4,161 mile distance in eight hours, fifteen minutes.

This special flight garnered most of the attention, but, in fact, in the week after the earthquake, Panagra had placed its facilities at the disposal of the Chilean government—both Panagra officials and Chilean government officials were well-schooled in the routine by now—and had transported 26,652 pounds of supplies into the stricken nation, using the regularly-scheduled all-cargo freighter run, as well as the freight capacity of regularly-scheduled passenger flights. This cargo was collected by the Church World Services and handed over to Panagra for transport.

On May 21 Captain Warren B. Smith died suddenly at his home in Miami. Loyal Domning recalls that:

> ... Smith had been a member of the Gates Flying Circus, walking wings and stunt flying. He crossed the States several times ferrying airplanes left over from WWI. Smitty joined the NYRBA (New York, Rio, and Buenos Aires) airline before Trippe got started. When PAA bought NYRBA, Smitty went to Panagra and made his home in Santiago, Chile, in 1931. He flew for Panagra from 1931 to January of 1965. He first flew Sikorsky amphibians for Pan American-Grace, flying from Panama to Talara, Peru. In 1932 he was appointed regional chief pilot in Chile. In 1939 Smith was decorated by the Chilean government for the same earthquake rescue missions that earned Fritz Sterling a decoration. In 1952 Smith returned to Miami to become operations assistant, a post

he held until his retirement.

The Chileans loved Smitty. He had made several rescue flights to earthquake-stricken cities. He was decorated several times by presidents of Chile, all of whom he knew personally. He was even the father of Chile's trout-stocking program and the sport of fly-fishing in that country. He always seemed to have small toys in his pockets for children. His proudest decoration, "Condor of the Andes," was bestowed when he completed 1,200 trans-Andean flights, all of which had been made through the 14,000-foot mountain passes before the introduction of pressurized airplanes that could fly above the peaks.

A friendly, unassuming man, his single voiced lament was that his poor health kept him from flying the jets.

Smith had been buried for three months when Chilean authorities received a letter he had written before his death. In it, he asked that his body be cremated and the ashes scattered in the "Corridor," the route from Santiago to Mendoza that included the Uspallata Pass. The Corridor was Smith's favorite place on earth, and with much fanfare, his body was exhumed and his wishes carried out. A squadron of fifteen Chilean Air Force jets accompanied a DC-3 to the pass. The commander-in-chief of the Chilean Air Force asked Noel Chaytor, the retired Chilean purser who had flown so many hours with Smith, to perform the rite. As the fighter jets dipped their wings, Chaytor opened the door of the DC-3 and scattered Smith's ashes.

On June 4 Panagra announced non-stop jet service from Buenos Aires to La Paz. Now there was non-stop service linking the *altiplano* and the *pampas* in both directions.

Panagra's safety record continued to be the best in South America. The airline had locked up the Inter-American Safety Award for twenty years now. Just as important to South Americans as safe flying was Panagra's response time in emergencies. To earthquake- or storm-ravaged natives, it seemed that a Panagra aircraft would loom out of the mist as soon as a reasonably flat surface could be cleared to land on. Using techniques developed in heavy-equipment mining lifts, Panagra aircraft could sometimes land on runways too short to permit a normal takeoff, and everyone would have to bustle about to lengthen or repair the strip before the parked aircraft began to pile up. Sometimes there was only the one airplane; the pilot had to get it up and off the ground again if there was even going to *be* a second load of relief supplies. Usually, once the landing site had been brought back to something like a near-normal state, the departing aircraft would carry as many injured victims as it could legally take—and frequently more—on the return trip.

With the advent of heavier aircraft, the cargo capacities were much larger, but the runway facilities had to be better, too. No longer did

Panagra aircraft fly into the most remote parts of a stricken nation. Panagra's role now was to bring large quantities of supplies over very long distances to a central distribution point. It was undoubtedly a more effective service, but a more impersonal one as well.

Panagra's emergency response routine swung into action in mid-August, when the worst storm in Chile's history devastated the country. Torrential rains and snows (this was mid-winter in Chile) left 110 persons dead and 10,000 homeless. Chilean President Eduardo Frei declared four-fifths of his nation a disaster area.

Panagra's first response, on August 17, was to collect its entire stock of blankets, stripping every aircraft and warehouse. The blankets—and an airline in those days owned a *lot* of blankets—were rushed to Santiago. Panagra President Andrew Shea also ordered company aircraft to transport relief supplies made available to it by various U.S. government agencies.

Within a week Panagra was part of a world-wide relief effort involving the U.S. government and civilian relief agencies. On August 23, for example, the *El Inter Americano* flight from Miami carried, in addition to passengers, 6,659 pounds of used fur coats and winter clothing donated by the Lutheran World Relief. In addition to supplying free cargo space on every regularly-scheduled southbound aircraft, Panagra had sent a special freighter to Chile, loaded with 18,737 pounds of blankets and winter clothing from the Catholic Relief Services.

On a happier note, Panagra transported, on September 21, some priceless pre-Columbian gold treasures from Peru. This was the first time that such national treasures had been legally removed from the country. The treasures went on display at the National Gallery in Washington, D.C., and then toured to other museums around the United States. The shipment had a special police guard upon leaving Lima, and a police escort upon arrival in Washington.

On October 15 Panagra announced an order for five more DC-8 jet transports, of the long-range Model 62 series. The order, totalling $42 million, made Panagra the first to add the most advanced jet in the world. One jet would be convertible from passenger to cargo configuration; four would be straight passenger aircraft. The aircraft, scheduled for delivery in early 1967, would be equipped with the slim, long-duct Pratt & Whitney JT3D-3B engines.

Again, on December 13, Panagra distributed more than 3,000 toys, games, and dolls to needy, orphaned, and hospitalized children along its route. Since the annual "toylift" began in 1953, Panagra had distributed more than 30,000 toys.

1966

By 1966 Panagra offered intercontinental jet service over a network in excess of 20,000 miles. Non-stop flights between New York and Lima took 8 hours, 40 minutes. It was 6 hours, 10 minutes between Miami and Lima. New direct service by Panagra and Pan Am allowed passengers to fly from San Francisco and Los Angeles to Lima, or the reverse, without change of plane. DC-8s, flying at 585 miles per hour and equipped with Fiesta Lounges, snack bars, and bed-sized sleeping berths provided a degree of luxury unheard of before or since.

Throughout 1966 and 1967 Pan Am and W. R. Grace quarreled over the future of Panagra. Pan Am appeared to want Panagra to stay just as it was, a small subsidiary of Pan Am's east-coast South American operations. Grace wanted the airline to be bigger, but with just 50% of the stock, couldn't force Pan Am's hand. Meanwhile, competition from national airlines within South America, from European airlines penetrating this lucrative market, and from other U.S. flag carriers, notably Braniff, was eroding Panagra's viability.

Having created and built the western South American routes, the radio stations, the weather reporting network, most of the runways, even the terminals in some cases, Panagra now saw other airlines come in to use the equipment without having to pay for it. Archaic CAB (now FAA) regulations, such as the one that required that Panagra maintain emergency fuel dumps all along its route, dumps that other airlines didn't pay to maintain, but used when needed without even reimbursing Panagra for the fuel, further hindered profitability.

When Grace, frustrated by Pan Am's behavior, decided simply to sell out its half of the airline, the end was inevitable. Cy Collins, by now a senior member of the Panagra staff, negotiated with Braniff for the sale of Panagra.

Braniff initially offered Pan American and W. R. Grace $11 million apiece for control of Panagra. At the same time, Braniff President Charles E. Beard notified the CAB that Braniff would oppose any attempt by Pan Am to buy out W. R. Grace's stock in the airline:

> Our offer is tangible evidence of both our support of the position of the United States as indicated by CAB action over the years in trying to establish a truly competitive U.S. flag service between the U.S. and South America, and our confidence in future travel between the U.S. and South America. The ownership by Pan American of Panagra would thwart the efforts of our government to put into effect the recently published Presidential policy supporting the competitive U.S. flag international services and would, in fact, create a practical monopoly of gigantic proportions. This is not in the public interest . . . .

"Panagra was a tremendously successful operation on a small base, when you remember that Pan Am and Grace each founded the company with a half-million dollar investment apiece, for a total start-up investment of one million dollars," Cy Collins recalled.

"They took $15 million each out of it when they sold it to Braniff, and in the meantime, they had been richly rewarded by substantial dividends. I think they totalled $7 or $8 million each in dividends, and they also got what we called Parent Company Fees.

"These fees, which Panagra paid in good and in bad years, were supposed to reflect what the parent company did for Panagra. It was payment for services rendered, that sort of thing. In the case of Grace, they did quite a lot. Grace, I think, was always on our side. In the case of Pan Am, we were paying for a portion of the Pan Am legal department, mostly for lawyers who were working against us. A similar amount was spent on various management types, most of whose time was spent in the U.S. in . . . well, let's just say it was not spent advancing the cause of Panagra.

"It was a difficult time, and it led to the decision by Peter Grace to sell his half of Panagra to Braniff. He decided, I think, to get out of South America entirely. He couldn't sell Grace Lines just then, though he did sell it later, but he could sell his half of Panagra.

"That left it up to Pan Am to try to find some way to avoid selling their half, and they couldn't. They knew they could never get full control—that had already been established in the courts. So my last activity with Panagra was to work out, under Andy Shea's direction, the merger of Panagra and Braniff.

"I spent a lot of time working in Dallas with Harding Lawrence. Harding was an interesting and very able guy, but I decided that I was not about to go to work for him, or to move to Dallas. I think I disappointed him. I know I disappointed all my friends in Panagra by taking a job with American Airlines, thereby staying in New York.

"It was a tough time, working out that merger. Harding had hired Henry Golightly, the famous aviation consultant, to help Braniff with the merger. Golightly and I had a talk one time. He said to me, 'Look, you've got to learn how to handle this guy Lawrence. I'll give you an example. He called me up a couple of months ago and said, "Henry, I've got a job for you. I'm buying Panagra, and I want you to work out the details of the merger." I said that my guys were awful busy, and what did Lawrence think the job was worth? He said, "Two or three hundred thousand."

"'Well, I badly needed the business. However, I said, 'Lawrence, I can't do it. My guys are tied up. I can't get into that little stuff. If you've got something that's a half-million or over, give me a ring." Two weeks later, Harding called me up and said, "Well, I think we're into something that's over a half-million, and I want you to do it.'

"So that's how Henry Golightly got the job of arranging the merger, which shows that being a consultant takes something more than knowledge. It takes a lot of moxie, and Henry Golightly had it. He understood how Harding worked.

"But it was a sad time, and I think that, in a way, we all regret the sale, even though some of the guys who went to work with Braniff had a good time there and did real well.

"It wasn't the same. We were part of a wonderful pioneering effort, and I don't think any of us will ever forget it. One of the reasons we can be proud of Panagra was that it was a damn good airline, even in the Pan Am family, where Wilbur Morrison ran the Latin American division.

"Wilbur and his men would travel on Panagra every so often. But more importantly, whenever Juan Trippe went to South America, he would always make a point of going one way on Panagra and the other way on Pan Am. Without exception, he would then write letters to Wilbur and all the guys running the Latin American division of Pan Am, asking how come Panagra was so much better. This rankled the Pan Am people considerably. They would respond that Panagra had four vice-presidents looking after their operation, and they had only one. 'Panagra's got all this top-heavy management,' they would say.

"That was true, but it was a source of some pride to us, and even the guys at Pan Am recognized that we were doing something right. Part of it was because guys like Andy Shea and Peter Grace were stubborn. When Peter thought there was something wrong with the meals, he didn't just sit there. He would write a report to Andy, and Andy would get hold of Ed Farrel, or Felix Larkin, or me, or whoever was down there, and say, 'What's going on here? Fix this up.' Believe me, it got fixed up.

"There was a tremendous amount of memo-writing. Panagra standards were very, very high, almost without regard to cost. We spent a lot of money, more money on food, I'm sure, than other airlines. Our payroll was low, but our maintenance was a very high expense. We had to pay Pan Am to do it at market rates. We got no discounts for anything they ever did for us.

"The fact that Panagra was a good airline and made good money for all but one or two years of its existence is also a credit to the tender loving care of the Grace people. Nobody realized it, but they were on top of it, managing us, making us perform even when we thought they were being silly and a pain in the neck. It was a shame that Grace had to get out of the airline business. They would have done very well in it, but the stock-holding arrangement of Panagra simply wouldn't permit it to continue."

Cy Collins never met Harold Harris at Panagra. "Having joined so late, I missed Harris's leadership and innovation. Years later, we were both active in the Wings Club in New York. It was Harris who came up with the idea for the annual 'Sight' lectures. 'Sight' meant 'hindsight,' 'foresight,' and 'insight.' Harris himself delivered one of the lectures, and the series has since been named the Harold Harris Sight Lectures.

"When we think about what Harold Harris did, designing the route structure, surveying the whole route, making it happen–I don't know how anybody could get along well enough with both Grace and Pan Am to do much for long, but he got it done. He got it started, and I guess, as they say, the rest is history."

At the end of the negotiations, Braniff paid Pan Am and W. R. Grace $15 million apiece for Panagra's equipment, routes, and other assets. Most of the personnel went to work for Braniff, although the merger of the two airlines created some overlaps, especially in office and ground-support functions.

The Panagra staff had known for some time that the end was in sight, but that didn't mean they had accepted it.

"Throughout the latter years of Panagra's existence, flight crews speculated and agonized endlessly over what might have happened in the way of expansion and progress of the company had we not been boxed into a corner by Juan Trippe of Pan American," Ernie Hummel recalled. "In crew cars, in the cockpits on long hops, we chewed over the horrible situation created by keeping Panagra south of Panama for so many years, blocking any hope of the company's launching out on its own."

Still, Hummel was intensely proud of the airline's accomplishments: "Panagra had been among the first to acquire the DC-6s, a marvelous aircraft with a very reliable engine. The DC-7s had an improved airframe, but a troublesome engine. Both aircraft were pressurized, and this meant more to Panagra than to most other airlines because of the ever-present Andes. The DC-8s, with their speed and high cruising altitudes, actually made the mountains seem small. Panagra's jump from Fairchilds to DC-8s staggers the imagination with regard to South American airline flying.

"But despite several well-intentioned and expensive efforts to break the lock on Panagra's expansion, it was never possible to do it. During these times, rumors and stories traveled over the airline like crazy. The flight radio officers gossiped interminably on the CW channels when they figured that no one but the FROs were listening. The pilots never stopped talking about it, and it was tremendously disappointing to all of us that the company wasn't allowed the expansion it rightfully deserved."

Frank Havelick agreed. "One of the great anomalies of the air industry in those days," he said, "was that if you wanted to go from South America to the U.S. on an American airline, you had to get off in Panama and seek another airline to come to the U.S. We, as an American company, had no right to go into our own country. Here was the second U.S. flag carrier, almost as old as Pan Am by a matter of months, and we never had the right to go into our own country."

Loyal Domning noted that the Through Flight Agreement that finally did allow Panagra into the United States added some 30% to the route miles just at the end of the airline's life. It was one of the last acts of a 40-year-long play, and Domning wrote his own summary of the story as his contribution for this book—a summary so interesting that it provides an excellent way of concluding:

> Panagra was fathered in 1928 by parents who, while needing each other badly, were each unwilling to yield any advantage to the other partner. The result was a 50-50 ownership. Neither could take any initiative that did not suit the other. The result of this stand-off was an agreement to divide the South American continent into two spheres of influence, with Pan American taking the east coast and Panagra the western side.
>
> W. R. Grace and Company had been quick to grasp the significance of an aerial link to the USA. The company had major commercial interests in all of the west coast countries of South America. The proffered facility of movement of people, mail, and goods would benefit their activities tremendously. As owners of a steamship line, they were concerned that such an airline might be formed by strangers and compete with their services. Harold Harris was offering them a double-edged opportunity, and they grasped it eagerly.
>
> Pan American also was eager to participate. Juan Trippe's ambition was to encircle the South American continent. At the time, he had not yet consolidated his positions on the East Coast of South America, being in a death-struggle with NYRBA (New York-Rio-Buenos Aires) Line and had his hands full. He saw the half ownership of Panagra as an effective block to significant competition on the Pacific side as well as a foot in the door to his eventual ambition. Trippe would not agree to Panagra's having a president. He wanted to maintain an appearance of its being a division of PAA. Thus, for the next decade, the company was run by two men. Vice President John McGregor was named general manager and was based in New York. Vice President Harold Harris ran the operations and everything else in South America from his office in the Grace Building in Lima.
>
> The initial investment of each company was $25,000 to study the feasibility of a west coast route. A Peruvian corporation was formed, but before long, in January of 1929, Pan American-Grace Airways was founded, and the parents increased the capital to $1,000,000. No additional funds were contributed to the company during its existence—until it was purchased by Braniff in 1967.
>
> In spite of the drawbacks of split ownership, the airline grew and prospered. Geography was favorable to Panagra. A string stretched over a globe from New York to Buenos Aires runs down

near to the Pacific coast. This was much shorter than PAA's route around Brazil, and, in the early days, it meant days saved. Moreover, Río de Janeiro was the only major city on the east coast route, whereas the capitals of Ecuador, Peru, Bolivia, Chile, Argentina, and Paraguay were on or near the western route.

Another weighty factor was the W. R. Grace Co. presence. Founded at Lima in the mid-1850s by William Russell Grace, the company had gradually expanded into all of the countries of western South America. Starting in the mercantile trade, Grace became a major factor in textiles, agriculture, sugar, mining, plus the importation of heavy machinery and a host of food and household products. Its major offices were in the capital cities, and it had agencies in every seaport and commercial center from Panama to Chile. It was no coincidence that the Panagra office in every community served by the airline was in the Grace Building. Panagra's South American headquarters for many years was in downtown Lima at the "Casa Grace."

Grace policy was never to take sides in any political conflict. As a result, it was not seriously affected by any of the numerous revolutions which made governments so short-lived in some countries. Its influence was sometimes critical in resolving crises which were bound to arise when a government official did not understand the reasons for some of the actions which the airline found necessary. Notably, Grace did not furnish its facilities in a spirit of pure beneficence. Panagra paid for all benefits, thereby providing a tidy income to its co-parent.

Another aspect of the situation that worked to Panagra's advantage was its nationality. The air network tied together pairs of neighbors which in every case had historic grievances and suspicions which made direct cooperation between them difficult, or worse. To form such a network under, for example, the Peruvian flag, would have been impossible at that time, even though all concerned recognized and desired the tremendous advantages of air service. The fact that Panagra was not a citizen of any of these countries was an important ingredient of its success.

Although the relationship between Trippe and Grace was always an uneasy one, PAA was a valuable partner in technical matters. Under Andre Priester, PAA's chief engineer, that company soon established a position of preeminence in airline operations and air navigation. Priester's engineering staff was strong, and PAA's relations with the airplane and engine manufacturers were close and respected. Panagra was given full access to all of the most advanced equipment and techniques, and was, from the start, one of the airlines that operated airplanes which were best suited to its demanding service conditions. Of course, this is made easier to understand by the fact that PAA was Panagra's exclusive purchasing agent in the United States, reaping a handsome commission on every deal.

Not the least of the many ingredients of Panagra's success was the fact that the split ownership left it free to manage its growth with little interference from its parents. When Trippe finally dropped his opposition to a president, in 1939, Harold Roig, a long-time Grace official, was installed under the condition that he could not vote on directorship decisions. Roig strengthened the organization. Douglas Campbell was named vice president, operations, and John Shannon was made vice president, engineering and maintenance. The Traffic and sales department was beefed up, both in New York and in Lima. The men who conducted Panagra's affairs were all well-seasoned by years of experience with South American airline operations. Not only was Panagra poised on the threshold of an explosive expansion, it had an organization well able to make it a solid one.

Another potent ingredient during the early years was the fact that Panagra enjoyed a monopoly on the Buenos Aires-Panama route. Elsewhere, with the disappearance of the Axis airlines and Aéropostale, there was no competition. As fast as airplanes could be bought up or leased, the demands of passengers, mail, and cargo filled them up.

The expansion was accelerated by the turbulence in Europe and the necessity to strengthen America's transportation and communications systems.

The war years were busy ones. The fleet had grown to 26 of the DC-3A type, a few leased from United and Pan Am, but most obtained either directly from the Douglas factory or from military production. Panagra was one of the first to order the DC-4; its colors had already been painted on the first airplane when the war broke out, it was commandeered by the Air Corps.

The war brought an abundance of multi-engined long range airplanes. Panagra had established its preference for Douglas aircraft and had ordered six DC-6s for delivery late in 1946. As interim equipment, a total of eleven DC-4s were either leased or purchased.

During the war, there was little time to worry about the fact that Panagra's route ended at the Panama Canal Zone. However, as soon as hostilities ended overseas, they broke out anew between Grace and PAA. Panagra now operated DC-4s which had the range needed to fly to Miami, and its board of directors tried unsuccessfully to win Trippe's approval to apply for an extension of its route. The matter reached the courts but was not resolved. At one point, Trippe offered Grace ten million dollars for Panagra. Peter Grace, tired of fighting with Juan, accepted, but the CAB rejected the deal, saying that if the routes were transferred, Braniff should have them.

In the long run, it was the political climate in Washington that would end Panagra's supremacy in South America. Harry Truman frowned on Juan Trippe's dominance of the international air routes and took advantage of the opportunity to give Braniff a route in 1947. It took twenty years, but in 1967, Braniff got it all by paying each partner fifteen million dollars.

In 1947 a compromise had been struck. Under the terms of the Through Flight Agreement, Panagra's airplanes and crews were to operate over PAA's Panama-Miami route. After extended negotiations between the pilots' associations of the respective airlines and much interplay with the Civil Aeronautics Board, the deal was put into operation. In a move that made travel on Panagra even more attractive, National Airlines signed an interchange agreement under which Panagra's airplanes (or PAA's, for that matter) would continue to New York with National's crews in the cockpits.

Implementation of the Through Flight Agreement marked a major turning point for Panagra. The added mileage meant more airplanes and more personnel. Miami became a crew base, and an exodus from South America began immediately. By 1960 Lima was just another city served by Panagra. All administrative and technical services had been transferred to Miami. The obstacle imposed by the terminus in Panama had been removed and, while no new air routes were obtained, the growth of the company quickly picked up speed.

The route to Miami added about 30% to the mainline operation. Its advent was especially timely as the greatly increased capacity of the DC-4 and DC-6, compared with the DC-3, foreshadowed a large reduction in the number of flight personnel required. Some of this reduction would still have been necessary had it not been possible to qualify the copilots as flight engineers. But in fact, Panagra was still hiring copilots as late as 1954.

1967

On Tuesday, January 31, 1967, Panagra's last flight took off from Lima and turned north to Miami. Six hours later, just three minutes late, Captain James R. McCleskey, rolled up to the gate in Miami. McCleskey climbed out and walked away without a backward glance. It was his last flight; the man who had served as a Panagra chief pilot was just two weeks away from his 60th birthday and mandatory retirement. When a customs official told him that, just this once, he would not have to go through the formalities, the pilot chuckled and said, "If I'd known that, I'd have smuggled in something."

McCleskey was one of the few Panagra employees who didn't go to work for Braniff. At the end, Panagra operated 15 round-trip flights weekly from Miami to South America. In all, Panagra employed some 1,300 persons throughout two continents; the Miami office alone employed some 150 people, including all of the air crews.

McCleskey himself boasted once of "never having made a headline." In more than 28,000 hours of flying he had never had an accident, although, he noted, "that's a long time sitting on your behind."

It was the second "last flight" that McCleskey had flown. In 1937 he had taken the last China National flight out of Shanghai, just half an hour before the Japanese Army seized the airfield.

The DC-8 (the El Inter Americano flight) was to be Panagra's last aircraft class.

EPILOGUE

An era, the era of the amateur hero, was passing. No one–pilots least of all–wanted air travel to be perceived as something dangerous and heroic. But, it *had* been in its youth. The aircraft had been primitive; the airports, communications, and navigational facilities were, too. The terrain over which Panagra pilots flew was some of the most challenging in the world. Most of the equipment had never been used at such high altitudes, and Panagra pilots had to be their own test pilots at times. It had been only through the most determined attention to the most minute details that Panagra pilots had achieved a safety record that airlines today would envy.

While not losing sight of the need for safety, these young men had a lot of fun despite flying for very long periods of time on some of the longer runs. Some of their work schedules would make today's FAA inspectors' hair turn white, yet there was never a complaint, from either the pilots or the mechanics. Those mechanics examined the airplanes meticulously between flights, aware that the slightest slip-up in ground maintenance would leave pilot and passengers at the mercy of the unforgiving Andes, where emergency airfields were few. The demise of Panagra marked the end of an age in aviation; individualism and youthful exuberance were to be replaced by regulation and technology.

In the end, Panagra's two great achievements had been to bring commercial aviation to a large part of South America and to show some of the best aspects of the U.S. and its people to the people of Latin America.

When South Americans remembered Panagra, it was not the unexpected profitability of the airline that they recalled, nor the innovative use of equipment that made it possible to fly over the second-highest range of mountains in the world. No, they remembered when a Panagra tri-motor was the only alternative to days of hellish road travel–if there *was* a road. They remembered how Panagra shortened from months to days the time it took an international letter to reach a small town in the jungle. They remembered a Panagra DC-3 performing a semi-crash landing at a shattered airstrip in a remote and earth-quake-struck village, its belly full of medicine and its cockpit full of hope. They remembered Warren B. Smith and those little toys he always picked up in Buenos Aires, Argentina, for the kids of Santiago, Chile.

And those are the best memories of all.

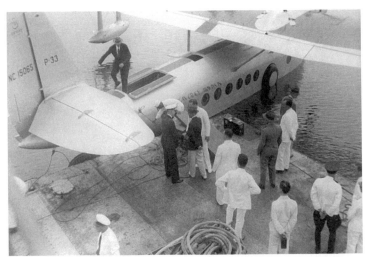

Panagra's first S-43 arriving in Butra, Peru, June 8, 1936, was greeted by Stuart Iglehart of W. R. Grace.

An S-43 engine being serviced.

A Panagra Lockheed Vega at Limatambo, 1930.

Sending up a weather balloon, Lima, early 1930s.

This Consolidated "Commodore" model 16 with 2 Hornet B-575 engines was bought from NYRBA Line and integrated into the Panagra fleet.

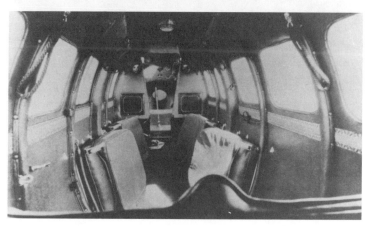

Interior of the Lockheed Vega, showing passenger seats covered in pigskin leather.

Jimmy Scholtz, Panagra manager in Lima for many years.

Carlos Velarda C., part of the Panagra management team during the '30s and '40s.

Guests at a luncheon given in honor of Harold R. Harris, vice president of Pan American-Grace Airways, at Roberto Dagnino's residence, "Villa Rosa," in Santiago on September 4, 1933. All Chilean aviation authorities were invited. Those shown here are, from left to right: Señor A. Alcaíno, chief lawyer of the Chilean aviation department; Cmmdr. Ignacio Aliaga, Director de Aeronáutica; Cmmdr. Manuel Francke, Director del Estado Mayor; Cmmdr. Luis Bassaure, Director of Material; Harris; Capt. Jorge Bate, chief, Cerrillos Airport; Cmmdr. Diego Aracena, director of the aviation school; Pilot Warren B. Smith, Pan American-Grace Airways; Cmmdr. Armando Castro; Roberto Dagnino; Pilot D. C. Beatty, Pan American-Grace Airways; Cmmdr. Francisco Garcia; and Capt. Rafael Saenz, director of L.A.N.

Peruvian President Augusto Leguía, U.S. Ambassador Moore, and Harold R. Harris celebrate another Panagra achievement in Lima in the early 1930s.

Captain Harold R. Harris (fourth from left) reviews the Panagra route map at Las Palmas Field, Lima, Peru, on February 17, 1930. W. H. Howell, secretary to Capt. Harris, is at Harris's left.

The arrival of Panagra's first air mail from the U.S. in Lima, Peru, May 19, 1929. The group includes President Augusto Leguía, Ambassador Moore, Admiral Loayza, Captain Grow, and Captain Harold R. Harris.

Interior of a Panagra passenger cabin on the occasion of the Peruvian "Fiestas Patrias," July 28, 1930. Passengers on this flight received a special light lunch and a small photo of the plane, signed by pilot, steward, and flight mechanic.

Customs inspection at Las Palmas Airport, Lima, in 1931. On the left, Ambassador Dearing and Mrs. Truxton Beale of Washington, D.C., watch other passengers having their baggage checked.

Panagra's Superintendent of Flight Attendants, Maureen Duane, and Director of Sales, Gordon McCoun.

Panagra advertising on a traffic direction stand in Mendoza, Argentina.

This Panagra Ford Tri-Motor was blessed and christened "Santa Rosa" in a ceremony at Lima, August 11, 1929. The group photo includes U.S. Chargé d'affaires Freddie Mayers (in top hat), Harold R. Harris, President Augusto Leguía, the presiding Archbishop, and President Leguía's daughter.

A Panagra plane crew and dispatchers (left to right): Jerry Vilicic, chief steward; José Ricardo Matallana, Lima traffic representative; Thomas Forrest Jardine, pilot; Carl Lindenbergh, flight mechanic; and Javier Buenaño, plane receiver.

Among Panagra's illustrious passengers was the world-famous humorist Will Rogers (third from left). Those with Rogers include Capt. Homer Farris, Ambassador Dearing, Capt. Harold R. Harris, and his son, Harold, Jr.

Actress Dolores del Rio christened "El Inter Americano" when Panagra inaugurated DC-6 service after World War II.

Ernest Hemingway, known for his world travels, was another famous Panagra passenger, shown here flanked by two flight attendants.

The rare loss of a Panagra plane was major news in 1945. A mechanic took the aircraft without authorization and without knowing how to fly. He crashed in the Pacific Ocean about ten kilometers off the Peruvian coastline.

This Panagra radio operator maintains vital communications from his station at Mt. Aconcagua in the 1930s.

F. H. Wang, in a dugout at San Blas, shows a typical water disembarkation.

Harold R. Harris meets with Mr. Naboa, vice president for air operations in Ecuador, January 19, 1937.

Capt. John Brumbaugh shows Panagra's new DC-6 to a young passenger.

Harold J. Roig, Pan American-Grace President, with Fernando Berkemeyer, Peruvian Ambassador to the U.S., and Capt. Douglas Campbell, Panagra pilot and senior vice president, being honored by the Peruvian government.

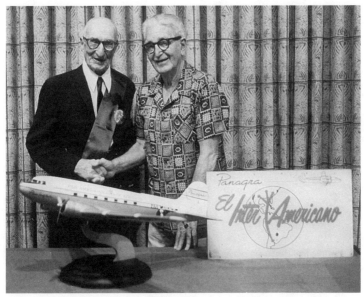

Late in life, Harold R. Harris and Douglas Campbell celebrate their many years of Panagra memories.

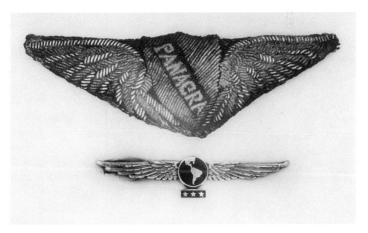

Two insignia worn with pride, the Panagra jacket emblem and the green and gold captain's wings.

INDEX

This index of key names and places is provided for the convenience of readers. However, no attempt has been made to be exhaustive. Pan American-Grace routes are listed only as they are mentioned in the text, and this should by no means be taken as a complete list of Panagra's flights or connections.

A

A-3, Navy attack bomber 203-204
Achilles, Frank L., Jr., "Kelly" 63, 67, 110, 125, 153
Aconcagua, Mount 5, 49, 60, 160
  photograph of 49, 60, 233
Aerial Experiment Association xvii
Aéropostale airlines 220
Aerovias del Ecuador 133, 135, 164
Aerovias Perunas S. A. (AVP) 70
Africa 128, 148
Air Corps. *See* Army Air Corps
Air Force Academy 208
Air Force Museum x
Air France 208
Alaska 29, 34
Albright, Ken 102
Albrook Field, Balboa, Panama 122, 124
Alcíano, Sr. A. 226
Aliaga, Ignacio 226
Allen, Eddie 191
Alluralde, Mr.
  Mendoza station chief 71-72
Amazon basin 46, 76
Amazon River 76
Ambato, Ecuador 173
American Airlines x, 98, 127, 199, 215
Anderson, Andy
  photograph displaying safety award 183
Andes xi, 48, 52, 175, 190, 202, 212, 223
  first night crossing 168
  flying across xv, 34, 61, 65, 69, 86, 154, 161
  foothills 185
  gold mining site 84, 89
  McArthur crossing 169
  Monturaqui Pass 50, 168-69
  photograph by Bill Krusen ii
  photograph of 6
Antofagasta, Chile 38, 53, 66, 159, 169, 195

"Cut-off route" 169
  El Inter Americano stop 167
  first exploratory flight to Salta 50
  hardship post 68
  new route to Salta 130-31
  weekly flight from New York 208
Antofagasta to Buenos Aires "Cut-off" route 178
Antofagasta to New York 187
Apurimac Canyon 84
Aracena, Commdr. Diego 226
Arajuno, Ecuador 123
Arequipa, Peru 72, 81, 84, 110, 130, 194
  airport 190
  Bates guest house 38
  from Panama 128
  generals' visit 37-38
  jewelry consigned to 166-67
  juncture point for North-South route 115
  new airport 71
  Prince of Wales's visit 44
  Reeve's flight to Lima 34
  revolutionaries in 45
Arequipa to Alpacay 88
Arequipa to La Paz
  voice-radio approval 174
Arequipa to Lima 130
Argentina 7, 33, 57-59, 61, 66, 68, 124, 132, 156, 160, 187, 219
  air mail 164
  and Upsallata Pass 51, 56
  'cabotage' traffic 163
  distributing toys 185
  films about 186
  government-built radio stations 168
  political instablity 46
  predicting weather 113
Argentina to Córdoba to Buenos Aires mail route 79
Argentine plains 34
Arica, Chile 35, 38, 45, 47, 110, 115
  added as stop on Diagonal 159
  escape route 44
Arica to Antofagasta 131
Arica to Uyuni 79
Armstrong, Del 190
Army Air Corps 123, 125, 220
  Engineering School 8
Army Flying School 10
Arnold, General Henry H. "Hap" 13-14, 128
Arosemena, Alcibiades, President of Panama 166